THE CHARTER AND ORDINANCES OF THE CITY OF RICHMOND.

PUBLISHED BY AUTHORITY OF THE COUNCIL.

RICHMOND:
JAMES E. GOODE, CITY PRINTER.
1875.

CONTENTS.

CHARTER OF THE CITY OF RICHMOND.

ORDINANCES OF THE CITY OF RICHMOND.

TITLE 1.

OF THE CITY GOVERNMENT.

TITLE 2.

OF THE REVENUE OF THE CITY.

TITLE 3.

CITY DEBT.

TITLE 4.

CITY PROPERTY.

TITLE 5.

HEALTH.

TITLE 6.

POLICE.

TITLE 7.

NUISANCES.

TITLE 8.

THE POOR.

TITLE 9.

EDUCATION.

TITLE 10.

HUSTINGS COURT, CITY ATTORNEY, AND JUSTICES OF THE PEACE.

TITLE 11.

CORONER AND SURVEYOR, AND ALLOWANCES TO JURORS.

TITLE 12.

OFFENCES.

TITLE 13.

RAILROADS AND THE IMPROVEMENT OF JAMES RIVER.

TITLE 14.

PUBLIC PRINTING, VIRGINIA VOLUNTEERS, PUBLIC INTERESTS, RETRENCHMENT AND REFORM.

TITLE 15.

TEMPORARY ORDINANCES STILL IN FORCE.

TITLE 16.

RECENT ORDINANCES.

TITLE 17.

ORDINANCES IN ALPHABETICAL ORDER.

ERRATA.

Page 45. In the subject of chapter 3, title 1, for "hustings court," read "*mayor.*"
81, section 3, line 8, for "sixth and seventh," read "*sixth, seventh and eighth.*"
291, line 3, after "pronounced," insert "*upon the foregoing ordinances.*"
324, (index) strike out the fourth entry under title "hustings court," relative to clerk's compensation for lists furnished commissioner.

BOUNDARIES OF THE CITY OF RICHMOND.

AN ACT

TO EXTEND AND DEFINE THE BOUNDARIES OF THE CITY OF RICHMOND.

Passed February 13, 1867.

1. Be it enacted by the general assembly, That the boundaries of the city of Richmond shall be extended and defined as follows: The said city of Richmond shall extend, on its southern boundary, to the line which now divides the counties of Henrico and Chesterfield, from a point in said dividing line which will be struck by the extension of the western line of the city limits, across the river to said dividing line, to a point in said dividing line which will be struck by the extension of the eastern line of the city limits, across the river, to said dividing line; and shall include all the territory lying between the present southern limits of said city and the said dividing line and between said western and eastern lines extended as aforesaid.

2. The other boundaries of said city shall be as follows: Beginning at a point in the line which divides the counties of Henrico and Chesterfield, which will be struck by the extension southwardly of the western line of Hollywood cemetery, and running thence northwardly to the southern line of the Clark's spring property, now belonging to the city of Richmond; thence along said line and the extension of the same to a point one hundred and fifty feet west of the western line of Randolph street; thence northwardly and on a

line parallel with said Randolph street, and one hundred and fifty feet from its western line, to a point on said line, one hundred and fifty feet southward from the southern line of Dover street on the Plank road, to a point one hundred and fifty feet west of the western line of a street on which Mr. John Carter resides, which is probably a continuation of Carter street; thence northwardly, crossing the Plank road, and on a line parallel with said Carter street, and one hundred and fifty feet westwardly from its western line, to the street or road which separates the farm of William C. Allen from the lands of the Richmond college, and continuing the same line through sundry lots and the lands of Nathaniel F. Bowe, to the northern margin of Bacon branch, one of the branches of Shockoe Creek; thence down the northern margin of Bacon branch by its meanders to the point where the present northern boundary of the city crosses the said branch, at or near the extended line of Seventh street, on the map of the city; thence eastwardly with the present boundary line, passing the corner on said boundary, marked C on said map, to a point on the west side of the County road leading from Valley street in said city to Chelsea or Bowling Green; thence down the centre of said road southwardly to Seventeenth or Valley street; thence along said Seventeenth or Valley street southwardly to the County road leading from said Seventeenth or Valley street to Fairfield; thence up and along the centre of said road eastwardly to a point one hundred and fifty feet eastward of the east line of Gamble street, extended northwardly, as the said street is laid down on the plan of Brown, Page and Gamble, commonly called McKenzie's Garden; thence southwardly and parallel with the said Gamble, Federal or Purcell streets one hundred and fifty feet eastward of the eastern lines of said streets, to a point in said line one hundred and fifty feet north of Venable street, as marked on Adam's plan; thence eastwardly and on a line one hundred and fifty feet northward of the north line of Venable street and parallel therewith, to a point one hundred and fifty feet northward of the north line of Q street; thence along a line eastwardly and parallel with said Q street, and one hundred and fifty feet therefrom, to a point one hundred and fifty feet eastward of Thirty-first street; thence southwardly and parallel with Thirty-first street, and one hundred and fifty feet therefrom, to a point one hundred and fifty feet north of the northern line of Marshall street on said plan; thence eastwardly and on a line one hundred and fifty feet northward of the north line of Marshall street, and parallel therewith, to a point on said line one hundred and fifty feet eastward of Thirty-fourth street; thence southwardly on a line parallel with Thirty-fourth street, and one hundred and fifty feet therefrom, to a point in said line one hundred and fifty feet north of the northern line of Main street extended; thence eastwardly and on a line parallel with said Main street so extended, and one hundred and fifty feet therefrom, until the said line meets a point one hundred and fifty feet eastward of the eastern line of Fulton street in the town of Fulton; thence along said line in a southwardly direction, and parallel with said Fulton street, until it strikes a point in said line one hundred and fifty feet southwardly of the south line of a street known as Orleans street; thence westwardly and on a line one hundred and fifty feet south of the southern line of said Orleans street, and one hundred and fifty feet therefrom, to James river, and thence across said river, continuing the same course, to the dividing line between the counties of Henrico and Chesterfield.

3. The inhabitants of the district of country lying between the present boundary of the city and the new boundary hereby established, shall not be liable, in their persons or property within the said district, for the period of five years from the passage of this act, for any portion of the debt contracted by the city of Richmond prior to the commencement of this act, or of the interest due and accruing thereon.

4. All taxes levied and collected upon persons and property within the limits hereby added to the city of Richmond shall, for the period of three years from the passage of this act, be applied to the improvement, protection and police of the district so annexed.

5. It shall be lawful for the sheriff or other collectors of the county of Henrico to collect and make distress for any public dues or officers' fees which shall remain unpaid by the inhabitants embraced within the limits of the extension of the corporation of the city of Richmond, at the time when this act shall commence and be in force, and shall be accountble for the same in like manner as if this act had never been passed.

6. The county levy for the year eighteen hundred and sixty-seven shall be collected within the limits added to the city of Richmond by this bill, by the authorities of Henrico county, and no taxes shall be collected from the persons or property within said limits by the authorities of the city of Richmond for the year eighteen hundred and sixty-seven.

7. The council of the city of Richmond shall provide for the representation in the council of the city of Richmond of the inhabitants of the territory embraced in said extension.

8. This act shall be in force from and after the first day of July, eighteen hundred and sixty-seven.

THE CHARTER OF THE CITY OF RICHMOND.

AN ACT

PROVIDING A CHARTER FOR THE CITY OF RICHMOND, APPROVED MAY 24, 1870; AS AMENDED BY ACTS OF JULY 11, 1871, MARCH 29, 1871, MARCH 29, 1873, AND APRIL 16, 1874.

CHAPTER I.

ELECTIONS.

1. Be it enacted by the general assembly, That the territory contained within the limits prescribed by the act passed February thirteenth, eighteen hundred and sixty-seven, and entitled an act to extend and define the boundaries of the city of Richmond, and by any act hereafter passed by the general assembly of this state, shall be deemed and taken as the city of Richmond; and the inhabitants of the city of Richmond, for all purposes for which towns and cities are incorporated in this commonwealth, shall continue to be one body politic, in fact and in name, under the style and denomination of The City of Richmond, and as such shall have, exercise, and enjoy all the rights, immunities, powers, and privileges, and be subject to all the duties and obligations now incumbent and appertaining to said city as a municipal incorporation. *City limits* *Corporate name* *Powers*

2. The administration and government of the said city shall be vested in one principal officer, to be styled the mayor; two boards, to be called respectively the common council and board of aldermen of the city of Richmond; and in such other boards and officers as are heireinafter provided for. *April 16, 1874.* *Administration and government*

3. The said city shall be divided into five wards, which number of wards the city council hereafter may increase as they may deem it expedient. Every such division shall be made in such manner as to include an equal number of voters *Wards*

in each ward, as nearly as conveniently may be, consistent with the well defined limits of each ward. Until such revision be made, the boundary lines of wards shall remain as now established.

July 11, 1870. Special elections, how ordered

4. Whenever any special election shall be ordered by the city council for any object not provided for in the general election laws of the state, they shall communicate their order for the same to the judge of the corporation court, and the same proceedings shall be had as are provided by the laws of the state for special elections to fill vacancies in any municipal office.

July 11, 1870. Municipal elections, when held

5. The election of municipal officers hereinafter mentioned, shall be held on the fourth Thursday in May, eighteen hundred and seventy, and on the fourth Thursday in May in every second year thereafter, except the election of city treasurer, who shall be elected on the said Thursday in every third year thereafter; and the said election shall be conducted under the provisions of the general election laws of the state.

July 11, 1870. Vacancies, how filled

6. In cases of vacancies arising in any municipal office herein provided to be filled at the first election that may be held thereafter in said city, it shall be the duty of the mayor forthwith, upon the happening of such vacancy or vacancies, to certify the fact of such vacancy or vacancies to the judge of the corporation court, who shall issue his writ for election to fill such vacancy or vacancies in the manner prescribed in the general election laws of the state.

July 11, 1870. Oath of office of mayor and members of council, before whom taken

7. The mayor and the members of the city council, before entering upon the duties of their respective offices, shall be respectively sworn in accordance with the laws of this state. Such oaths may be administered to the mayor elect by any judge of a court of record commissioned to hold any such court within said city; and the members of the city council by the mayor, being himself first sworn as aforesaid, or by any judge of any court of record as aforesaid; and a certificate of such oaths having been respectively taken, shall be filed with the city clerk, and entered upon the journal of the city council.

Other officers

Every other person elected or appointed to any office under this act, or under any law or ordinance of the city council, shall, before he enters upon the duties of said office, take and subscribe said oath, and such other oaths as may be required by law or ordinance, before the mayor or city clerk, the said clerk having himself been first sworn by said mayor, or a judge of a court of record as aforesaid; and a certificate of the same shall be filed in the office of said city clerk. If any person, elected or appointed to any office in said city, shall neglect to take such oath for forty days after receiving notice of his election or appointment, or shall neglect, for the like space of time, to give such securities as may be required of him by the city council, as hereinafter provided, or as may be hereafter required by any law or ordinance, he shall be considered as having declined such office, and the same shall be deemed vacant; and whenever any such vacancy shall occur, another election shall be ordered or another appointment made, according to the directions of this act.

City clerk, certificates filed with

CHAPTER II.

MAYOR.

8. The mayor shall be elected by the qualified voters of the city of Richmond for the term of two years, and until his successor shall be elected, and qualify; and no person shall be qualified to hold the office of mayor except such as shall be qualified to hold office under the constitution of this state. His salary shall be fixed by the city council, payable at stated periods; and he shall receive no other compensation or emolument whatsoever; and no regulations diminishing such compensation, after it has been once fixed, shall be made to take effect until after the expiration of the term for which the mayor then in office shall have been elected. The salary of the mayor, when fixed, shall so continue until changed by the city council as aforesaid.

Mayor, how elected and term of office

Who may hold such office

Salary

9. He shall, by virtue of his office, possess all the jurisdiction and exercise all the powers and authority, in criminal cases, of a justice of the peace of said city, in addition to the powers hereby given to him by virtue of this act, or that may hereafter be given to him by virtue of any other act of assembly; but he shall receive no fees for his services as such justice of the peace.

His jurisdiction and powers

Shall receive no fees

10. It shall be his duty to communicate to the city council annually, as soon as may be after the commencement of the fiscal year, and oftener if he shall deem it expedient, or be required by said council, a general statement of the situation and condition of the city in relation to its government, finances

General statement to council

and improvement, with such recommendations as he may deem proper.

His powers over subordinate officers

11. He shall exercise a constant supervision over the conduct of all subordinate officers, have power and authority to investigate their acts, have access to all books and documents in their offices, and may examine said officers and their subordinates on oath. He shall also have power to suspend or remove such officers for misconduct in office, or neglect of duty, to be specified in the order of suspension or removal; but no such removal shall be made without reasonable notice to the officer complained of, and an opportunity afforded him to be heard in his defence. On the removal or suspension of such officer or officers, the mayor shall report the same, with his reasons therefor, to the city council, at their next stated meeting.

Shall not remove subordinate without notice

Removal or suspension to be reported to council

April 16, 1874. When president of council shall act as mayor

12. In case of the absence or inability of the mayor, the president of the board of aldermen shall possess the same powers and discharge the municipal duties of the mayor during such absence or inability.

Vacancy, how filled

13. In case a vacancy shall occur in the office of mayor, the city council shall elect a qualified person to supply the vacancy until the first general election which may be held in the city thereafter, when the vacancy shall be filled by election for the unexpired term.

CHAPTER III.

THE CITY COUNCIL.

April 16, 1874. Common council and board of aldermen; their election and terms of office, &c

14. The council of the city of Richmond shall be formed of two distinct branches: one of these shall be called the common council, and shall consist of five members from each ward, to be elected every two years; the other shall be called the board of aldermen, and shall consist of three members from each ward, to be elected every four years. The members of the board of common council and aldermen shall be residents of their respective wards, and shall not be less than twenty-one years of age. They shall be elected by the electors of their respective wards. Upon the assembling of the members of the board of aldermen, so elected, they shall be divided into two equal classes, to be numbered by lot. The term of service of the members of the first class shall expire

with that of the members of the common council elected at the first election after the passage of this act, and the term of service of the members of the second class shall expire with that of the members of the common council elected at the second election after the passage of this act, and this alternation shall continue, so that one-half of the members of the board of aldermen, may be chosen every two years.

15. When any vacancy shall occur in either branch by death, resignation, removal from the ward, failure to qualify, or from any other cause, the branch in which such vacancy occurs shall elect a qualified person to supply the vacancy until the next election for members of the council, which may be held in the city, when the vacancy shall be filled by election. April 16, 1874. Vacancies; how filled

16. Each branch of the council shall elect one of its members to act as president, who shall preside at its meetings, and continue in office for two years; and when from any cause he shall be absent, a president pro tempore shall be appointed, who shall preside during the absence of the president. The president or the president pro tempore, who shall preside when the proceedings of a previous meeting are read, shall sign the same. The president of each branch shall have power at any time to call a meeting of his branch of the council; and in case of his absence, sickness, disability or refusal, either branch may be convened by the order, in writing, of any three members of the branch. April 16, 1874. President; his term of office. Who shall sign proceedings when read. Called meetings

17. Each branch shall have authority to adopt such rules and to appoint such officers and clerks as it may deem proper for the regulation of its proceedings and for the convenient transaction of business; to compel the attendance of absent members; to punish its members for disorderly behavior; and, by a vote of two-thirds of its members, to expel a member for malfeasance or misfeasance in office. Each branch shall keep a journal of its proceedings, and its meetings shall be open, except when the public welfare shall require secrecy. April 16, 1874. Rules, officer and clerks. Power over the members. Journal

18. A majority of the members of each branch shall constitute a quorum for the transaction of business. On all ordinances or resolutions appropriating money, exceeding the sum of one hundred dollars, imposing taxes, or authorizing the borrowing of money, the yeas and nays shall be entered on the journal of each branch respectively. No vote shall April 16, 1874. Quorum. Yeas and nays when to be recorded

When vote reconsidered

be reconsidered or rescinded at any special meeting, unless at such special meeting there be present as large a number of members as were present when such vote was taken. No ordinance or resolution appropriating money exceeding the sum of one thousand dollars, imposing taxes, or authorizing the borrowing of money, shall be passed by the two branches on the same day, nor shall any such ordinance or resolution be valid unless at least three days intervene between its passage by the said branches respectively.

What ordinances or resolutions shall not be passed on same day by both branches

Intervention of three days required to make valid

Powers of city council

19. The city council shall have, subject to the provisions herein contained, the control and management of the fiscal and municipal affairs of the city, and of all property, real and personal, belonging to the said city; and may make such ordinances, orders and by-laws, relating to the same, as it shall deem proper and necessary. They shall likewise have the power to make such ordinances, by-laws, orders and regulations, as they may deem desirable to carry out the following powers, which are hereby vested in them:

Markets, &c

I. To establish markets in and for said city; appoint clerks and proper officers therefor; prescribe the times and places for holding the same; provide suitable buildings therefor, and to enforce such regulations as shall be necessary or proper to present huckstering, forestalling and regrating.

Work-houses, &c

II. To erect or provide, in or near the city, suitable workhonses, houses of correction or reformation, and houses for the reception and maintenance of the poor and destitute.

Poor of the city

They shall possess and exercise exclusive authority over all persons within the limits of the city, receiving or entitled to the benefits of the poor laws; appoint officers and other persons connected with the aforesaid institutions, and regulate pauperism within the limits of the city; and the council, through the agencies it shall appoint for the direction and management of the poor of the city, shall exercise the powers and perform the duties vested by law in overseers of the poor.

Public buildings, squares and parks

III. To erect and keep in order all public buildings necessary or proper for said city; to open, regulate and ornament public squares and parks.

City prison

IV. To erect within said city a city prison, and said prison may contain such apartments as shall be necessary for the safe keeping and employment of all persons confined therein.

V. To establish or enlarge water works and gas works within or without the limits of the said city; contract and agree with the owners of any land for the use or purchase thereof, or may have the same condemned for the location, extension or enlargement of their said works, the pipes connected therewith, or any of the fixtures or appurtenances thereof. They shall have power to protect from injury, by adequate penalties, the said works, pipes, fixtures and land, or anything connected therewith, within or without the limits of said city, and to prevent the pollution of the water in the river, by prohibiting the throwing of filth or offensive matter therein above the said water works, within one mile above said water works.

Water and gas works

Protection from injury

VI. To establish, construct and keep in order, alter or remove, landings, wharves and docks, on lands belonging to the city; and to lay and collect a reasonable duty on vessels coming to and using the same, and to regulate the manner of using other wharves and landings within the corporate limits; to prevent or remove all obstructions in and upon any landings, wharves or docks. They may also appoint port wardens for the port of said city, prescribe their duties, and fix their fees or compensation.

Landings, wharves and docks

Port wardens

VII. To close or extend, widen or narrow, lay out and graduate, pave, and otherwise improve, streets and public alleys in the city, and have them properly lighted and kept in good order; and they shall have over any street or alley in the city, which has been or may be ceded to the city, like authority as over other streets or alleys. They may build bridges in, and culverts under, said streets; and may prevent or remove any structure, obstruction or encroachment over, or under, or in a street or alley, or any sidewalk thereof, and may have shade trees planted along the said streets; and no company shall occupy with its works the streets of the city, without the consent of the council. In the meantime, no order shall be made, and no injunction shall be awarded, by any court or judge, to stay the proceedings of the city in the prosecution of their works, unless it be manifest that they, their officers, agents, or servants, are transcending the authority given them by this act, and that the interposition of the court is necessary to prevent injury that cannot be adequately compensated in damages.

Streets and public alleys

Bridges and culverts

Shade trees

Occupation of streets

No injunction against city, except when

Cumbering of streets, &c

VIII. To prevent the cumbering of streets, avenues, walks, public squares, lanes, alleys, or bridges, in any matter whatever.

City railways

IX. To authorize the laying down of city railway tracks, and the running of horse cars thereon, in the streets of the city, under such regulations as they may prescribe.

Route and grade of railroad, locomotives, &c

X. To determine and designate the route and grade of any railroad to be laid in said city, and to restrain and regulate the rate and speed of locomotives, engines and cars, upon the railroads within the said city, and may wholly exclude the said engines or cars, if they please: provided, no contract be thereby violated.

Breadth of wagon tires, &c

XI. To regulate and prescribe the breadth of tires upon the wheels of wagons, carts, and vehicles of heavy draught used upon the streets of said city: provided, however, that this section shall not apply to vehicles coming into and not owned in said city.

Gauging and inspection of liquors, &c

Weighing hay, &c

XII. To require spirituous liquors, wine, oil, molasses, vinegar, and spirits of turpentine, in casks, to be guaged and inspected; and may make sueh provision for the weighing of hay, fodder, oats, shucks, or other long forage, as will not be in conflict with the act passed the twenty-second of March, eighteen hundred and forty-seven, to prevent the authorities of said city from laying and collecting a tax on the bales of hay sent by the farmers of the state to said city. They may also provide for measuring corn, oats, grain, coal, stone, wood, lumber, boards, potatoes, and other articles for sale or barter.

Measuring grain, &c

Sealing weights and measures

XIII. To require every merchant, retailer, trader, and dealer in merchandise, or property of any description, which is sold by measure or weight, to cause their weights and measures to be sealed by the city sealer, and to be subject to his inspection; and may impose penalties for any violation of any such ordinance.

Military companies, agricultural and mechanical societies, &c

XIV. To grant aid to military companies and regiments organized within the city; to societies or associations for the advancement of agriculture and the mechanic arts; to scientific, literary and benevolent societies: provided, such societies or associations are located in or near the city, or in the case of agricultural societies, shall hold their fairs in or near the city; and to provide or aid in support of public libraries and public schools.

XV. To secure the inhabitants from contagious, infectious, or other dangerous diseases; to establish, erect, and regulate hospitals; to provide for and force the removal of patients to said hospitals; for the appointment and organization of a board of health for said city, with the authority necessary for the prompt and efficient performance of its duties.

Contagious diseases, hospitals and board of health

XVI. To provide, in or near the city, lands to be appropriated, improved, and kept in order, as places for the interment of the dead, and may charge for the use of ground in said places of interment, and may regulate the same; may prevent the burial of dead in the city, except in the public burial grounds; may regulate burials in said grounds, and may require the keeping and return of bills of mortality by the keepers or owners of all cemeteries.

Burial grounds

XVII. To establish a quarantine ground for the city; but if said ground shall extend below the eastern boundary of the city on the river, the assent of the county court of Henrico shall be first obtained.

Quarantine

XVIII. To require and compel the abatement and removal of all nuisances within said city, at the expense of the person or persons causing the same, or the owner or owners of the ground whereon the same shall be; to prevent or regulate slaughter-houses and soap and candle factories within said city, or the exercise of any dangerous, offensive, or unhealthy business, trade, or employment therein, and to regulate the transportation of coal and other articles through the streets of the city.

Abatement of nuisances

Slaughter houses, soap and candle factories

XIX. If any ground in the said city shall be subject to be covered by stagnant water, or if the owner or owners, occupier or occupiers thereof, shall permit any offensive or unwholesome substance to remain or accumulate therein, the council may cause such ground to be filled up, raised, or drained, or may cause such substances to be covered or to be removed therefrom, and may collect the expense of so doing from the said owner or owners, occupier or occupiers, or any of them, by distress and sale, in the same manner in which taxes, levied upon real estate for the benefit of said city, are authorized to be collected: provided, that reasonable notice shall be first given to the said owners or their agents. In case of non-resident owners, who have no agent in said city, such notice may be given by publication for not less than four weeks in any newspaper printed in said city.

Stagnant water, filth, &c., how removed

Notice to owner

Powder magazines, &c

XX. To direct the location of all buildings for storing gunpowder or other combustible substances, and to regulate the sale and use of gunpowder, fire-crackers or fire-works manufactured or prepared therefrom, kerosene oil, nitro-glycerine, camphine, burning fluid, or other combustible material; to regulate the exhibition of fire-works, the discharge of fire-arms, the use of candles and lights in barns, stables and other buildings, and to restrain the making of bonfires in streets and yards.

Fireworks, &c

Hogs, dogs, &c

XXI. To prevent hogs, dogs, and other animals from running at large in the city, and may subject the same to such confiscations, regulations, and taxes, as they may deem proper; and the council may prohibit the raising or keeping of hogs in the city.

Fast driving, flying kites, abuse of animals, &c

XXII. To prevent the riding or driving of horses or other animals at an improper speed; to prevent the flying of kites, throwing stones, or the engaging in any employment or sports in the streets or public alleys, dangerous or annoying to passengers, and to prohibit and punish the abuse of animals.

Drunkards, vagrants, &c

XXIII. To restrain and punish drunkards, vagrants, mendicants, and street beggars.

Prevention of vice and immorality, gaming houses, &c

XXIV. To prevent vice and immorality; to preserve public peace and good order; to prevent and quell riots, disturbances, and disorderly assemblages; to suppress houses of ill-fame and gaming houses; to prevent lewd, indecent, and disorderly conduct or exhibitions in the city, and to expel therefrom persons guilty of such conduct who shall not have resided therein as much as one year.

Vending liquors without license, &c

XXV. To forbid and prevent the vending or other disposition of liquors and intoxicating drinks, to be drunk in any canal boat, store, or other place not duly licensed; and to forbid the selling, or given to be drunk, any intoxicating liquors to any child or young person without the consent of his or her parents or guardian; and for any violation of any such ordinance, may impose fines in addition to those prescribed by the laws of the state.

Prevention of improper persons coming into the city, &c

XXVI. To prevent the coming into the city, from beyond the limits of the state, of persons having no ostensible means of support, or of persons who may be dangerous to the peace and safety of the city; and for this purpose may require any railroad company, or the captain or master of any vessel bringing such passengers to Richmond, to enter into bond, with satisfactory security, that such persons shall not become chargeable to the city for one year, or may compel such company, captain, or master to take them back from whence they came, and compel the persons to leave the city if they have not been in the city more than thirty days before the order is given.

20. Where, by the provision of this act, the city council have authority to pass ordinances on any subject, they may prescribe any penalty, not exceeding five hundred dollars (except where a penalty is herein otherwise provided for), for a violation thereof, and may provide that the offender, on failing to pay the penalty recovered, shall be imprisoned in the jail of said city for any term not exceeding three calendar months; which penalties may be prosecuted and recovered, with costs, in the name of the city of Richmond. And the city council may subject the parent or guardian of any minor, or the master or mistress of any apprentice, to any such penalty for any such offence committed by such minor or apprentice.

Power of council to prescribe penalties and imprisonment

21. No ordinance hereafter passed by the city council, for the violation of which any penalty is imposed, shall take effect until the same shall have been published for five days consecutively in one of the daily newspapers of said city, to be designated by the said council. A record or entry made by the clerk of said city, or a copy of such record or entry, duly certified by him, shall be prima facie evidence of the time of such first publication; and all laws, regulations and ordinances of the city council may be read in evidence in all courts of justice, and in all proceedings before any officer, body, or board in which it shall be necessary to refer thereto, either from a copy thereof certified by the clerk of said city, or from the volume of ordinances printed by the authority of the city council.

April 16, 1874. Publication of ordinances

How used as evidence

22. The council shall not take or use any private property for streets or other public purpose without making to the owner or owners thereof just compensation for the same. But in all cases where the said city cannot by agreement obtain title to the ground necessary for such purposes, it shall be lawful for the said city to apply to and obtain from the circuit or county court of the county in which the land shall be situated, or to the proper court of the city having jurisdiction of such matters, if the subject lies within this city,

Private property, how taken for public purpose

for authority to condemn the same; which shall be applied for and proceeded with as provided by law.

Where building or fence encroaches upon street, how removed

23. In every case where a street in said city has been or shall be encroached upon by any fence, building, or otherwise, the city council may require the owner or owners, if known, and if unknown, the occupant or occupants of the premises so encroaching, to remove the same. If such removal shall not be made within the time ordered by the council, they may impose a penalty of five dollars for each and every day that it is allowed to continue thereafter, and may cause the encroachment to be removed, and collect from the owner all reasonable charges therefor, with costs, by the same processes that they are hereinafter empowered to collect taxes. No encroachment upon any street, however long continued, shall constitute an adverse possession to, or confer any rights upon, the person claiming thereunder, as against said city.

Penalty

No length of encroachment to give adverse possession

Five years public use of street, &c. to vest right of city therein

24. Whenever any street, alley, or lane, shall have been opened to and used as such by the public for the period of five years, the same shall thereby become a street, alley, or lane, for all purposes, and the city shall have the same authority and jurisdiction over, and right and interest therein, as they have by law over the streets, alleys and lanes laid out by it. And any street or alley reserved in the division or sub-division into lots of any portion of the territory within the corporate limits of the city, by a plat or plan of record, shall be deemed and held to be dedicating to the public use; and the council shall have authority, upon the petition of any person interested therein, to open such street or alley, or any portion of the same. No agreement between, or release of interest by, the persons owning the lands immedidiately contiguous to any such alley or street, whether the same has been opened and used by the public or not, shall avail or operate to abolish said alley or street as to divest the interest of the public therein, or the authority of the council over the same.

Street or alley reserved in record plat deemed to be public

No agreement between contiguous owners to divest public use

How expense of new street, &c., to be determined

25. Whenever any new street shall be laid out, a street graded or paved, a culvert built, or any other public improvement whatsoever made, the city council may determine what portion, if any, of the expenses thereof ought to be paid from the public treasury, and what portion by the owners of real estate benefited, or may order and direct that the whole

expense be assessed upon the owners of real estate benefited thereby. But no such public improvement shall be made to be defrayed in whole or in part by a local assessment, until first requested by a petition signed by at least a majority of the owners of property to be assessed for such improvement, or unless at least three-fourths of all the council shall concur in voting any improvement to be expedient, or in determining to make the same after allegations have been heard; in which case, no petition or request shall be necessary. The council shall have the same powers to collect such local assessments for improvements as are hereinafter vested in them for the collection of taxes.

When public improvement to be made by local assessment

Collection of local assessment

26. The city council shall grant and pay to all city officers, clerks, and assistants, elected or appointed under or in pursuance of this act, such salaries or compensation as the said city council may from time to time deem proper, or shall be fixed by this or any other act of assembly hereafter enacted.

Salaries of city officers

27. If any person, having been an officer of said city, shall not, within ten days after he shall have vacated or been removed from office, and upon notification and request of the city clerk, or within such time thereafter as the city council shall allow, deliver over to his successor in office all the property, books, and papers belonging to the city or appertaining to such office, in his possession or under his control, he shall forfeit and pay to the city the sum of five hundred dollars, to be sued for and recovered with cost. And all books, records, and documents used in any such office by virtue of any provisions of this act, or of any ordinance or order of the city council, or any superior officer of said city, shall be deemed the property of said city and appertain to said office, and the chief officer thereof shall be responsible therefor.

Penalty for failure of former officer to deliver to his successor all public property, &c., under his charge, &c

CHAPTER IV.

CITY OFFICERS.

28. There shall be one auditor, one city treasurer, one collector of city taxes, one commissioner of the revenue, one city attorney, one city engineer, one city clerk, and such clerks and assistants as the city council may see fit, by ordinance, to prescribe and furnish.

City officers

July 11, 1870. Additional officers and clerks

29. The council may appoint such officers and clerk's as they may deem proper, in addition to those herein provided for, and define their powers and prescribe their duties and compensation, and may take from any of the officers, and so forth, appointed, bonds, with sureties, in such penalties as to the council may seem fit, payable to the city by its corporate name, with condition for the faithful performance of said duties. All officers appointed by the council may be removed from office at its pleasure. In case of vacancies occurring in any municipal office, when it is not herein otherwise provided, the city council shall elect a qualified person to fill such office during the unexpired term.

Removals by council

Elections to fill vacancies

Liabilities of such officers, their securities, &c., on their official bonds

Jurisdiction over same

30. The parties to bonds taken in pursuance of the preceding section, their heirs, devisees, executors and administrators, shall be subject to the same proceedings on the said bonds for enforcing the conditions and terms thereof, by motion or otherwise, before the circuit court of the city of Richmond, or any other courts held in the city which may succeed to the civil common law jurisdiction of said court, that collectors of the county levy and their securities are or shall be subject to, on their bonds, for enforcing payment of the county levies.

July 11, 1870. City auditor; his term

31. The city auditor shall be elected by the qualified voters of the city of Richmond. He shall hold his office for the term of two years, and until his successor be elected and qualify, unless sooner removed. He shall hold his office in such place as may be designated and prescribed by the city council. He shall give bond, with sureties, to the amount of not less than thirty thousand dollars, which shall be determined by the city council, before he enters upon the duties of his office; said bond to be approved by the said city council, entered on their record, and filed in the office of the city clerk. The said auditor shall open and keep, in a neat and methodical manner, a complete set of books, under the direction of the city council, wherein shall be stated, among other things, the appropriations of the year for each distinct object and branch of expenditure, and also the receipts from each and every source of revenue, so far as he can ascertain the same. Said books, and all papers, vouchers, contracts, bonds, receipts, and other things, kept in said office, shall be subject to the examination of the mayor, the members of the city council, or any committee or committees thereof.

Penalty of bond

What books and accounts he shall keep

32. The said auditor shall be charged with and exercise a general supervision over all the officers of the city charged in any manner with the receipt, collection, or disbursement of the city revenues, and the collection and return of such revenues into the city treasury. He shall have charge of all deeds, mortgages, contracts, judgments, notes, bonds, debts, choses in action, belonging to the said city, except such as are confided to the custody of the city clerk, and such other papers as may be committed to his care by the city council, by ordinance or otherwise.

Charge of auditor over city revenue officers

Custody of city deeds, contracts, &c.

33. The said auditor shall have power to examine all accounts, claims and demands for or against the said city; and no money shall be drawn from the treasury or paid by the city to any person, except as herein otherwise provided, unless that balance due or payable be first settled and adjusted by the said auditor; and for the purpose of ascertaining the true state of any balance or balances so due, he shall have, and is hereby clothed with, full power and authority to administer an oath or oaths to the claimant or claimants, or any other person or persons, whom he may think proper to examine as to any fact, matter, or thing concerning the correctness of any account, claim, or demand presented; and the person so sworn shall, if he swear falsely, be guilty of wilful and corrupt perjury, and be subject to punishment by imprisonment in the penitentiary for not less than one nor more than five years.

He shall audit all claims against the city &c

He may administer oaths

34. All money found to be due and payable by the said auditor to any person, shall be drawn by said auditor by warrant on the treasurer, stating the particular fund or appropriation to which the same is chargeable and the person to whom payable; and no money shall be drawn from the treasury except on the warrant of the auditor, as aforesaid. But the auditor is forbidden to issue his warrant for the payment of any money in excess of the appropriation on account of which said money is drawn.

How money found due by auditor paid

No warrant to be issued in excess of appropriation

35. It shall be the duty of said auditor, as nearly as may be, to charge all officers in the receipt of revenues or moneys of the city, with the whole amount, from time to time, of such receipts; he shall also require of all officers in recept of city moneys that they shall submit reports thereof, with vouchers and receipts of payment therefor into the city treasury, weekly or monthly, or as often as he shall see fit to re-

Revenue officers, how charged

Reports to auditor, how often

Notice to delinquent officer

quire the same by any regulation which he may adopt; and if any such officer shall neglect to make an adjustment of his accounts, when required as aforesaid, and to pay over such moneys so received, it shall then be the duty of said auditor to issue notice in writing, directed to such officer and his securities, requiring him or them, within ten days, to make settlement of his said account with the auditor, and to pay over the balance of moneys found to be due and in his hands belonging to the said city, according to the books of said auditor; and in case of the refusal or neglect of such officer to adjust his said accounts or pay over said balance to the treasurer as required, it shall then be the duty of said auditor to make report of the delinquency of such officer to the mayor, who shall at once suspend him from office, proceed forthwith to institute the necessary proceeding for the removal of such officer from office, and immediately on his removal, institute suit in the name of said city against him and his securities to recover the balance of moneys so found to be due and in his hands belonging to said city.

Delinquency reported to mayor, who has power to suspend, &c

Auditor's annual statement

36. The auditor shall make out an annual statement, as soon as possible after the end of each fiscal year, giving a full and detailed statement of all the receipts and expenditures during the said year. The said statement shall also detail the liabilities and expenditures during the year, the liabilities and resources of said city, the condition of all unexpended appropriations and contracts unfulfilled, the balances of money then remaining in the treasury, with all sums due and outstanding, the names of all persons who may have become defaulters to the city, and the amounts in their hands unaccounted for, and all other things necessary to exhibit the true financial condition of the city.

Annual estimates to council

37. The auditor shall annually submit to the city council, at their first stated meeting after the beginning of the fiscal year, a report of the estimates necessary, as nearly as may be, to defray the expenses of the city government during the current fiscal year. He shall in said report class the different objects and branches of said city expenditure, giving, as nearly as may be, the amount required for each; and for this purpose he is authorized to require of all city officers and heads of departments their statements of the condition and expense of their respective departments and offices, with any proposed improvement, and the probable expense thereof,

Auditor may require heads of departments to make statements to him of contracts already made and unfinished, and the amount of unexpended appropriations of the preceding year. He shall also in such report show the aggregate income of the preceding fiscal year, from all sources; the amount of liabilities outstanding upon which interest is to be paid, and of bonds and city debts payable during the year, when due and where payable, so that the city council may fully understand the money exigencies and demands of the city for the current year.

What auditor's report shall show

38. In addition to the other duties of the said auditor, it is hereby made his duty, on the last day of each and every month, to make out a monthly statement, giving a full and detailed account of all moneys received, from what sources and on what account received, and of all moneys ordered to be paid or drawn for by warrant by him, and on what account the same has been paid; and shall deliver said statement to the said city council at their next meeting, to be filed, after the adjournment of said council, by the city clerk with the papers belonging to his office.

Auditor's monthly statement

39. There shall be elected by the qualified voters of the city of Richmond, in the same manner as is provided hereinbefore for the election of mayor of said city, at the first charter election, and every three years thereafter, one city treasurer, who shall hold his office for the term of three years, and until his successor be elected and qualified, unless sooner removed from office. He shall give bond, with sureties, to the amount of not less than one hundred thousand dollars; said bond to be approved by the city council, entered on their records, and filed in the city clerk's office.

City treasurer

His bond

40. The said treasurer shall receive all moneys belonging to the city, and shall keep his office in some place designated by the council. He shall have the custody of the corporate seal. He shall keep his books and accounts in such manner as the city council may prescribe, and such books and accounts shall always be subject to the inspection of the mayor and any member of the city council, or any committee or committees thereof.

His duties; keeper of seal, &c

41. No money shall be paid out by the treasurer except upon the warrant of the auditor, issued as hereinbefore provided, and he shall keep a separate account of each fund or appropriation, and the debits or credits belonging thereto.

How money paid out

How money paid to treasurer

42. All moneys to be paid into the treasury of the city, except the bills for gas and water, and such other assessments as the city council may so ordain, shall be paid by the person liable to pay the same, or his agent, to the treasurer, in the following manner: a warrant shall first be obtained from the auditor, directing the treasurer to receive the sum to be paid, specifying on what account the payment is to be made. Upon the payment of the money to the treasurer, he shall give a receipt for the same, which shall be carried to the auditor, and his receipt therefor shall be the acquittance of the party making the payment. Bills for gas and water, and such other assessments as the city council may so ordain, shall be paid directly to the treasurer, who shall keep an account thereof, and make daily reports of such receipts to the auditor.

Gas and water bills

Treasurer's monthly account

43. The treasurer shall, at the end of each and every month, and oftener if required, render an account to the auditor, showing the state of treasury at the date of such account, and the balance of moneys in the treasury. He shall also, if required so to do by the auditor, accompany such account with a statement of all moneys received into the treasury, and on what account, with a list of all warrants redeemed and paid by him during the month.

Treasurer's annual report to council

44. The treasurer shall also report to the city council, at the end of each fiscal year, and oftener if required, a full and detailed account of all receipts and expenditures during the preceding fiscal year, and the state of the treasury. He shall also keep a register of all warrants, their date, amount, number, the fund from which paid, and the person to whom paid, specifying also the time of payment; and all such warrants shall be examined, at the time of making such annual report to the city council, by a committee thereof, who shall examine and compare the same with the books of the auditor, and report discrepancies, if any, to the city council.

Register of warrants

Special funds

45. All moneys received on any special assessment shall be held by the treasurer as a special fund, to be applied to the payment for which the assessment was made; and said money shall be used for no other purpose whatsoever.

Where funds kept

46. The treasurer may be required to keep all moneys in his hands belonging to the city in such place or places of deposit as the city council may, by ordinance, provide, order, establish, or direct. Such moneys shall be kept distinct and

separate from his own moneys; and he is hereby expressly prohibited from using, either directly or indirectly, the corporation money, or warrants in his custody and keeping, for his own use and benefit, or that of any person or persons whomsoever; and any violation of this provision shall subject him to immediate removal from office. In case of his removal, the city council shall elect a qualified person to fill said office until the next general election which may be held in the city, when the qualified voters of said city shall, as in other cases, fill such vacancy by an election of a successor, who shall hold his office for the remainder, if any, of the unexpired term of the officer removed.

Penalty for personal use

If removed, vacancy filled by council till election

47. There shall be elected by the qualified voters of the city of Richmond, one collector of the city taxes, who shall hold his office for the period of two years, and until his successor shall be elected and qualify, unless sooner removed from office. He shall give bond, with sureties, to the amount of not less than fifty thousand dollars—said bond to be approved by the city council, entered on their records, and filed in the office of the city clerk.

July 11, 1870. Collector of city taxes; term of office

Penalty of bond, &c

48. Said collector shall collect all taxes and assessments which may be levied by said city, and perform such other duties as may be herein prescribed or ordained by the city council. He shall keep his office in such place as may be designated and prescribed by the city council, and shall keep in his said office, besides his collection and revenue warrants, such other books, vouchers, records, and accounts, as the city council may direct and prescribe, all of which shall be subject to the inspection and examination of the mayor, the members of the city council, or any committee or committees thereof.

His duties, &c

His books, &c. to be inspected by mayor

49. The said collector shall make report in writing, under oath, to the auditor, weekly, or oftener if required, the amount of all moneys collected by him, and shall pay the same into the city treasury in the manner hereinbefore provided. At the end of each fiscal year he shall submit to the city council a statement of all moneys by him collected during the year, and the particular warrant, assessment, or account upon which collected, and the balance of moneys uncollected on the warrants in his hands or returned to the auditor, and a copy of such statement shall also be filed with the auditor of said city.

Collector's weekly report to auditor

His annual report to council

3

July 11, 1870. Money not to be kept in his hands; penalty therefor

50. The said collector is expressly prohibited from keeping the money of the city in his hands, or in the hands of any person or corporation, to his use, beyond the time prescribed for the payment of the same into the city treasury, and any violation of this provision shall subject him to immediate removal from office.

Collector to sell real estate for non-payment of taxes

51. It shall be the duty of said collector to conduct all the proceedings and render all the service necessary to perfect the sale and transfer of real estate in said city, where the same shall be sold or advertised for sale for the non-payment of any tax or assessment imposed by the city council, as hereinafter provided.

Collector's deputies

52. The said collector may, with the consent of the city council, appoint a deputy or deputies, who may be removed from office by the said collector, by the mayor, or by the city council. During the continuance in office of the said collector, a deputy of his may discharge any of the duties of the office of collector; but the collector and his sureties shall be liable therefor.

Penalty for collector's selling land for which he has received taxes

53. If the said collector shall receive any money for taxes or assessments, giving a receipt therefor, for any land or parcel of land, and afterwards sell the same, at any sale for taxes or assessments, for the tax or assessment which has been so paid and receipted for by himself or his deputy, he and his sureties shall be liable to the holder of the certificate given to the purchaser at the sale for double the amount on the face of the certificate, to be demanded within three years from the date of sale, and recovered in any court having jurisdiction of the amount; and the city shall in no case be liable to the holder of such certificate.

July 11, 1870. Commissioner of revenue

54. There shall be elected by the qualified voters of the city of Richmond, one commissioner of the revenue, who shall hold his office for the period of two years, and until his successor shall be elected and qualify, unless sooner removed from office. He shall give bond with sureties, to the amount of not less than five thousand dollars; said bond to be approved by the city council, entered on their record, and filed in the office of the city clerk. In case a vacancy shall occur in the office of commissioner of the revenue, the city council shall elect a qualified person to fill said office until the next general election which may be held in the city, when the vacancy shall be filled by election for the unexpired term.

His bond, where filed

Vacancy, how filled

55. The said commissioner of the revenue shall perform all the duties in relation to the assessment of property for the purpose of levying city taxes that may be ordered by the city council. He shall keep his office in such place as may be designated and prescribed by the city council, and shall keep therein such books, schedules, and records, and in such manner as the mayor and city council may direct and prescribe; which books, records, and other papers shall be subject to the inspection and examination of the mayor, the members of the city council, or any committee or committees thereof, and of the collector of city taxes. His duties

56. To aid the commissioner of the revenue in his duties, the clerks of the several courts of the city of Richmond and of the county of Henrico shall, as required respectively, deliver to him such lists as are mentioned in the seventh and eighth sections of the thirty-fifth chapter of the Code of Virginia of eighteen hundred and sixty, as far as may relate to lands in said city. Clerks of Richmond and Henrico courts to deliver to him list of deeds, &c

57. As soon as said commissioner of the revenue shall have ascertained the value of all the real and personal property taxable in said city, he shall make complete schedules of the same, and leave them in his office open to the inspection and examination of all persons interested therein; and he shall give notice by six days' publication in two of the daily newspapers of said city of the time and place, when and where such inspection and examination may be made. Said schedules shall be kept open for the period of ten days from the time of the first publication of such notice, so that any person feeling aggrieved by the assessment of his or her property, may appear and make his or her objection. The said commissioner of the revenue shall hear and consider all objections which may be made, and shall have power to alter, add to, take from, and otherwise correct and revise his assessment; and he shall have power to examine any person on oath as to the value of his personal property, and also to examine under oath such other persons as witnesses in relation thereto as he may deem proper, and for that purpose may administer oaths and issue process to compel the attendance of witnesses before him. Any person feeling aggrieved at the decision of the said commissioner of the revenue may appeal to the city council, whose decision shall be final. Any person who shall refuse to make under oath a full disclosure of all the facts Commissioner's schedule How inspection of schedule had How long schedule kept open Commissioner's power as to schedule Party aggrieved may appeal to council Penalty for failure to give commissioner information

necessary to enable said commissioner of the revenue to make a fair and just assessment of his personal taxable property, when duly called upon by said commissioner of the revenue so to do, or to answer such questions as may be put to him in relation thereto, shall be assessed a gross sum, in the judgment of the commissioner of the revenue, double the correct assessment of his personal taxable property.

Commissioner's assistants

58. The said commissioner of the revenue may, with the consent of the city council, appoint an assistant or assistants, who may be removed from office by the said commissioner, by the mayor, or by the city council. During the continuance in office of the said commissioner, an assistant of his may discharge any of the duties of the office of commissioner; but the commissioner and his sureties shall be liable therefor.

July 11, 1870. City attorney

His term, compensation, duties, &c

59. The city council shall appoint a suitable and proper person, who shall be the attorney and counsel for the corporation, who shall hold his office for the term of two years, unless sooner removed, and until his successor shall be appointed and qualify. He shall receive such compensation as the council may determine, to be paid by the city. Said attorney shall have the management, charge, and control of all the law business of the corporation and the departments thereof, and of all the law business in which the city shall be interested; shall draw all leases, deeds, and legal papers for the same, and be the legal adviser of the mayor, city council, or any committee thereof, and of the several departments of said corporation; and when required, shall furnish written opinions upon any subjects involving questions of law submitted to him by them. He shall appear as counsel for the said corporation in any civil case in which it is interested, depending in any court in the city of Richmond; and when the constitutionality or validity of any ordinance is brought in issue in any penal prosecution, or when the mayor shall direct a prosecution for a nuisance, he shall appear for the prosecution when the case shall come into court. He shall perform such other duties as are or may be required of him for the city by any ordinance or resolution of the city council.

May authorize another to appear for him

60. He shall have power and authority, from time to time, during his continuance in office, with the consent of the mayor, to authorize an attorney or other person to appear

for him in his name and on behalf of said corporation, and conduct and defend suits and proceedings in all courts and places.

61. Said attorney for the corporation shall keep his office in such place as the city council may direct, and shall keep therein a docket of all the cases to which the city may be a party in any court of record, in which shall be briefly entered all steps taken in such causes; and said docket shall at all times be open to the inspection of the mayor, the members of the city council, and the city auditor. His office and docket

62. There shall be appointed by the city council one engineer for the city, who shall hold his office for the period of two years, and until his successor shall be appointed and qualify, unless sooner removed from office. He shall give bond, with sureties, to the amount of not less than five thousand dollars, said bond to be approved by the city council and filed in the office of the city clerk. July 11, 1870. Engineer of city; his term, bond, &c

63. The said engineer shall have such assistants and clerks as the city council may allow and approve; but such assistants or clerks may be removed at any time by the mayor or by the city council. His assistants and clerks

64. The said engineer shall be the general superintendent of the streets, culverts, public buildings, and all public improvements. He shall make such surveys, reports, drawings, plans, specifications and estimates as the city council may require of him, and do, in relation thereto, whatever else it may direct. All surveys or other acts, which shall be made or done by said engineer, shall be as valid and effectual as if the same were done by a surveyor of a county. He shall keep his office in such place as the city council may direct, and shall keep therein all maps, drawings and papers pertaining to his office. He shall keep a record of all his proceedings, and a set of books, in which shall be entered, under appropriate heads, the receipts and expenditures of his department; and all the books and papers of his office shall be open at all times to the inspection of the mayor, to the members of the city council, or to any committee or committees thereof. His duties His surveys valid His office, records, &c

65. There shall be one city clerk appointed by the city council, who shall hold his office for the period of two years, and until his successor shall be appointed and qualified, unless sooner removed from office by the city council. City clerk

April 16, 1874. His duties

66. The said city clerk shall attend the meetings of the common council, and keep a record of its proceedings. He shall keep all papers that by the provisions of this act, or by direction of the city council, or either of its branches, are required to be kept or filed with him. It shall also be his duty to make and present to the mayor a transcript of every ordinance, resolution or order passed by both of the branches of the city council. He shall likewise transmit to the auditor a transcript of all ordinances, resolutions or orders appropriating money, or authorizing the payment of money, the issue of bonds or notes; and to the heads of all departments of the city government all ordinances, resolutions or orders relating to their departments. He shall likewise give information to parties presenting communications or petitions to the city council of the final action of the council on such communications or petitions. He shall publish such reports and ordinances as the city council are required by this act to publish, and such other reports and ordinances as the said council may direct, and shall, in general, perform such other acts and duties as the city council, or either branch thereof, may from time to time require of him.

Transcript of ordinances, &c. to mayor

To auditor

He shall inform parties interested of final action of council

He shall publish reports and ordinances

April 16, 1874. City council may contract loans redeemable within thirty-four years

67. The city council may, in the name and for the use of the city, contract loans, or cause to be issued certificates of debt or bond; but such loans, certificates or bonds shall not be irredeemable for a period greater than thirty-four years: provided, however, that they shall not contract such loans or issue such certificates of debt or bonds for the purpose of subscribing to the stock, or appropriating money or bonds for the benefit of any company incorporated for a work of internal improvement or other purposes, without first being authorized so to do by three-fourths of the legal voters of the city voting on the question; and the council shall, when such debt or loan is created, provide a sinking fund for the payment of the same. Neither shall the city endorse the bonds of any such company without the same authority: provided, however, that the said council may issue or cause to be issued bonds for other purposes than those for railroads or internal improvement companies; but the bonds or interest bearing debt of the city of Richmond shall not in the aggregate exceed eighteen per centum of the assessed value of the taxable real estate of said city, and any excess of such bonded or interest bearing debt over and above the limit

Proviso

herein prescribed, which may be created or issued in violation of this provision, shall be void as to said city.

68. There shall be set apart, annually, from the accruing revenues of the city, a sum not less than one per centum of the city debt existing at the commencement of this act. The fund thus set apart shall be called the sinking fund; and shall be applied to the payment or purchase of the principal of the city debt. If no part be redeemable, then the residue of the sinking fund shall be invested in the bonds or certificates of debt of the city, and applied to the payment of the city debt as it shall become redeemable. Whenever hereafter there shall be contracted by the city any debt not payable within the next twelve months, there shall be set apart annually for thirty-four years, or until the debt is paid, a sum exceeding by one per centum the aggregate amount of the annual interest agreed to be paid thereon at the time of its contraction, which sum shall be applied and invested towards the payment of such debt in the same manner as hereinbefore provided for the present existing debt of the city.

July 11, 1870. Sinking fund; how provided

69. For the execution of its powers and duties, the city council may raise annually, by taxes and assessments in said city, such sums of money as they shall deem necessary to defray the expenses of the same, and in such manner as they shall deem expedient, in accordance with the laws of this state and the United States: provided, however, that they shall impose no tax on the bonds of said city, nor on any capital invested in real estate or employed in manufacture outside the city limits, although the person or persons engaged in said business or manufacture have a place of business in said city. Neither shall they impose any tax at the same time upon the stock of a corporation and upon the dividends thereon; nor upon any capital, interest, income, or dividends when a license or other tax is imposed upon the business in which the capital is employed, or upon the principal money, credit, or stock from which the interest, income, or dividend is derived. Said taxes shall be equal and uniform upon all property, both real and personal. The capital invested in all business operations shall be assessed and taxed as other property. Assessments upon all stock shall be according to the market value thereof.

Taxation

Proviso

Things not to be taxed

Taxes to be equal and uniform

Stock assessed at market value

70. The city council may grant or refuse licenses, and may require taxes to be paid on such licenses, to agents of insu-

Licenses

rance companies whose principal office is not located in said city; to auctioneers; to public, theatrical, or other performances or shows; to keepers of billiard tables, ten-pin alleys, and pistol galleries; to hawkers and pedlers in the city, or persons to sell goods by sample therein; to agents for the sale or renting of real estate; to commission merchants, and all other business which cannot be reached by the ad valorem system under the preceding section. They may also grant or refuse such license to all sellers of wine or spirituous or fermented liquors, and require taxes to be paid on such license, in addition to other taxes imposed.

Licenses on liquors

Taxes on wagons, &c

71. The council may grant or refuse licenses to owners or keepers of wagons, drays, carts, hacks, and other wheeled carriages kept or employed in the city for hire, and may require the owners or keepers of wagons, drays and carts, using them in the city, to take out a license therefor, and may require taxes to be paid thereon, and subject the same to such regulations as they may deem proper, and prescribe their fees and compensation.

Council may vest in collector powers of sheriff to collect taxes

72. The council may vest in the collector of the city taxes, and of assessments for the use of water, gas, or other purposes, any or all of the powers which are now or may hereafter be vested in a sheriff as collector of the state taxes; may prescribe the mode of his proceeding, and the mode of proceeding against him for the failure to perform his duties.

May prescribe his mode of proceeding, and proceeding against him

All goods, &c. liable for taxes; trust or mortgage no bar while goods remain in hands of grantor, or otherwise

73. All goods and chattels, wheresoever found, may be distrained and sold for taxes assessed and due thereon; and no deed of trust or mortgage upon goods or chattels shall prevent the same from being distrained and sold for taxes assessed against the grantor in such deed while such goods and chattels remain in the grantor's possession; nor shall any such deed prevent the goods and chattels conveyed from being distrained and sold for taxes assessed thereon, no matter in whose possession they may be found.

Where tenant or fiduciary pays taxes

74. Any payment of taxes made by the tenant, unless under an express contract contained in his lease, shall be a credit against the person to whom he owes the rent, and where any tax is paid by a fiduciary on the interest of profit of moneys of an estate invested under an order of court or otherwise, the tax shall be refunded out of such estate.

Lien on real estate for taxes

75. There shall be a lien on real estate for the city taxes as assessed thereon from the commencement of the year for

which they were assessed. The city council may require real estate in the city, delinquent for the non-payment of taxes, to be sold for said taxes, with interest thereon at the rate of twelve per centum per annum, and such per centum as they may prescribe for charges. Such real estate shall be sold, and may be redeemed under the provisions hereinafter made.

How delinquent land sold

76. The collector of city taxes shall, under the direction of the city council, cause a notice of the time and place of such sale to be published, in all the daily newspapers published in said city, at least ten days previous to such sale; and he shall also cause to be published in one or more of said daily papers, on some day not more than twenty days nor less than ten days previous to such sale, a list of the several parcels of real estate so to be sold, in the same manner as the same is described in the assessment rolls in which the said tax or assessment is imposed thereon, together with the name of the person to whom each parcel is assessed, and the amount of the tax or assessment thereon.

Notice of such sale

77. If such tax or assessment, and the per. centage, interest, and expenses aforesaid, be not paid previous to the day for which said sale was advertised, or on some day immediately thereafter, to which said sale may be adjourned, the collector shall proceed to make sale, accordingly, of the said several parcels of real estate, or so much thereof as may be necessary, to the highest bidder; and the sale may be adjourned from day to day until it shall be completed. On such sale the collector shall execute to the purchaser a certificate of sale, in which the property purchased shall be described, and the aggregate amount of tax or assessment, with charges and expenses specified; but the collector shall not for himself, either directly or indirectly, purchase any real estate so sold.

How such sale made

Certificate of sale

78. If at any such sale no bid shall be made for any such parcel of land, or such bid shall not be equal to the tax or assessment, with interest and charges, then the same shall be struck off to the city. On such sale the collector shall execute to the city a certificate of sale, in which the property purchased shall be described, and the aggregate amount of tax or assessment, with charges and expenses specified, and shall deposit such certificate with the auditor.

When city may become purchaser

How and within what period such estate may be redeemed

79. The owner of any real estate so sold, his heirs or assigns, or any person having a right to charge such real estate for a debt, may redeem the same by paying to the purchaser, his heirs or assigns, within two years from the sale thereof, the amount for which the same was sold, and such additional taxes thereon as may have been paid by the purchaser, his heirs or assigns; or, if purchased by the city, with such additional sums as would have accrued for taxes thereon if the same had not been purchased for the city, with interest on the said purchase money and taxes at the rate of twelve per centum per annum from the time that the same may have been so paid; or the same may be paid within the said two years to the city treasurer in any case in which the purchaser, his heirs or assigns, may refuse to receive the same, or may not reside or cannot be found in the city of Richmond.

Rights of persons under disability; how saved

80. Any infant, married woman, insane person, or person imprisoned, whose real estate may have been so sold, or his heirs, may redeem the same by paying to the purchaser, his heirs or assigns, within two years after the removal of the disability, the amount for which the same was so sold, with the necessary charges incurred by the purchaser, his heirs or assigns, in obtaining the title under the sale, and such additional taxes on the estate as may have been paid by the purchaser, his heirs or assigns, and the appraised value of any improvement that may have been made thereon, with interest on the said items, at the rate of twelve per centum per annum from the time the same may have been paid. Upon such payment within two years after the removal of such disability, the purchaser, his heirs or assigns, shall, at the cost of the original owner, his heirs or assigns, convey to him or them, by deed with special warranty, the real estate so sold.

Deed to purchaser of such estate; how executed, and within what time

Deed to assignee or heirs

81. The purchaser of any real estate, sold for taxes and not redeemed, shall, after the expiration of two years from the sale, obtain from the city auditor a deed conveying the same, wherein shall be set forth what appears in his office in relation to the sale. When the purchaser has assigned the benefit of his purchase, the deed may, with his assent, evidenced by his joining therein, or by a writing annexed thereto, be executed to his assignee. If the purchaser shall have died, his heirs or assigns may move the court of hustings of

said city to order the auditor to execute a deed to such heirs or assigns.

82. When the purchaser of any real estate, sold for taxes, his heirs or assigns, shall have obtained a deed therefor, and within sixty days from the date of such deed shall have caused the same to be recorded, such estate shall stand vested in the grantee in such deed as was vested in the party assessed with the taxes (on account whereof the sale was made) at the commencement of the year for which the said taxes were assessed, notwithstanding any irregularity in the proceedings under which the said grantee claims title, unless such irregularity appear on the face of the proceedings. And if it be alleged that the taxes, for the non-payment of which the sale was made, were not in arrear, the party making such allegation must establish the truth thereof by proving that the taxes were paid.

Effect of such deed, if recorded within sixty days

Onus probandi

83. In case that any real estate, struck off to the city as hereinbefore provided, shall not be redeemed within the time specified, the city auditor shall, within sixty days after the expiration of two years from the sale, cause to be recorded such certificate of sale, with his oath that the same has not been redeemed, and thereupon the said corporation, or their assignees, shall acquire an absolute title to the same in fee. The said certificate may be acknowledged, or proved, and recorded in the same manner that deeds are recorded, and the said certificate, or the record thereof, or a copy of said record, duly authenticated, shall, in all courts and places, be presumptive evidence of the facts therein stated and of the regularity and correctness of such sale, and of all proceedings prior thereto.

When city becomes purchaser, how it may acquire title

Effect of certificate of sale as evidence

CHAPTER VI.

POLICE AND FIRE DEPARTMENTS.

84. The police department of the city of Richmond shall be under the general control and management of police commissioners thereof, who shall consist of the mayor, the president of the city council, and the police justice, and shall constitute a board of police commissioners for said city; of which board the mayor shall be president, and shall have a

July 11, 1870. Police department, how controlled

Board of police commissioners

How constituted

Quorum

By-laws, &c

casting vote. Any two of said commissioners shall form a quorum for the transaction of any business. Said board may adopt rules and by-laws for the government thereof, and also may establish, promulgate, and enforce proper rules, regulations and orders for the good government and discipline of said police force: provided, that said rules, regulations and orders shall not in any way conflict with any ordinance of the city council, or of the provisions of this act, or the constitution and laws of this state or of the United States.

Meetings of said board

85. The said police commissioners, after taking the oath of office as such commissioners, shall meet at the office of the mayor, or other suitable place, at such time as may be expedient, and as they shall from time to time designate, and on special occasions, as the mayor may, in writing, appoint. They shall perform the duties of said office without any compensation, reward, or salary therefor from said city, except that nothing herein shall in any way conflict with the payment of the salary elewhere provided to be paid to the said mayor and police justice for their services in their respective offices.

July 11, 1870. To appoint policemen, officers, &c

86. It shall be the duty of said police commissioners to select from among the electors of said city, and appoint by warrant of appointment, bearing the signatures of all three of said commissioners, to be immediately filed with the city clerk, so many permanent policemen, officers, and patrolmen as may be authorized by the city council; and said board shall also appoint, with the approval of the city council, one chief of police, who shall hold office for the term of two years, through whom said board may promulgate all rules, regulations, and orders to the whole force, and who shall have immediate direction and control of said force, subject, however, at all times, to the rules, regulations, and orders of said board, and to the orders of the mayor: provided, that the orders of such single commissioner do not conflict with the rules, regulations, or orders of said board then in force; and said chief and each policeman of said police force, appointed in manner as aforesaid, may hold his respective office during the term of good behavior, or until said board, by unanimous vote, shall remove him; but in case of misconduct on the part of such chief or any member of said police force, then he may be removed by the decision of a majority of said board, as hereinafter provided, or by the city council.

To appoint chief of police, with approval of council

Of removals

87. In times of exigency, said commissioners, or a majority of them, or any one of them, if the others should be absent from the city or unable to act, may appoint temporarily, without authority from the city council, a suitable number of additional policemen for such time as shall appear necessary; not, however, to extend beyond the time of the next meeting of the city council. Additional policemen; how appointed for exigency

88. The mayor, at any time, upon charges being preferred, or upon finding said chief or any other member of said police force guilty of misconduct, shall have power to suspend such member from service until the board of commissioners shall convene and take action in the matter: provided, however, that such member shall not remain so suspended for a longer period than thirty days without an opportunity of being heard in his defence; and upon hearing the proofs in the case, a majority of said commissioners may discharge or restore such member, in accordance with the decision of the majority of such board thereon; and the pay or salary of such member shall cease from the time of suspension to the time of restoration to service, unless otherwise ordered by said board of commissioners in their written decision, which shall be filed with the city clerk; and any violation of the rules, regulations, or orders of the board, or orders of any superior, shall be good cause for dismissal. Power of mayor to suspend any member of police force; how long Pay during suspension

89. The salary or pay of said chief and policemen shall be determined by the city council, and all bills of expense on account of the police department shall be audited by at least two of said commissioners. Salary and pay of police; how determined, &c

90. The said chief of police and every policeman duly appointed as aforesaid, shall have issued to him a warrant of appointment, signed by the president of the board and countersigned by the city clerk, stating the date of his appointment, which shall be his commission; and he shall take such oath as the city council may ordain, and subscribe the same in a book to be kept for that purpose by the said city clerk Warrant of appointment of police force Qualification

91. The said chief of police and policemen shall generally have power to do whatever may be necessary to preserve the good order and peace of said city, and to secure its inhabitants from personal violence and their property from loss and injury. Such number of the said police force as the board of police commissioners may designate shall, in criminal cases, have the same powers and duties, and be subject Powers of police force

to the same penalties that are prescribed by law as to constables.

Uniform, badges and arms of force

92. The said board of commissioners may prescribe such uniform and badges for the police force as they may deem proper, and direct in what manner they shall be armed. And if any person other than a policeman shall publicly wear such uniform and badges as may be prescribed as aforesaid, he may be subjected to such fine, not exceeding the sum of one hundred dollars, as the city council may ordain.

Penalty for others than police wearing badges, &c

Former police to vacate unless reappointed

93. As soon as said commissioners shall have entered upon the discharge of their duties, and appointments of police are made in the manner as herein provided, then all the policemen and the chief of police, who shall be in service previous thereto, shall immediately vacate their offices respectively, unless reappointed as herein provided.

Fire department; how organized, &c

94. The city council may organize and maintain a fire department for said city, and appoint a chief engineer and assistants, with any or all of the powers which have been or may be vested by law in such officers. They may also make rules and regulations for the government of the officers and men of said fire department; may prescribe their respective duties in case of fire or alarms of fire; may direct the dresses or badges of authority to be worn by them; may prescribe and regulate the time and manner of their exercise; shall fix their pay, and may impose reasonable fines for the breach of any such regulations. They may also make such ordinances as they may deem proper to extinguish and prevent fires, prevent property from being stolen, and to compel citizens to render assistance to the fire department in case of need.

Rules, regulations, pay, &c

Control over erection of wooden buildings, &c

95. For the purpose of guarding against the calamities of fire, the city council may, from time to time, designate such portions and parts of the said city as it shall think proper within which no buildings of wood shall be erected, and may regulate the manner of construction of all buildings. They may prohibit the erection of wooden buildings in any portion of the city without permission obtained from them, and shall, on the petition of the owner or owners of not less than one-fourth of the ground included in any square of the city, prohibit the erection in such square of any building, or addition to any building, unless the outer walls thereof be made of brick and mortar, or stone and mortar, or some other fire

proof material; and may provide for the removal of any such building or addition which shall be erected contrary to such prohibition, at the expense of the builder or owner thereof. And if any building shall have been commenced before said petitions can be acted on by the council, or if a building in progress appears clearly to be unsafe, the council may have such buildings taken down.

Power to remove buildings not fire-proof

96. Whenever any building in the said city shall be on fire, it shall be the duty of and be lawful for the chief engineer to order and direct such building, or any other building which he may deem hazardous and likely to communicate fire to other buildings, or any part of such buildings, to be pulled down and destroyed; and no action shall be maintained against any person or against the said city therefor. But any person interested in any such building so destroyed or injured may, within three months thereafter, apply to the city council to assess and pay the damages he has sustained. At the expiration of the three months, if any such application shall have been made in writing, the city council shall either pay the said claimant such sum as shall be agreed upon by them and the said claimant for such damages, or if no such agreement shall be effected, shall proceed to ascertain the amount of such damages, and shall provide for the appraisal, assessment, collection, and payment of the same in the same manner as is provided for the ascertainment, assessment, collection, and payment of damages sustained by the taking of land for purposes of public improvement.

Control of chief engineer over buildings on fire, &c

Application for damages for destruction of such buildings; how made, &c

97. The commissioners appointed to appraise and assess the damages incurred by the said claimant, by the pulling down or destruction of such building, or any part thereof, by the direction of the said officers of the city, as above provided, shall take into account the probability of the same having been destroyed or injured by fire if it had not been so pulled down or destroyed, and may report that no damages should equitably be allowed to such claimant. Whenever a report shall be made and finally confirmed, in the said proceedings for appraising and assessing the damages, a compliance with the terms thereof by the city council shall be deemed a full satisfaction of all said damages of the said claimant. But any party feeling aggrieved thereby, may appeal to the circuit court for the city of Richmond, which court, in taking jurisdiction thereof, shall be controlled by

Commissioners to appraise such damages; their duties

Their report

Appeal to circuit court

the laws regulating assessment of damages to real estate in other cases.

CHAPTER VII.

THE JUDICIARY.

Clerks for circuit, hustings and chancery courts; term of office

98. There shall be elected by the qualified voters of said city, at the first charter election, and every six years thereafter, one clerk for the circuit court, one clerk for the hustings court, and one clerk for the chancery court of the city of Richmond, who shall serve for the period of six years, and until their successors be elected and qualify. They shall receive, in compensation for their services, the fees and emoluments allowed by law to clerks of the circuit courts.

Fees, &c

Commonwealth's attorney

99. There shall be elected at the first charter election, and every two years thereafter, by the qualified voters of said city, one commonwealth's attorney for the circuit court, who shall also prosecute in all cases in the hustings court of the city of Richmond. He shall hold his office for a term of two years, and until his successor be elected and qualify, unless sooner removed, and shall receive such compensation for his services as may be prescribed by law.

Sheriff; term of office, bond, &c

100. There shall be elected at the first charter election, and every two years thereafter, by the qualified voters of said city, one sheriff of the city of Richmond, who shall, before entering upon the duties of his office, give bond, with good security, in a penalty of not less than one hundred thousand dollars nor more than three hundred thousand dollars, as shall be required by the judge before whom he shall execute the same, whose powers and duties, liability, responsibility, emoluments, and term of office shall be, so far as not inconsistent with the provisions of this act, the same as now provided by law in respect to the sheriff of the city of Richmond.

Sergeant; term of office

101. There shall be elected at the first charter election, and every two years thereafter, by the qualified voters of said city, one city sergeant, who shall serve for two years, and until his successor be elected and qualify, unless sooner removed. He shall keep his office in such place as the city council may provide and appoint, and shall receive such compensation for his services as the city council shall determine.

Before entering upon the duties of his office, the said city sergeant shall give bond and security in such amount as the said city council shall determine; which bond shall be approved by the said council, entered on their records, and filed in the office of the city clerk. Compensation and bond

102. The said sergeant shall attend the terms of the court of hustings, and act as the officer thereof. He shall also, in all respects, except as to the collection of taxes, have the same powers and authority, and shall perform the duties, and be subject to the same liabilities and penalties, and be proceeded against in the same manner as sheriffs. His powers and duties

103. There shall be elected by the qualified voters of the city of Richmond at the first charter election, one high constable for said city, who shall hold his office for the term of two years, and until his successor be appointed and qualify, unless sooner removed from office. Said high constable shall keep his office in such convenient place in the city as may be designated by the city council, and shall receive such compensation for his services as the said council shall determine. He shall in civil cases have the same powers and duties, and be subject to the same penalties, as are prescribed by law to other constables, and shall perform such duties as the city council may ordain, not in conflict with the provisions of this act, the laws of this state, or the laws of the United States. April 16, 1874. High constable; term of office. Compensation, powers and duties

104. Before entering upon the duties of his office, the said high constable shall give bond and security, in such amount as shall be required by the city council, for the faithful discharge of the duties of his office; which bond shall be approved by the said council, entered on their record, and filed in the office of the city clerk. Said high constable may appoint one or more deputies to attend to and execute the duties of his office; but the sureties on the bond of the high constable shall be equally liable for the acts of the deputy or deputies as for those of their principal. His bond. His deputies

105. The sergeant of the city of Richmond shall be the officer of the hustings court, and the sheriff of the city of Richmond shall be the officer of the circuit court, and also of the chancery court. Sergeant to attend hustings, and sheriff the circuit and chancery courts

106. There shall be appointed by the city council one police justice, who shall hold his office for the term of two years, and until his successor shall be elected and qualify, unless July 11, 1870. Police justice; his appointment, jurisdiction and powers

sooner removed from office. The police justice shall hold a court daily in said city (Sundays excepted), in such place as the city council may provide and appoint. The jurisdiction of the court shall extend to all cases arising within the jurisdictional limits of the city, of which a justice of the peace may take cognizance under the laws of the state, and to all cases arising under the charter or ordinances of the city, or where there is a claim against the city or a person therein, if it does not exceed one hundred dollars, exclusive of interest; and the judgment shall be final in all civil cases where the matter in controversy, exclusive of costs, is not more than twenty dollars. He shall have such other powers and jurisdiction as may be conferred upon him by the city council, not in conflict with the constitution and laws of the United States, and of the state of Virginia. The city council may provide for the appointment of such clerks and officers for said court of the police justice, and make such rules for the government of said court, as they may find proper. If any person who has been duly summoned as a witness to attend and give evidence before the police justice, touching any matter or thing pending before him under the charter or any ordinances of the city, shall fail to attend in obedience to the said summons, he or she may be fined, at the discretion of the said justice, in a sum not exceeding twenty dollars.

His clerks and officers

Fine upon witness for non-attendance

July 11, 1870. Justices of peace; three in each ward, elected for two years

107. There shall be elected by the qualified voters of each ward, three justices of the peace for each ward of the said city, who shall be residents of their respective wards, and shall hold office for the term of two years, and until their successors be elected and qualify, unless sooner removed from office. They shall be designated by the city council as first, second, third, et cetera, justices. The said justices of the peace shall be conservators of the peace within the limits of the corporation of Richmond, and shall have the same powers and duties within said limits as are provided by law in respect to justices of the peace in the counties of this state in their respective counties, except that nothing herein contained shall be construed as vesting in said justices any portion of the jurisdiction given by this act to the police justice. Whenever the police justice shall be absent from the city, or unable, from any cause, to hold his court, the same shall be holden by a justice of the peace, to be desig-

Their designation

Powers and duties

Council to designate one to act as police justice in his absence

nated by the council. And when the said court shall be holden by a justice of the peace six or more days in succession, he shall be entitled to receive therefor the same compensation, pro rata, that may be prescribed as salary to the police justice.

108. Any officer, who by the provisions of the charter of Richmond is required to be elected or appointed by the city council, shall be elected or appointed by the two branches in joint meeting. The president of the board of aldermen shall preside at such joint meeting, and each member of the two branches shall be entitled to one vote in all joint meetings of the two boards.

April 16, 1874. Officers to be elected by the two branches in joint meeting

President board of aldermen to preside, &c

109. All ordinances, resolutions and acts of the city council shall be signed by the president of each branch, and shall be presented to the mayor for his approval, who, if he objects thereto, shall, within five days after it shall have been presented to him for his assent, return it to that branch of the city council in which it originated, with his objection in writing, and if a majority of the whole number of the members of each branch shall be of opinion that the ordinance, resolution or act ought to be passed, it shall, notwithstanding the objections of the mayor, become a law.

April 16, 1874. Ordinances, resolutions and acts of city council; how signed and approved

Veto power vested in mayor, &c

110. The board of aldermen may appoint a clerk, who shall attend the meetings of said board, and keep a record of its proceedings, and shall perform such other acts and duties as the said board may from time to time require of him.

April 16, 1874. Board of aldermen may appoint a clerk, &c

111. All acts and parts of acts in conflict with this act, are hereby repealed.

Inconsistent acts repealed

112. This act shall be in force from its passage.

Commencement

THE
ORDINANCES OF THE CITY OF RICHMOND.

WHEREAS it is expedient that the general ordinances of the city of Richmond should be arranged in appropriate titles, chapters and sections; that the amendments thereto made since the last revision should be ingrafted therein, and that any inconsistencies should be corrected; therefore,

Be it ordained by the council of the city of Richmond, in manner and form following, that is to say: *

Title 1.

OF THE CITY GOVERNMENT.

CHAPTER I.

OF THE WARDS OF THE CITY.

1. Clay ward shall include that portion of the city bounded as follows: Commencing at a point on the corporation line on April 17, 1871.

* This ordaining preamble is left as it was in the Ordinances of 1869. It will of course have no effect without an enacting statute at the end of the collection, such as was adopted at that time.

April 17, 1871. the south side of James river, in a direct line with the centre of Belvidere street; thence northwardly along the centre of Belvidere street to the centre of Main street; thence eastwardly along the centre of Main street to the centre of Adams street; thence northwardly along the centre of Adams street to the centre of Leigh street; thence westwardly along the centre of Leigh street to the corporation line; thence southwardly along the corporation line to the beginning.

2. Monroe ward shall include that portion of the city bounded as follows: Commencing at a point on the corporation line on the south side of James river, in a direct line with the centre of Belvidere street; thence northwardly along the centre of Belvidere street to the centre of Main street; thence eastwardly along the centre of Main street to the centre of Adams street; thence northwardly along the centre of Adams street to the centre of Leigh street; thence westwardly along the centre of Leigh street to the centre of St. Peter's street; thence northwardly along the centre of St. Peter's street to the centre of Jackson street; thence eastwardly along the centre of Jackson street to the centre of Fifth street; thence southwardly along the centre of Fifth street to the northern margin of the James river and Kanawha canal; thence westwardly along the northern margin of the said canal to the centre of Tate street; thence southwardly along the centre of Tate street to the corporation line; thence westwardly along the corporation line to the beginning.

3. Madison ward shall include that portion of the city bounded as follows: Commencing at a point on the corporation line on the south side of James river, in a direct line with the centre of Tate street; thence northwardly along the centre of Tate street to the northern bank of the James river and Kanawha canal; thence eastwardly along the bank of the said canal to the centre of Fifth street; thence northwardly along the centre of Fifth street to the centre of the ravine next north of Jackson street; thence eastwardly along the centre of said ravine to the junction of Balding and Concord streets, and in a line with the centre of Twelfth street; thence southwardly along the centre of Twelfth street to the corporation line; thence westwardly along the corportion line to the beginning.

4. Jefferson ward shall include that portion of the city bounded as follows: Commencing at a point on the corporation line on the south side of James river, in a direct line with the centre of Twelfth street; thence northwardly along the centre of Twelfth street to the centre of Clay street; thence eastwardly along the centre of Clay street to the centre of Thirteenth street; thence southwardly along the centre of Thirteenth street to the centre of Marshall street; thence eastwardly along the centre of Marshall street to the centre of College street; thence southwardly along the centre of College street to the centre of Broad street; thence eastwardly along the centre of Broad street to the centre of Eighteenth street; thence northwardly along the centre of Eighteenth street to the corporation line; thence eastwardly along the corporation line to a point opposite the centre of Pink street; thence southwardly along the centre of Pink street to the centre of Burton street; thence eastwardly along the centre of Burton street to the centre of Twenty-fourth street; thence southwardly along the centre of Twenty-fourth street to the centre of Broad street; thence eastwardly along the centre of Broad street to the centre of Twenty-fifth street; thence southwardly along the centre of Twenty-fifth street to the corporation line; thence westwardly along the corporation line to the beginning. April 17, 1871.

5. Marshall ward shall include that portion of the city bounded as follows: Commencing at a point on the corporation line on the south side of James river, in a direct line with the centre of Twenty-fifth street; thence northwardly along the centre of Twenty-fifth street to the centre of Broad street; thence westwardly along the centre of Broad street to the centre of Twenty-fourth street; thence northwardly along the centre of Twenty-fourth street to the centre of Burton street; thence westwardly along the centre of Burton street to the centre of Pink street; thence northwardly along the centre of Pink street to the corporation line; thence eastwardly along the corporation line to the beginning.

6. Jackson ward shall include that portion of the city bounded as follows: Commencing at a point on the corporation line opposite the centre of Eighteenth street; thence southwardly along the centre of Eighteenth street to the centre of Broad street; theuce westwardly along the centre

April 17, 1871. of Broad street to the centre of College street; thence northwardly along the centre of College street to the centre of Marshall street; thence westwardly along the centre of Marshall street to the centre of Thirteenth street; thence northwardly along the centre of Thirteenth street to the centre of Clay street; thence westwardly along the centre of Clay street to the centre of Twelfth street; thence northwardly along the centre of Twelfth street to the centre of Concord and Balding streets, at a point opposite the centre of the ravine north of Ellett street; thence westwardly up the centre of said ravine to the centre of Fifth street; thence southwardly along the centre of Fifth street to the centre of Jackson street; thence westwardly along the centre of Jackson street to the centre of St. Peter's street; thence southwardly along the centre of St. Peter's street to the centre of Leigh street; thence westwardly along the centre of Leigh street to the corporation line; thence northwardly along the corporation line to the northern margin of Bacon's Quarter Branch; thence eastwardly along the said branch and the corporation line to the beginning.

CHAPTER II.*

OF ELECTION PRECINCTS IN THE SEVERAL WARDS.

Clay Ward—First, second and third precincts.
Monroe Ward—First, second, third and fourth precincts.
Madison Ward—First, second, third and fourth precincts.
Jefferson Ward—First, second, third and fourth precincts.
Marshall Ward—First, second and third precincts.
Jackson Wdrd—First, second and third precincts.

The wards of this city are hereby divided into election precincts, bounded respectively as follows:

Clay Ward.

April 21, 1871. First Precinct: Commencing at a point on the corporation line on the south side of James river, opposite the centre of

*Chapter II, of the Ordinances of 1869, was "Of Elections." Its provisions have been superseded by the state election laws, Code of 1873, p. 143, et seq. The ordinance here substituted was passed April 21, 1871.

The whole machinery of the charter elections is now provided by the state laws referred to; and for the services of the different officers engaged about them, specific allowances are therein made, to be paid out of the treasury of the city. This state law of elections is distinctly accepted for the city by the new charter, thus fixing it, if it was not already fixed, as the law of the corporation on the whole subject; as certainly re-

Belvidere street; thence northwardly along the centre of Belvidere street to the centre of Main street; thence eastwardly along the centre of Main street to the centre of Henry street; thence northwardly along the centre of Henry street to the centre of Broad street; thence westwardly along the centre of Broad street to the corporation line; thence southwardly along the corporation line to the beginning. April 21, 1871.

Second Precinct: Commencing at the centre of Broad and Henry streets; thence northwardly along the centre of Henry street to the centre of Leigh street; thence westwardly along the centre of Leigh street to the corporation line; thence southwardly along the corporation line to a point opposite the centre of Broad street; thence eastwardly along the centre of Broad street to the beginning.

Third Precinct: Commencing at the centre of Main and Henry streets; thence northwardly along the centre of Henry street to the centre of Leigh street; thence eastwardly along the centre of Leigh street to the centre of Adams street; thence southwardly along the centre of Adams street to the centre of Main street; thence westwardly along the centre of Main street to the beginning.

Monroe Ward.

First Precinct: Commencing at a point on the corporation line on the south side of James river, opposite the centre of Belvidere street; thence northwardly along the centre of Belvidere street to the centre of Main street; thence eastwardly along the centre of Main street to the centre of Fifth street; thence southwardly along the centre of Fifth street to the northern margin of the James river and Kanawha canal; thence westwardly along the bank of said canal to a

quiring the payments allowed therein as it does the observance of any of its other provisions. But though the law requires payment by the city of the amounts thus allowed, and cannot be satisfied with less, it of course does not restrict the council to those amounts. The provisions of the old ordinance on this subject, however, which were adopted as early, certainly, as the revisal of 1869, are no longer binding; and if the council does not see fit to pass a new ordinance, the occasions as they arise can probably be as well provided for by resolutions, making such allowances as may be deemed just in each case. It may be proper to note here, as what was the mind of the council in 1869, that the payments required by that ordinance were: for each commissioner of election three dollars per day, and for each writer five dollars per day. These were the only officers to whom allowances were made in the ordinance. The conductor (who was then an officer of the police, and not paid for this service,) was, under the direction of the council, to provide the necessary conveniences for the occasion, and to present his bill therefor to the council for payment. Judges of election and registrars were not named in that ordinance.

April 21, 1871. point opposite the centre of Tate street; thence southwardly along the centre of Tate street to the corporation line; thence westwardly along said corporation line to the beginning.

Second Precinct: Commencing at the centre of Fifth and Main streets thence westwardly along the centre of Main street to the centre of Adams street; thence northwardly along the centre of Adams street to the centre of Broad street; thence eastwardly along the centre of Broad street to the centre of Fifth street; thence southwardly along the centre of Fifth street to the beginning.

Third Precinct: Commencing at the centre of Broad and Adams streets; thence northwardly along the centre of Adams street to the centre of Leigh street; thence westwardly along the centre of Leigh street to the centre of St. Peter street; thence northwardly along the centre of St. Peter street to the centre of Jackson street; thence eastwardly along the centre of Jackson street to the centre of Second street; thence southwardly along the centre of Second street to the centre of Broad street; thence westwardly along the centre of Broad street to the beginning.

Fourth Precinct: Commencing at the centre of Broad and Second streets; thence northwardly along the centre of Second street to the centre of Jackson street; thence eastwardly along the centre of Jackson street to the centre of Fifth street; theence southwardly along the centre of Fifth street to the centre of Broad street; thence westwardly along the centre of Broad street to the beginning.

Madison Ward.

First Precinct: Commencing at the centre of Broad and Fifth streets; thence northwardly along the centre of Fifth street to the centre of the ravine north of Jackson street; thence eastwardly along the centre of said ravine to a point opposite the centre of Eighth street; thence southwardly along the centre of Eighth street to the centre of Broad street; thence westwardly along the centre of Broad street to the beginning.

Second Precinct: Commencing at the centre of Broad and Eighth streets; thence northwardly along the centre of Eighth street to the ravine north of Ellett street; thence eastwardly along the centre of said ravine to its junction with the centre of Twelfth street; thence southwardly along the centre of Twelfth street to the centre of Broad street; thence westwardly along the centre of Broad street to the beginning. April 21, 1871.

Third Precinct: Commencing at the centre of Main and Fifth streets; thence northwardly along the centre of Fifth street to the centre of Broad street; thence eastwardly along the centre of Broad street to the centre of Twelfth street; thence southwardly along the centre of Twelfth street to the centre of Main street; thence westwardly along the centre of Main street to the beginning.

Fourth Precinct: Commencing at a point on the corporation line on the south side of James river, opposite the centre of Tate street; thence northwardly along the centre of said Tate street to the northern bank of the James river and Kanawha canal; thence eastwardly along the bank of said canal to the centre of Fifth street; thence northwardly along the centre of Fifth street to the centre of Main street; thence eastwardly along the centre of Main street to the centre of Twelfth street; thence southwardly along the centre of Twelfth street to the corporation line; thence westwardly along the corporation line to the beginning.

Jefferson Ward.

First Precinct: Commencing at a point on the corporation line on the south side of James river, opposite the centre of Twelfth street; thence northwardly along the centre of Twelfth street to the centre of Clay street; thence eastwardly along the centre of Clay street to the centre of Thirteenth street; thence southwardly along the centre of Thirteenth street to the centre of Marshall street; thence eastwardly along the centre of Marshall street to the centre of College street; thence eastwardly along the centre of College street to the centre of Broad street; thence eastwardly along the centre of Broad street to the centre of Fifteenth street; thence southwardly along the centre of Fifteenth street to the corporation line, and westwardly along said corporation line to the beginning.

Second Precinct: Commencing at a point on the corporation line on the south side of James river, opposite the centre of Fifteenth street; thence northwardly along the centre of Fifteenth street to the centre of Broad street; thence eastwardly along the centre of Broad street to the centre of

April 21, 1871. Twentieth street; thence southwardly along the centre of Twentieth street to the corporation line; thence westwardly along the corporation line to the beginning.

Third Precinct: Commencing at a point on the corporation line on the south side of James river, opposite the centre of Twentieth street; thence northwardly along the centre of Twentieth street to the centre of Broad street; thence eastwardly along the centre of Broad street to the centre of Twenty-fifth street; thence southwardly along the centre of Twenty-fifth street to the corporation line; thence westwardly along the corporation line to the beginning.

Fourth Precinct: Commencing at the centre of Broad and Eighteenth streets; thence northwardly along the centre of Eighteenth street to the corporation line; thence eastwardly along the corporation line to a point opposite the centre of Pink street; thence southwardly along the centre of Pink street to the centre of Burton street; thence eastwardly along the centre of Burton street to the centre of Twenty-fourth street; thence southwardly along the centre of Twenty-fourth street to the centre of Broad street; thence westwardly along the centre of Broad street to the beginning.

Marshall Ward.

First Precinct: Commencing at a point on the corporation line on the south side of James river, opposite Twenty-fifth street; thence northwardly along the centre of Twenty-fifth street to the centre of Main street; thence eastwardly along the centre of Main street to the centre of Rocketts street; thence southwardly along the centre of Rocketts street to the centre of Williamsburg avenue; thence along the centre of Williamsburg avenue to its junction with the York river railroad; thence eastwardly along said railroad to the corporation line; thence southwardly along said corporation line and with its angles to the beginning.

Second Precinct: Commencing at the centre of Main and Twenty-fifth streets; thence northwardly along the centre of Twenty-fifth street to the centre of Broad street; thence westwardly along the centre of Broad street to the centre of Twenty-fourth street; thence northwardly along the centre of Twenty-fourth street to the centre of Clay street; thence eastwardly along the centre of Clay street to the corporation line; thence southwardly along the corporation line to its junction with the York river railroad; thence westwardly along the said railroad to its junction with the Williamsburg avenue; thence westwardly along the centre of Williamsburg avenue to the centre of Rocketts street; thence northwardly along the centre of Rocketts street to the centre of Main street; thence westwardly along the centre of Main street to the beginning. April 21, 1871.

Third Precinct: Commencing at the centre of Clay and Twenty-fourth streets; thence northwardly along the centre of Twenty-fourth street to the centre of Burton street; thence westwardly along the centre of Burton street to the centre of Pink street; thence northwardly along the centre of Pink street to the corporation line; thence eastwardly along the corporation line, and its angles, to a point opposite Clay street; thence westwardly along the centre of Clay street to the beginning.

Jackson Ward.

First Precinct: Commencing at the centre of Jackson and St. James street; thence westwardly along the centre of Jackson street to the centre of St. Peter street; thence southwardly along the centre of St. Peter street to the centre of Leigh street; thence westwardly along the centre of Leigh street to the corporation line; thence northwardly along the corporation line to the northern margin of Bacon's Quarter branch; thence eastwardly along said branch, with its meanders, to a point opposite the centre of St. James street; thence southwardly along the centre of St. James street to the beginning.

Second Precinct: Commencing at the centre of Jackson and St. James streets; thence northwardly along the centre of St. James street to the corporation line; thence eastwardly along the corporation line to a point where Shockoe creek leaves the corporation line; thence southwardly along said creek to a point opposite the centre of the ravine north of Ellett street; thence westwardly along the centre of said ravine to the centre of Fifth street; thence southwardly along the centre of Fifth street to the centre of Jackson street; thence westwardly along the centre of Jackson street to the beginning.

Third Precinct: Commencing at a point on the corporation line opposite the centre of Eighteenth street; thence south-

April 21, 1871. wardly along the centre of Eighteenth street to the centre of Broad street; thence westwardly along the centre of Broad street to the centre of College street; thence northwardly along the centre of College street to the centre of Marshall street; thence westwardly along the centre of Marshall street to the centre of Thirteenth street; thence northwardly along the centre of Thirteenth street to the centre of Clay street; thence westwardly along the centre of Clay street to the centre of Twelfth street; thence northwardly along the centre of Twelfth street to its junction with Shockoe creek; thence along Shockoe creek to its junction with the corporation line; thence eastwardly along the corporation line and its angles to the beginning.

CHAPTER III.*

OF THE MAYOR.

June 15, 1870. 1. It shall be the duty of the mayor to see that the laws of the state and the ordinances of the city be faithfully executed. He shall exercise a constant supervision and control over the conduct of all subordinate officers, and receive and examine into all complaints against them for neglect of duty. He shall recommend to the council such measures as he shall deem expedient; and, in general, maintain the peace and good order, and advance the prosperity of the city.

2. It shall be the duty of the mayor to communicate to the city council annually, as soon as may be after the commencement of the fiscal year, and oftener if he shall deem it expedient, or be required by the city council, a general statement of the situation and condition of the city in relation to its government, finances and improvement, with such recommendations as he may deem proper.

---

*Chapter III, of 1869, was "Of the Election of Judge of the Court of Hustings," most of the provisions of, which have been superseded by the state law—Code of 1873, ch. 49, § 2. What remains in force of the old chapter III, will be found in the chapter 'Concerning the Hustings Court," under title 10 of this collection.

3. It shall be the duty of the mayor in all cases, when he shall suspend or remove a subordinate officer, under the provisions of the constitution of the state, to report the same to the council at their next stated meeting, with his reasons therefor. June 15, 1870.

4. The mayor shall exercise all the powers and authority in criminal cases of a justice of the peace, but he shall receive no fees for such services. He shall also perform such other duties, and exercise such other powers, as are enjoined or conferred upon him by the constitution or laws of the state, or that may be required of him by any ordinance or resolution of the council.

5. In case of the absence or inability of the mayor, the president of the city council shall possess the same powers, and discharge the municipal duties of the mayor during such absence or inability.

CHAPTER IV.*

OF ANNUAL REPORTS, TERMS OF OFFICERS, AND FORFEITURES OF OFFICE.

1. The auditor, treasurer, city engineer, superintendent of the gas works, the superintendent of the water works, the superintendent of the alms house, and the chief engineer of the fire department, shall, on or before the fifteenth day of February in each year, forward the annual reports of their several departments to the mayor, who shall transmit the same to the city council, with his message, as soon as may be after the commencement of the fiscal year. Nov. 11, 1872.

2. The official terms of all officers hereafter elected or appointed by the city council, shall extend from the date of such election or appointment, which shall be made at the June 11, 1872.

*In the compilation of 1869, chapter IV was, "Of Contested Elections," a subject since provided for by the state law—Code of 1873, ch. IX, § 9. In the stead of that subject, the chapter contains certain important general provisions relating to city officers, passed at the dates noted in the margin.

June 11, 1872. first joint meeting in July,* or as soon thereafter as practicable, to the first day of July in the second year thereafter, or until their successors shall have been elected or appointed and qualified, respectively; except the clerk in the office of the city treasurer, whose term shall extend to the first day of July in the third year thereafter, or until his successor shall have been elected or appointed and qualified: provided, however, that the right of removal from office shall remain, in every case, as set forth in the ordinances reserving such right, and in the charter of the city. And every vacancy occurring, whether by removal or otherwise, shall be filled for the unexpired term.†

Sept. 9, 1872. 3. Any person holding any office or post of profit, trust or emolument, to which he may have been elected under the city charter, by the city council or otherwise, or appointed by any committee thereof, who may be sentenced for felony by any court of this state or of the United States, shall, by such sentence, forfeit his post, and be thenceforth incapable of acting therein under his previous election or appointment. And though a pardon be afterward granted him, such pardon shall not avoid the forfeiture.

---

* The wording of the ordinance here was, "at the first regular meeting in July." The present charter, and the practice of the council, require joint meetings for all such elections.

† The provisions of this section now rule as to the time of appointment and terms of all officers elected or appointed by the city council; and the first six sections of the fifth chapter, make provision for whatever relates to the qualification of *all* city officers; except as to the penalty and approval of the bond, and except also a very few cases of special oaths and special conditions in bonds, and a few in which the entry of the bond on the records of the council is ordered. The duty of the council to fill all vacancies occurring in offices of their appointment, is clearly expressed and made mandatory in the charter—see especially section 29. Its power to remove all its appointees at pleasure, is also fully assured by the same section of the charter. A considerable part of the often repeated directions in the old ordinances, on the subjects of time of appointment, term of office, qualification and filling vacancies, has therefore been omitted in the ensuing chapters, and the several cases of officers to be appointed by the council left, when the way was clear, to be controlled by the general provisions of this section and the succeeding chapter, and the directions of the charter. It would be a further improvement to make this change more sweeping, and in every such case (with the exceptions before indicated as to bonds and special oaths) simply to require that the officer shall be appointed by the council, and then proceed at once to the duties, &c., of the office. The special proviso of this section, "that the right of removal from office shall remain, in every case, as set forth in the ordinances reserving such right, and in the charter of the city," now seems to stand in the way, not only as to the right of removal, but as to the term of office, because when the right is asserted, it is generally in connection with the term, the common form being that the officer shall hold his office "for the term of two years, &c., unless sooner removed." But it is submitted that the whole proviso is now unnecessary, and might be stricken out with advantage. When the right of removal by the council is as broad and general as it is made by the charter, it seems worse than useless to reserve the right for particular cases.

4. That if any such post, or the deputation thereof, either in whole or in part, shall be sold or let to farm, or contracted to be sold or let to farm, by any person holding or expecting to hold the same, such person, and the person who may buy or take to farm, or contract to buy or take to farm, shall, each of them, be forever disabled from holding such post or deputation. Sept. 9, 1872.

5. It shall not be lawful for any salaried officer of the city government, personally or through an agent, to contract for, or sell supplies of food, machinery, or any other article for the use of said city, or to be in any way interested in any such contract. June 11, 1872.

6. Any officer who shall be guilty of violating the last preceding section, shall be fined not less than one hundred nor more than five hundred dollars, and shall be deemed guilty of misconduct in office, and removed therefrom.

CHAPTER V.*

OF OFFICIAL OATHS AND BONDS, AND THE SEAL OF THE CITY.

Oaths.

1. Every person elected to the office of mayor of the city, or member of the city council, shall, in accordance with the laws of this state, take the following oath, before entering upon the duties of his office: Ordinances 1869 ch. 5, § 1. Charter, § 7.

"I, ——— ———, do declare myself a citizen of the commonwealth of Virginia, and do solemnly swear (or affirm) that I will support and maintain the constitution and laws of the United States, and the constitution and laws of the state of Virginia; that I recognize and accept the civil and political equality of all men before the law; and that I will faithfully perform the duty of ————, to the best of my ability. So help me God." Code of 1873, ch. 12, § 1.

* Compiled from the Ordinances of 1869, and a subsequent ordinance, the new charter, and the Code of 1873, as noted in the margin. See note to chapter IV, § 2, as to the general effect of this chapter.

Charter, § 7. Such oath may be administered to the mayor elect by any judge of a court of record, commissioned to hold any such court within said city; and to the members of the city council by the mayor, being himself first sworn as aforesaid, or by any judge of any court of record, as aforesaid; and certificates of such oath having been respectively taken, shall be filed with the city clerk, and entered upon the journal of the city council.

Charter, § 7. 2. Every other person elected or appointed to any office under the charter of the city, or under any law, or ordinance of the city council, shall, before he enters upon the duties of said office, take and subscribe said oath, and such other oaths as may be prescribed by law or ordinance, before the mayor or city clerk, the said clerk having himself been first sworn by said mayor, or a judge of a court of record, as aforesaid; and a certificate of the same shall be filed in the office of said city clerk.

Ordinances 1869 ch. 5, § 4. Code 1873, ch. 12, § 5. 3, If any person required to take an oath shall declare that he has religious scruples as to the propriety of taking an oath, he may make a solemn affirmation, which shall have in all respects the same effect as an oath.

Ordinances 1869 ch. 5, § 2. Charter, § 7. 4. If any person, elected or appointed as aforesaid to any office in this city, shall act in his office before taking the oath hereinbefore prescribed, and such other oath or oaths as may be prescribed in qualification for such office by law or by ordinance of the council, and filing a certificate thereof with the city clerk, he shall pay a fine of not less than one nor more than twenty dollars for each day on which he so acts.

Charter, § 7. 5. If any person, elected or appointed to any office in this city, shall neglect to take such oath or oaths for forty days, after receiving notice of his election or appointment, or shall neglect for the like space of time to give such securities as may be required of him by the city council, as provided in the charter, or as may be hereafter required by any law or ordinance, he shall be considered as having declined such office, and the same shall be deemed vacant; and whenever any such vacancy shall occur, another election shall be ordered, or another appointment made, according to the directions of the charter.

Bonds.

6. Every bond required by any ordinance, to be taken or approved by the city council, or any other body or person acting under the authority of the city government, shall, unless otherwise provided, be made payable to "The City of Richmond," with surety deemed sufficient by the body or person before whom it is taken. Every such bond, required of any person elected or appointed to any office, post or trust, shall, unless otherwise provided, be with condition for the faithful discharge by him of the duties of his office or trust; and, unless otherwise directed or authorized by the city council, shall be returned to the city clerk, and preserved by him. Ordinances 1869 ch. 5, § 6.

Seal.

7. From and after the first day of October, eighteen hundred and seventy-two, the seal of the city of Richmond shall be represented by a design, within a circle, one and three-quarter inches in diameter, within which shall be represented a sitting female figure, clothed in classic costume, wearing a mural crown, in her left hand a bundle of tobacco leaves, which rest upon her lap; at her feet, a river flowing to her left, on the banks of which are shown mining operations, iron works and a steam engine; towards which her extended right hand is pointed. Above her head the motto, "Sic itur ad astra," and in the exergue this inscription, Sept. 9, 1872

RICHMOND, VA.,
FOUNDED BY
WILLIAM BYRD,
MDCCXXXVII,

in Roman characters.

8. From and after the date named in the seventh section, no other design or seal shall be used for the city of Richmond, and no paper issued with municipal authority, which requires the seal of the city, shall be valid, unless the seal described in the seventh section shall be affixed to the same.*

---

*By the Charter, § 40, and chapter X, § 11, of the Ordinances, the treasurer is made the keeper of the seal. For tax on seal, see chapter XIII, § 26.

CHAPTER VI.

OF SALARIES OF OFFICERS.

Passed June 9, 1873, to take effect July 1, 1873

1. The several officers of the city hereinafter mentioned, shall receive, annually, the following sums, that is to say:

The mayor of the city, twenty-five hundred dollars.

The treasurer, two thousand dollars.

The clerk in the treasurer's office, fifteen hundred dollars.

The auditor, eighteen hundred dollars.

The clerk in the auditor's office, fifteen hundred dollars.

The engineer of the city, two thousand dollars.

The superintendent of the gas works, eighteen hundred dollars.

The inspector of gas works, fifteen hundred dollars.

The superintendent of water works, eighteen hundred dollars.

The assistant superintendent of water works, twelve hundred and fifty dollars.

The superintendent of the pump house, twelve hundred dollars.

The assistant superintendent of the pump house, one thousand dollars.

The clerk of the first market, one thousand dollars; and for sweeping, white-washing, &c., of building and grounds, seven hundred and fifty dollars.

The clerk of the second market, one thousand dollars; and for sweeping, white-washing, &c., of building and grounds, seven hundred and fifty dollars.

The chief engineer of the fire department, one thousand dollars.

The commanders of fire companies, each, two hundred and fifty dollars.

The engineers of the steam fire engines, each one thousand and eighty dollars.

The foremen of fire companies, each, one hundred and eighty-seven dollars and fifty cents.

The firemen of the steam fire engines, each, seven hundred and eighty dollars. June 9, 1873.

The hostlers of the steam fire engines, each, seven hundred and eighty dollars.

The other firemen, each, one hundred and twenty-five dollars.

The superintendent of the alms house, hospital and Shockoe Hill burying ground, one thousand dollars; and he shall have, in addition thereto, the use of the house provided for the superintendent, and his fuel, gas and water free of cost; and he shall have the privilege of taking supplies for his family from the provisions purchased for the alms house at the prices given for them.

2. The officers of the city shall be paid monthly, except the commissioner of the revenue, who shall be paid as provided by the ordinance concerning the assessment of taxes. Ordiaances 1869 ch. 6, §§ 2, 3, 4.

3. A person elected to any office under the charter of the city, who may be prevented from qualifying at the usual time, by a contested election, shall, upon being declared duly elected and qualifying, be entitled to the salary from the time when he would have entered upon his office if there had been no contest.

4. All other officers and employees of the city shall receive the salaries or compensation provided by the ordinances of the city or resolutions of the city council.

5. The salaries of all city officers, who receive a fixed compensation for their services, including all officers and employees in the police force, fire, gas and water departments of said city, shall be established by the city council, annually,* in the month of July, or, if not then acted on by the city council, shall remain as prescribed by ordinances or resolutions in force on the first day of that month; and the salaries or compensation thus established, shall neither be increased nor diminished by the said council, during the then current municipal year, and no extra compensation shall ever be allowed to any such officer or employee in any department of the city government, over and above that provided in the manner aforesaid. March 20, 1871.

* The time prescribed in this ordinance for establishing salaries, was "at the first annual regular meeting" of the council in the month of July. For the words quoted, the single word *annually* is substituted above, as more consistent with the present order of meetings. Other changes in the phraseology of this clause of the section are made, to remove obscurities, and to render it consistent with subsequent action of the council.

CHAPTER VII.*

OF THE CITY CLERK, AND ENROLLMENT OF ORDINANCES.

City Clerk.

June 15, 1872. Charter, §.66.

1. There shall be a city clerk, who shall be appointed by the city council, and shall hold his office for the period of two years, and until his successor shall be appointed and qualify, unless sooner removed from office by the council.† He shall, in his office, file all papers, and preserve all books and papers which, by the provisions of the ordinances, or by the direction of the city council, or either of its branches, are required to be filed with or kept by him.

Feb. 20, 1871.

2. He shall attend the meetings of the common council, and enter correctly its proceedings, and in a book kept for the purpose, record all the ordinances. The book of such proceedings, and the book of ordinances, shall be kept by him, with indexes referring to the different matters therein, and they shall be open at all times to the inspection of any member of the city council. He shall act as clerk to such committees of the council as shall require such service; and no committee shall appoint any clerk or other assistant, without the consent of the city council. He shall make copies of or extracts from any thing in said books when and as often as he may be required so to do by either branch of the council, or by either president or any chairman of any committee. He may also make like copies or extracts, upon the request of any other person desiring the same, and may demand and receive from such other person a reasonable compensation therefor.

June 15, 1870. Charter, § 66.

3. He shall regularly furnish the chairman of each committee with a copy of the resolution constituting it, and of

* In the Ordinances of 1869, this chapter contained the Rules of the Council.

† See note on chapter IV, § 2.

all resolutions referring matters to his committee. It shall also be his duty, immediately after the close of each session of the council, to make and present to the mayor a transcript of every ordinance, resolution and order, passed by both branches of the city council. He shall in like manner transmit to the auditor a transcript of all ordinances, resolutions or orders appropriating money, or authorizing the payment of money, the issue of bonds or notes; and to the heads of all departments of the city government all ordinances, resolutions or orders relating to their departments. He shall also give notice to the parties presenting communications or petitions to the city council, of the final action of the council on such communications or petitions. June 15, 1870. Charter, § 66.

4. He shall publish, in such manner as may be directed, all reports and ordinances which he may be required by the ordinances to publish, and such other reports and ordinances as the city council may direct. And he shall in general perform such other acts and duties as the city council, or either branch thereof, may from time to time require of him.

5. The said city clerk shall receive, in full compensation for all public services rendered by him, a salary of two thousand dollars per annum. May 13, 1872.

Enrollment of Ordinances, &c.

6. The style in which ordinances shall be passed shall be: Be it ordained by the council of the city of Richmond. That in which joint resolutions shall be passed shall be: Be it resolved by the council of the city of Richmond, (the board of aldermen, or the common council, as the case may be, concurring.) A joint resolution shall always provide for the concurrence of the other branch of the council from that in which it is introduced; and all other resolutions shall be considered as referring only to that branch in which they originate and are passed. July 24, 1874.

7. As soon as any ordinance or joint resolution shall have passed both branches of the city council, it shall be enrolled by the city clerk, with his certificate of the date of its passage, on large folio record paper, which he shall procure and keep on hand for the purpose, and shall then be signed first by the president of the branch in which it originated, and then by the president of the other branch, and then be submitted by said clerk to the mayor for his signature. The re-

July 24, 1874. turn of any ordinance or joint resolution by the mayor to the clerk of the body in which it originated, within five days after it has been thus submitted to him, shall be considered the return of the same to the body itself within five days, as provided for in the charter. If the mayor shall sign the same, the city clerk shall file the same away, and communicate the fact of the signature thereof to the branch in which it originated, in writing. If such ordinance or joint resolution be refused signature by the mayor, and afterward be passed over his veto, or if it become law by virtue of not having been returned within five days, then it shall be the duty of the city clerk to append a certificate of such fact to said ordinance or joint resolution; which certificate shall be signed by the presidents of the two branches, and the city clerk, and shall be filed with the other ordinances and joint resolutions which have become laws.

8. The city clerk shall keep an index of such ordinances or joint resolutions as have passed, and on the first day of January, eighteen hundred and seventy-six, shall arrange them according to their appropriate subjects, classifying and collecting them together, and shall have them bound in one or more volumes, as may be necessary, marked: Ordinances, from July, 1874, to January, 1876; and he shall index, collect and classify, and have bound, the ordinances and joint resolutions for every year thereafter up to the first day of January of each year, so as to have all the corporate acts of each year in a separate volume or volumes, properly and plainly marked.

9. These ordinances and joint resolutions, thus certified, signed and enrolled, shall be taken to be the records of the corporation of the same; and the city clerk shall cause the same to be annually printed.

CHAPTER VIII.*

THE POLICE JUSTICE.

1. There shall be elected by the city council a police justice, who shall hold his office for the term of two years, unless sooner removed, and until his successor shall be elected and qualify.† The said police justice shall hold a court daily, except Sundays, in said city, in such place as the city council may designate. The jurisdiction of the court shall extend to all cases arising within the jurisdictional limits of the city, of which a justice of the peace may take cognizance under the laws of the state, and to all cases arising under the charter or ordinances of the city, or where there is a claim against the city, or a person therein, if it does not exceed one hundred dollars, exclusive of interest; and the judgment shall be final, in all civil cases, when the matter in controversy, exclusive of costs, is not more than twenty dollars. June 15, 1870. Charter, § 106.

2. The police justice shall nominate to the city council three persons as a clerk, and from the number thus nominated the city council shall elect one to serve as clerk of the police justice. The said clerk shall perform such duties as may be required of him by the police justice, and shall also act as clerk or secretary to the board of police commissioners. June 15, 1870.

3. The police justice shall not be entitled to receive any fees as a justice of the peace, but shall receive, in full compensation for his services, a salary of two thousand dollars per annum. The clerk of the police justice shall receive, in March 20, 1871.

* Sections 1 to 10, of this chapter, as here given, were passed June 15, 1870, substituting "Chapter VIII, of the Mayor's Court," in the compilation of 1869, notes in the margin of these sections indicating the dates of subsequent changes. The remaining sections of the chapter are from an ordinance "concerning a janitor of the police court building," passed March 25th, 1872.

† See note on chapter IV, § 2.

March 20, 1871. full compensation for his services, a salary of one thousand dollars per annum.

July 11, 1870. 4. All the fines and penalties imposed by the said police justice, and all the moneys that shall be paid to or received by him as such, shall belong to the city; and the said police justice shall report on oath to the city council, at the first regular meeting thereof in each month, during the term for which he shall be elected, the number and names of persons fined by him, and the names of persons against whom judgment shall have been rendered by him for any penalty or penalties respectively, and all moneys collected or received by him as such police justice for fines and penalties, or otherwise; and also all disbursements made by him in abating nuisances, paying the necessary expenses of prisoners confined in the station houses awaiting examination before him, and other expenses incident to his office. The disbursements in every case must be supported by proper vouchers. After these reports have been submitted to and approved by the city council, the city clerk shall file them successively, as they are received, with the other papers and documents belonging to his office. The said police justice shall, on the first Monday in each and every month during his term of office, pay to the city treasurer all moneys received by him, hereinbefore declared to belong to the city. Any neglect to comply with the provisions of this section shall be good ground for the removal from office of said police justice.

June 15, 1870. 5. It shall be the duty of the police justice, on the first Monday in June, and the first Monday in December, in every year, to deliver an account, verified by his oath, to the city council, of all moneys, goods, wares and merchandize, then remaining unclaimed in the custody of his court, and immediately thereafter to give notice daily, for two successive weeks, in two of the newspapers printed in the city, to all persons interested or claiming such property, that unless claimed by the owner, with satisfactory proof of such ownership, before a specified day, the same shall be sold at public auction to the highest bidder. On the day, and at the place specified in said notice, all property remaining unclaimed, except money, shall be sold at auction by said police justice, or under his direction. If any goods, wares, merchandize and chattels of a perishable nature, or which shall be expensive to keep, shall at any time remain unclaimed in the custody of said court, it shall be lawful for said police justice to sell the same at public auction, at such time, and after such notice, as to him shall seem proper. The said police justice shall, immediately after the sale of any property in accordance herewith, pay to the city treasurer, as aforesaid, all money remaining unclaimed in his hands as such police justice, and all moneys received by him upon such sale, after deducting the expenses thereof. June 15, 1870.

6. It shall be the dnty of said police justice, whenever he shall obtain possession of any stolen property, on his receiving satisfactory proof of property from the owner, to deliver such property to the owner thereof on his paying all necessary and reasonable expenses which may have been incurred for the preservation or sustenance of such property. But no property shall be sold or delivered in pursuance of this or the preceding section, if the commonwealth's attorney for the city shall direct that it shall remain unsold or undelivered for the purpose of being used as evidence in the administration of justice.

7. All dockets and other books kept by said police justice, shall at all times be subject to the inspection or examination of the city attorney, the city council, or any member thereof.

8. It shall be the duty of the board of police commissioners, when so requested by the said police justice, to detail one or more of the city police to attend the court of said police justice, and perform such duties therein as may be required by the same.*

9. If any person who has been duly summoned as a witness to attend and give evidence before the police justice touching any matter or thing pending before him under the charter, or any ordinance of the city, shall fail to attend in obedience to the said summons, he or she may be fined, at the discretion of the police justice, in a sum not exceeding twenty dollars.

10. At the first meeting of the city council in the month of July in each year, or as soon thereafter as practicable, the council shall designate first, second, third, and so forth, jus- August 26, 1872. Charter, § 107.

* There is some doubt whether this section should remain. If the appointment of janitor, under the subsequent ordinance, (sections 11, &c., of this chapter,) was intended to give all the service in his court that the police justice could properly call for, this section should be repealed. But perhaps the section was purposely retained to provide for occasions when the justice might need additional service of this kind.

August 26, 1872. Charter, § 107. tices of the peace of the city. And whenever the police justice shall be absent from the city, or unable from any cause to hold his court, the same shall be holden by a justice of the peace to be designated by the city council. And when the said court shall be holden by a justice of the peace six or more days in succession, he shall be entitled to receive therefor the same compensation, pro rata, that is prescribed as salary to the police justice.

March 25, 1872. 11. There shall be elected by the city council a janitor of the police court building,* who shall hold his office for two years, unless sooner removed by the council, the mayor, or the police justice. The said janitor shall have charge of the police court building, and the furniture and other property contained therein, and be held responsible for the safe-keeping and proper protection of the same. He shall have the care of keeping, cleaning, warming and lighting the said building.

12. He shall attend all courts held by the police justice, and shall perform such other services as may be required of him by the police justice.

13. The said janitor shall have the power and authority of a policeman, and shall receive in compensation for his services a salary of sixty dollars per month.

CHAPTER IX.†

OF THE SERGEANT—AT—ARMS OF THE COMMON COUNCIL AND BOARD OF ALDERMEN.

July 13, 1874, to take effect from July 1, 1874. 1. There shall be one sergeant-at-arms for the two branches of the city council, to be elected by their joint vote, who shall continue in office for two years, unless sooner removed. He shall attend upon each branch during its sessions, and shall execute its commands, together with all such process issued by its authority as shall be directed to him by the

* See note on chapter IV, § 2.

† Approved at the date given in the margin, the object of the ordinance being to substitute this for chapter IX, "Of the Messenger of the Council," in the Ordinances of 1869.

president. He shall, under the direction of the president, have charge of the police of the hall, and shall prevent any interruption of the business of the body by disorder within or without. He shall distribute among the members all papers printed for their use, and shall render such assistance during the session of the body as will promote the comfort of the members and facilitate the business of the body. He shall announce to the president all messages sent from the mayor or other branch. He shall also attend on the meetings of the committees of the city council, act as the messenger of the city clerk, and deliver in person all notices and summonses issued by him to the members of either branch of the council, or the committees thereof. He shall act as the superintendent of the city hall building and council chamber, and be responsible for the safe-keeping and proper protection of the property contained therein. He shall also superintend the cleansing, warming, and lighting the said city hall and council chamber. He shall have the power and authority of a sergeant of police within and around the city hall and council chamber. He shall have charge of the library belonging to the board of aldermen and common council, and permit no book belonging to the same to be taken from the chamber, without the direction of the board or common council. He shall receive as compensation for his services the sum of one thousand five hundred dollars per annum. July 13, 1874.

2. The ordinance concerning the messenger of the council is hereby repealed.

3. This ordinance shall take effect from the first day of July, eighteen hundred and seventy-four.

CHAPTER X.

OF THE AUDITOR AND TREASURER OF THE CITY.

City Auditor.

Dec. 5, 1870. 1. The person elected to the office of auditor shall, before acting in his office, give bond with security in the sum of thirty thousand dollars, to be approved by the city council and entered on their records.*

2. The auditor shall open and keep, in a neat and methodical manner, a complete set of books, under the direction of the city council, wherein shall be stated, among other things, the appropriations of the year for each distinct object and branch of expenditure, and also the receipts in detail from each and every source of revenue, so far as he can ascertain the same. Said books, and all papers, vouchers, contracts, bonds, receipts, and other things kept in said office, shall be subject to the examination of the mayor, the members of the city council, or any committee or committees thereof.

3. The said auditor shall be charged with and exercise a general supervision over all the officers of the city charged in any manner with the receipt, collection or disbursement of the city revenues, and the collection and return of such revenues into the city treasury. He shall have charge of all deeds, mortgages, contracts, judgments, notes, bonds, debts, choses in action, belonging to the said city, except such as

* See note on chapter IV, § 2.

are confided to the custody of the city clerk, and such other papers as may be committed to his care by the city council, by ordinance or otherwise. Dec. 5, 1870.

4. The said auditor shall examine all accounts, claims and demands, for or against the said city; and no money, shall be drawn from the treasury, or paid by the city to any person, except as herein otherwise provided, unless that balance due or payable be first settled and adjusted by the said auditor; and for the purpose of ascertaining the true state of any balance or balances so due, he shall have, and is hereby clothed with full power and authority, to administer an oath or oaths to the claimant or claimants, or any other person or persons, whom he may think proper to examine as to any fact, matter or thing, concerning the correctness of any account, claim or demand presented; and the person so sworn shall, if he swear falsely, be guilty of wilful and corrupt perjury, and be subject to punishment by imprisonment in the penitentiary for not less than one nor more than five years.

5. All money found to be due and payable by the said auditor to any person, shall be drawn by said auditor by warrant on the treasurer, stating the particular fund or appropriation to which the same is chargeable, and the person to whom payable; and no money shall be drawn from the treasury except on the warrant of the auditor, as aforesaid. But the auditor is forbidden to issue his warrant for the payment of any money in excess of the appropriation on account of which said money is drawn, or unless the bill filed in his office shall show for what articles furnished or services rendered, the warrant is issued.

6. It shall be the duty of said auditor, as nearly as may be, to charge all officers in the receipt of revenues or moneys of the city, with the whole amount, from time to time, of such receipts; he shall also require of all officers in receipt of city moneys, that they shall submit reports thereof, with vouchers and receipts of payment therefor into the city treasury, weekly or monthly, or as often as he shall see fit to require the same by any regulation which he may adopt; and if any such officer shall neglect to make an adjustment of his accounts, when required as aforesaid, and to pay over such moneys so received, it shall then be the duty of said auditor to issue notice in writing, directed to such officer and his securities, requiring him or them, within ten days, to make

Dec. 5, 1870. settlement of his said account with the auditor, and to pay over the balance of moneys found to be due and in his hands belonging to the said city, according to the books of said auditor; and in case of the refusal or neglect of such officer to adjust his said accounts, or pay over said balance to the treasurer as required, it shall then be the duty of said auditor to make report of the delinquency of such officer to the mayor, who shall at once suspend him from office, proceed forthwith to institute the necessary proceedings for the removal of such officer from office, and immediately on his removal, institute suit in the name of said city against him and his securities, to recover the balance of moneys so found to be due and in his hands belonging to said city.

7. The auditor shall make out an annual statement, as soon as possible after the end of each fiscal year, giving a full and detailed statement of all the receipts and expenditures during the said year. The said statement shall also detail the liabilities and expenditures during the year, the liabilities and resources of said city, the condition of all unexpended appropriations and contracts unfulfilled, the balances of money then remaining in the treasury, with all sums due and outstanding, the names of all persons who may have become defaulters to the city, and the amounts in their hands unaccounted for, and all other things necessary to exhibit the true financial condition of the city.

8. The auditor shall annually submit to the city council, at their first stated meeting after the beginning of the fiscal year, a report of the estimates necessary, as nearly as may be, to defray the expenses of the city government during the current fiscal year. He shall, in said report, class the different objects and branches of said city expenditure, giving, as nearly as may be, the amount required for each; and for this purpose he is authorized to require of all city officers and heads of departments, their statements of the condition and expense of their respective departments and offices, with any proposed improvement, and the probable expense thereof, of contracts already made and unfinished, and the amount of unexpended appropriations of the preceding year. He shall also in such report show the aggregate income of the preceding fiscal year, from all sources; the amount of liabilities outstanding upon which interest is to be paid, and of bonds and city debts payable during the year, when due and where

payable, so that the city council may fully understand the money exigencies and demands of the city for the current year. Dec. 5, 1870.

9. In addition to the other duties of the said auditor, it is hereby made his duty, on the last day of each and every month, to make out a monthly statement, giving a full and detailed account of all moneys received, from what sources and on what account received, and of all moneys ordered to be paid or drawn for by warrant by him, and on what account the same have been paid; and shall deliver said statement to the said city council at their next meeting, to be filed after the adjournment of said council, by the city clerk, with the papers belonging to his office.

City Treasurer.

10. The person elected to the office of treasurer shall, before acting in his office, give bond with security in the sum of one hundred thousand dollars, to be approved by the city council, and entered on their records.*

11. The treasurer shall receive all moneys belonging to Charter, § 40. the city, and shall keep his office in some place designated by the city council. He shall have the custody of the corporate seal. He shall keep his books and accounts in such manner as the city council may prescribe, and such books and accounts shall always be subject to the inspection of the mayor and any member of the city council, or any committee or committees thereof.

12. No money shall be paid out by the treasurer except Dec. 5, 1870. upon the warrant of the auditor, issued as hereinbefore provided, and he shall keep a separate account of each fund or appropriation, and the debits or credits belonging thereto, corresponding as nearly as possible with those kept by the auditor.

13. All moneys to be paid into the treasury of the city, except the bills for gas and water, and such other assessments as the city council may so ordain, shall be paid by the person liable to pay the same, or his agent, to the treasurer, in the following manner: a warrant shall first be obtained from the auditor, directing the treasurer to receive the sum to be paid, specifying on what account the payment is to be made. Upon the payment of the money to the treasurer, he

* See note to chapter IV, § 2.

Dec. 5, 1870. shall give a receipt for the same, which shall be carried to the auditor, and his receipt therefor shall be the acquittance of the party making the payment. Bills for gas and water, and such other assessments as the city council may so ordain, shall be paid directly to the treasurer, who shall keep an account thereof, and make daily reports of accurate copies of such receipts to the auditor.

14. The treasurer shall, at the end of each and every month, and oftener if required, render an account to the auditor, showing the state of the treasury at the date of such account, and the balance of moneys in the treasury. He shall also, if required so to do by the auditor, accompany such account with a statement of all moneys received into the treasury, and on what account, with a list of all warrants redeemed and paid by him during the month.

15. The treasurer shall also report to the city council, at the end of each fiscal year, and oftener if required, a full and detailed account of all receipts and expenditures during the preceding fiscal year, and the state of the treasury. He shall also keep a register of all warrants, their date, amount, number, the fund from which paid, and the person to whom paid, specifying also the time of payment; and all such warrants shall be examined, at the time of making such annual report to the city council, by a committee thereof, who shall examine and compare the same with the books of the auditor, and report discrepancies, if any, to the city council.

16. All moneys received on any special assessment, shall be held by the treasurer as a special fund, to be applied to the payment for which the assessment was made; and said money shall be used for no other purpose whatsoever.

17. The treasurer may be required to keep all moneys in his hands, belonging to the city, in such place or places of deposit as the city council may by ordinance provide, order, establish or direct. Such moneys shall be kept distinct and separate from his own moneys; and he is hereby expressly prohibited from using, either directly or indirectly, the corporation money or warrants in his custody and keeping, for his own use and benefit, or that of any person or persons whomsoever; and any violation of this provision shall subject him to immediate removal from office. In case of his removal, the city council shall elect a qualified person to fill said office until the next general election which may be held

in the city, when the qualified voters of said city shall, as in other cases, fill such vacancy by an election of a successor, who shall hold his office for the remainder, if any, of the unexpired term of the officer removed. Charter, § 46.

Auditor and Treasurer.

18. The city council shall, as soon as practicable after the auditor and treasurer have qualified respectively, elect one clerk for each officer; but such clerks shall not enter upon the discharge of their duties until they shall have taken an oath before the city clerk for the faithful performance of the duties required, and shall have given bond in the sum of five thousand dollars each, with sureties approved by the city council. The clerks so appointed may be removed at any time by the city council. Dec. 5, 1870.

19. The hours for transacting business in the offices of the treasurer and auditor, shall be as follows: From eight A. M., until three P. M., from the first day of April until the first day of October, and from nine A. M., until three P. M., during the rest of the year; and the treasurer and the auditor shall be required to be present in the offices assigned them by the city council, and attend to their official business, during these hours; and if either of these officers shall engage in any regular business which shall require or cause him to neglect his office habitually during business hours, the city council shall inflict such penalty as to them shall seem proper. Sept. 18, 1871.

Title 2.

OF THE REVENUE OF THE CITY.

CHAPTER XI.*

CONCERNING THE RECEIVING AND PAYING MONEY AT THE TREASURY.

Ordinances 1869 ch. 11, §§ 3 to 5, and 7 to 23.

1. All moneys, if over one hundred dollars, received by the treasurer under the thirteenth section of the tenth chapter, up to Wednesday, at two o'clock of each week, shall be de-

---

* Part of the original contents of this chapter has been drawn into chapter X, just preceding, passed December 5, 1870. The first two sections of chapter XI, of 1869, were thus transferred in a modified form, section 13 of chapter X being the substitute for them. The provisions of the sixth section of chapter XI, (1869,) will also be found in section 21, of the 24th section in sections 7 and 8, and of the 25th in sections 14 and 15, of chapter X of this collection. Most of the provisions of this chapter X, are also to be found in the new charter.

Chapter XI, as here given, contains all the sections of that chapter in the Ordinances of 1869, which have not been superseded or substituted by sections in chapter X.

posited by him on that day in one of the banks of this city, to the credit of the city, and so all moneys, if over one hundred dollars, received by him up to Saturday, at two o'clock, of each week, shall be deposited in like manner. Ordinances 1869

2. Any person bound to pay money into the city treasury, who shall pay the same otherwise than according to the thirteenth section of the tenth chapter, shall remain liable for such money, and be subject to every fine, forfeiture or penalty to which he would have been subject if he had not paid the same.

3. All money paid into bank, in pursuance of the first section of this ordinance, shall stand on the books of the banks to the credit of the city. But the treasurer shall have no authority to draw any of said money, except by his check, drawn upon a warrant issued by the auditor. If any money in bank, to the credit of the city as aforesaid, shall be paid otherwise than upon his check, drawn upon such warrant, the payment shall not be valid against the city.

4. The proceedings of each of said officers shall be entered in books kept for the purpose, and the books, vouchers and papers properly arranged and preserved.

5. The committee on accounts shall examine the accounts for the necessary contingent expenses of each of said officers, and report to the city council for payment such as they may approve.

6. When it is necessary for either of said officers to be absent from the city or from his office, on account of sickness, the other shall be informed thereof. During such absence, the duties of the officer so absent shall be performed by the clerk in his office.

7. The said officers and their sureties shall be liable for any default or breach of duty of their clerks, respectively, during their absence, in performing the duties of said absent officers.

8. The fiscal year shall commence on the first day of February, and end on the last day of January.

9. Any person having a claim against the city of Richmond, for salary as an officer of the city, or for interest upon bonds of the city, may apply to the auditor, and he shall allow so much on account thereof as may appear to be due.

10. All the claims authorized by ordinance to be paid on the order of a committee, shall be drawn on the auditor, and all other claims against the city shall be presented to the city

Ordinances 1869 council, and such of them as shall be allowed, for the amount allowed, shall be certified by the city clerk to the auditor, and these claims shall be entered upon his books.

11. After any claim is allowed under this chapter, a warrant shall be issued by the auditor for the sum to be paid, which shall be signed by the auditor and attested by his clerk.* Every warrant shall express the particular head of general revenue or expenditure on account of which the money is received or paid.

12. There shall be kept on the books of the auditor's office an account against the treasurer; a separate account for each of the subjects on which there are standing committees of the city council; an account with each officer or agent of the city to whom advances may be made by order of any committee; and such other accounts as may be necessary to exhibit plainly the condition of every branch of the revenue and expenditures of the city.

13. On the last day of each quarter of the fiscal year, the auditor shall compare the books of his office with those in the treasurer's, and strike the balance on his books, showing the amount of money in the treasury; which balance he shall carry forward to the next quarter.

14. All unsettled accounts on the books of the auditor, shall be balanced on the last day of each fiscal year, and the balances brought forward on the first day of the new fiscal year. For this purpose there shall be a general ledger of accounts, which shall be kept so as to show all the balances due to or from the city.

15. The auditor shall, in books kept for the purpose, keep a register of all city property; and also of all bonds or certificates of debt issued by the city.

16. The treasurer on his books shall state the accounts of money received and paid, so as to show distinctly the net produce of each branch of the revenue, and the whole amount thereof, and also the amount of disbursements.

17. He shall keep a list of the warrants drawn upon the treasury in every fiscal year, numbered from one upwards.

18. The treasurer shall furnish the auditor, at the expiration of each quarter of the fiscal year, with a list of the re-

* This requirement of attestation by the clerk seems inconsistent with the second section of this and the thirteenth section of the preceding chapter; but probably the inconsistency is not material.

ceipts, and a list of the payments, at the treasury, during such quarter, showing the number, date and amount of each warrant, and in whose name the money was received, or the warrant issued, placing in separate columns the amount of each warrant under which money was received or paid in a different year from that in which it was issued. The auditor may, however, dispense with such lists at the end of any particular quarter, if he finds that the purpose thereof can be as well attained by examining the treasurer's books for each quarter. **Ordinances 1869**

19. The treasurer shall keep a general ledger of accounts, into which he shall post all the receipts and disbursements at his office, arranging the disbursements under the heads to which they properly belong. There shall be opened on the said ledger a general account of receipts and disbursements, which, on the last day of each quarter of the fiscal year he shall compare with the books kept by the auditor. After they are made to correspond, he shall strike the balance on said account, showing the amount at that time in the treasury; which balance shall be carried forward to the general account for the next quarter.

20. He shall keep accounts on the books of his office with the different banks in which the money of the city is deposited, on which accounts balances shall be struck at the same periods, showing the amount in bank to the credit of the city at the end of each year.

CHAPTER XII.*

CONCERNING THE ASSESSMENT OF TAXES.

Charter, § 54. 1. The person elected to the office of commissioner of the revenue shall, before entering upon the duties of his office, give bond, with sureties, in the sum of five thousand dollars, to be approved by the city council, and entered on their records.†

Ordinances 1869 ch. 12, § 1. 2. The commissioner may appoint one or more deputies, and may take from each of them such security as he may approve, not exceeding the sum of two thousand dollars; and said commissioner shall be liable upon his official bond for the acts of his deputies.

---

* Of this chapter, section 1 is, in substance, from the charter, § 54; section 2 is transferred from the Ordinances of 1869, chapter XII; section 3 is as amended and reordained April 22, 1872; sections 4 to 28, and 30 to 34, were passed February 23, 1874, being sections 1 to 31 of that ordinance; and sections 29, 35 and 36, are from the Ordinances of 1869, chapter XII, answering to sections 31, 35 and 36, of that chapter. The ordinance of February 23, 1874, was passed as a separate chapter; but having no repealing clause, it left the other sections mentioned still in force.

† See note on chapter IV, § 2.

3. The clerk of the chancery court of the city of Richmond, and the clerk of the county court of Henrico, shall be paid annually, the former one hundred dollars, and the latter fifteen dollars; and the clerk of the circuit court of the city of Richmond shall be paid annually ten dollars; upon the certificate of the commissioner of the revenue that they have respectively delivered to him such lists as are mentioned in the sixth and seventh sections of the thirty-fifth chapter of the Code of Virginia, edition of eighteen hundred and sixty, so far as may relate to lands in this city: provided, that if such lists be not furnished by the clerk of said chancery court on or before the tenth day of January, in any year, his compensation therefor shall be fixed at the sum of fifteen dollars. Any party interested may procure, at his costs, and deliver to the commissioner, an abstract from the land office of any grant issued therefrom for lands in this city, or a statement from the clerk of any court of any such judgment, decree or order,* as is mentioned in said seventh* section, or of proceedings under chapter fifty-six of the Code, edition of eighteen hundred and sixty, accompanied by evidence of the payment required by that chapter to vest title.

April 22, 1872.

Code 1873, ch. 33, §§ 16, 17.

Code of 1873, ch. 56.

4. The commissioner shall, as soon as may be after the first day of the fiscal year, ascertain, and in a book (called the land-book) enter separately each parcel of real estate in the city, and enter in as many separate columns as may be necessary, the name of the owner of the freehold, his place of residence, (described, where it can be done, with reference to some particular street or part of a ward,) the nature of his estate, whether in fee or for life, (charging, in the case of a lot leased for a term of years on ground rent, the lot with all improvements thereon, not to the lessee but to the tenant for life, or fee simple owner, under whom the lessee holds,) the number of the lot, the street on which it fronts, and the number of feet that the lot or part of a lot charged, fronts thereon; the value of the buildings on the land, and the value of the land, including buildings; and from whom, when and how the owner derived the land; making transfers on his land-book according to the lists, statements and abstracts furnished by the clerks of Richmond city and Henrico county, or any record evidence furnished by a party interested, or any satis-

Feb. 23, 1874.

* This word *order* should probably be *devise;* the section *eighth* of the ordinance should be *seventh*, as above.

Feb. 23, 1874. factory evidence of mistake in previous entries, and making a note and explanation of each alteration made from the preceding book, showing why and upon what authority it was made. He shall also, in said book, insert a list of all buildings erected in the city during the preceding year, stating as to each building for what use it is intended, the materials of which it is constructed, and the number of stories.

5. In ascertaining the value, the commissioner shall be governed by the valuation for the next preceding year, except in cases of gross mistake, or when otherwise directed by any ordinance or resolution of the city council. He shall add the value of any old building omitted, and of any addition to or improvement on an old building, and of any new building.

6. When a lot becomes the property of different owners in several parcels, the value at which the whole had been assessed, shall be distributed amongst the several parcels, having regard to the value of each parcel compared with that of the whole lot.

7. When real estate is sold for taxes, the commissioner shall, in his land-book, transfer the land sold to the purchaser, and shall continue the same in his name until it shall be redeemed. If any land be purchased for the city, it shall be entered in a separate list at the end of the book. When, however, any land so sold is redeemed, it shall be re-tranferred to the former owner or his grantee.

8. The commissioner, in making out his land-book, shall correct any mistake in the land-book of the preceding year, upon satisfactory evidence thereof. But land which has been correctly charged to one person, shall not be transferred to another without evidence as hereinbefore required, except that when the owner dies intestate, the commissioner may ascertain who are the heirs of the intestate, and charge the land to such heirs.

9. The commissioner (when he takes the list of taxable personal property) shall carry with him the land-book of the preceding year, and the entry of land charged to any person resident, or having an agent within the city, shall be shown to such person or his agent, who shall be required to state, on oath, whether the same be correctly entered; whether any part thereof ought to be transferred to any other person; and if so, to whom, and the nature of the evidence to au-

thorize such transfer; also, to state whether any other land in the city ought to be charged to such resident or non-resident, and to describe the same, as well as to give a description of any of the lands charged to such resident or non-resident, which may not be correctly entered. Any such resident or agent failing to comply with such requisition, shall forfeit twenty dollars. Feb. 23, 1874.

10. No new building shall be assessed until it be so far finished as to be fit for use.

11. In assessing the value of all manufacturing establishments, mills or iron works, all machinery and fixtures attached thereto, shall be included.

12. Each person, of full age and sound mind, not a married woman, shall list the personal property in his possession or care subject to taxation, situate in the city, and the subjects and persons on account of which he is chargeable. The property of a minor shall be listed by his guardian, father, mother, or any other person having charge of the property; of a wife, by her trustee, husband, or by herself; of a deceased person, idiot or lunatic, by the personal representative or committee; of a person for whom property is held in trust by the trustee, if in the city, if not, by the cestui que trust, or his or her father or husband; of a corporation whose assets are in the hands of agents, receivers or factors, by such agents, receivers or factors, of every company, firm, body politic or corporate, by the principal accounting officer, partner or agent thereof.

13. The commissioner shall, as soon as may be after the first day of the fiscal year, ascertain, by personal application, and in a book (called the personal property book) enter: First. The name of every male inhabitant of the city who has attained the age of twenty-one years, recording in separate columns those that are white and those who are not white. Second. The name of each person, whether living in or out of the city, who, in his own right, or as personal representative, committee, trustee, guardian or agent, is possessed of any personal property in the city subject to taxation, showing, in each case, in what character he is possessed of the same. Third. The name of every bank, insurance company, or other incorporated company, located or doing business in the city.

Feb. 23, 1874. 14. He shall, at the same time, in said book, enter the names: First. Of each person or firm carrying on the business of merchant, trader or shopkeeper, and not exclusively engaged in the sale of agricultural products or stock of his own growth or raising. Second. Of every person or firm engaged in the business of a manufacturer, whether of flour, iron, engines, tobacco, machinery, or any other kind of manufacture. Third. Of each banker, stock-broker, or other broker, and of each agent of a company or corporation located out of the city. Fourth. Of each person or firm carrying on the business of auctioneer. Fifth. Of each practising physician, lawyer, dentist, artist, architect, veterinary surgeon, barber, baker, plumber, measurer or inspector of lumber. Sixth. Of all keepers of ordinaries, of houses of private entertainment, of private boarding houses, of cookshops, eating houses, and lager beer or other drinking saloons. Seventh. Of all persons who sell at private sale or rent out houses, or procure employment for labor, for profit, whether auctioneers or not. Eighth. Of all keepers of livery stables, and the number of stalls in each. Ninth. Of all dealers in horses or mules, or cattle, sheep or hogs. Tenth. Of all owners of theatres and buildings, or rooms kept for shows, lectures or public exhibitions. Eleventh. Of all owners or keepers of wagons, drays, carts, hacks, and other wheeled carriages, kept or employed in the city for hire, and the owners or keepers of wagons, drays and carts not kept for hire.

15. The commissioner shall state plainly in his book the peculiar character in which a person or firm is listed; when corporations or agents of corporations are listed, the nature of the business of each; when a merchant is listed, whether he sells by wholesale or retail, on his own account or on commission, and whether he sells spirituous liquors; when manufacturers are listed, the nature of their business; and when auctioneers or brokers are listed, whether they do a general business as such, or are confined to a particular subject.

16. The commissioner shall presume that all persons prosecuting any business by virtue of a license, are applicants for a continuance of the privilege, and list them accordingly. If any other person, either before or after the commencement of the license year, shall desire to engage in a business for which a license is required, he shall report to the commis-

sioner, and through him make application to the committee on finance. If he shall engage in such business before obtaining a license, in addition to any other penalties to which he may be subject, the city council may require him to pay a double tax, as the price of a license to prosecute his business for the residue of the year. Feb. 23, 1874.

17. The commissioner shall, from time to time, before the completion of his annual report, return to the committee on finance, partial alphabetical lists of persons liable to a license tax for the ensuing year, with all facts necessary to determine their classification; and, with such annual report, shall return to the auditor a complete alphabetical list of all such persons. Thereafter, he shall make similar reports to the committee on finance, at least once a month, and more frequently as occasion may require, communicating in all such reports, all violations which may come to his knowledge, of the requirements of the revenue law, by persons prosecuting business without license.

18. Whenever the commissioner shall have reason to doubt whether any person carrying on business liable to a license tax is permanently located in the city, he shall hand to the collector for immediate collection the account against such person for such tax.

19. The commissioner shall ascertain from each person or firm the market value, on the first day of the fiscal year: First. Of all his personal property in the city, except family portraits and private library. Second. Of his capital employed in business and not invested in real estate, or employed in manufacturing outside the city. Third. Of all his shares in corporations or other joint stock companies located in the city, not otherwise assessed for city taxes. Fourth. Of all his bonds or certificates of debt of any country, state, county, municipal or other public corporation, other than the United States, the state of Virginia, or the city of Richmond.

20. He shall ascertain, from each person residing in the city, the amount of all solvent bonds and securities, other than those mentioned in the preceding section, and of all solvent, liquidated and certain demands and claims, however evidenced, or wherever the debtor may live, owing and coming to such person, whether due or not, on the first day of the fiscal year, deducting from the aggregate amount thereof

Feb. 23, 1874. the amount of all such bonds, securities, liquidated claims and demands owing to others from such person as principal debtor; but in neither case shall unsettled book accounts be included. The aggregate of principal and interest shall constitute the amount of a bond or claim due and payable. The present value, after deducting the legal interest, shall constitute the amount of a bond or claim not yet due and payable, and which bears no interest.

21. He shall ascertain from the proper officers of all corporations and joint stock companies, except companies incorporated for the purpose of internal improvement, and banking associations organized under the laws of the United States, or incorporated under the authority of the state of Virginia, the amount of their capital and assets, not exempt from taxation, excluding that invested in real estate, or machinery or fixtures attached thereto, or in manufactures outside of the city, and shall require such officers of all banking associations to report the number of the shares in their respective companies, and the market value of each share on the first day of the fiscal year.

22. The commissioner shall call, in person or by his deputy, upon every person in the city required to render a list of property, moneys, credits or other subjects of taxation; and shall furnish forms for lists and valuations. Every such person shall return statements according to such forms, and annex thereto valuations of the property, verified, if required, by oath, taken and subscribed before the commissioner or some other officer authorized to administer an oath, to be appended to every such statement, to the following effect, viz: "I do solemnly swear, that, to the best of my knowledge and belief, the annexed statements are true, and the valuations not below the fair cash value of the property, and that I have not omitted any subjects or persons on account of which I am chargeable with taxes. So help me God." The auditor shall furnish to the commissioner as many printed copies of such forms as may be necessary, with the required oath printed on the back. The lists received from the tax-payers shall be filed by the commissioner with the auditor.

23. If any person be absent from the city at the time the commissioner calls, (and there be no person on the premises authorized to act for him,) the commissioner may leave at his residence or place of business, proper forms, to enable him

to make out the statements aforesaid; and it shall be the duty of such person, within twenty days thereafter, or as soon as he returns to the city, to return to the commissioner such lists, with valuations, verified by affidavit, as hereinbefore required. Feb. 23, 1874.

24. If the commissioner is not satisfied with the tax-payer's valuation of the property, he may, upon his own view, or such information as he may obtain or possess, adopt what he deems a fair and proper valuation thereof: provided, that where it is practicable, he shall give an opportunity to the tax-payer to be heard before his books are returned to the auditor.

25. If any person, after being furnished with the proper forms, shall fail, for twenty days, to return the lists in the manner prescribed, he shall forfeit not less than ten nor more than fifty dollars. If any person shall refuse to exhibit to the commissioner any property listed, or required to be listed, in order that a fair valuation thereof may be assessed, he shall pay a fine of not less than twenty nor more than one hundred dollars, and he shall be assessed by the commissioner with such property at the highest valuation.

26. No tax shall be assessed upon any real or personal property belonging to the state of Virginia, the United States, or the county of Henrico, or upon any such property belonging to or held in trust for the benefit of any church, or association of churches, religious society, orphan asylum, or other charitable institution, or any college, theological seminary, academy, free school, or public library, or upon any such property held by or in trust for any society of Free Masons, Odd Fellows, Sons of Temperance, Knights of Pythias, or similar benevolent associations, and exclusively employed for charitable and benevolent purposes, or upon any private library; and no license tax shall be required of any tract society, or religious organization, for the privilege of publishing and selling religious papers, pamphlets and books.

27. The commissioner shall keep a separate record for each ward, alphabetically arranged, and opposite to the name of each tax-payer in the ward of his residence or place of business, shall extend the amount of taxes assessed against him.

28. If the commissioner shall ascertain that any person, or any real or personal property which should have been assessed for taxation in previous years, has been omitted, he

Feb. 23, 1874. shall list the same, making a proper assessment of value of property omitted; and in addition to the taxes for the current year, shall charge the taxes for each year, not exceeding five, for which the assessment thereof shall have been omitted, adding thereon interest at the rate of six per centum from the first day of July of each year. The real estate upon which any such arrears of taxes may be due, shall not be liable therefor, if the same shall have been transferred for value to a bona fide purchaser without notice of such arrears.

Ordinances 1869 ch. 12, § 31. 29. When, in consequence of the failure or refusal of any person to give to the commissioner an account of his property and state the value thereof, or produce the same to the commissioner to be valued by him, as required by this ordinance, the list thereof shall have been obtained too late to be placed upon the commissioner's books of personal property for the year in which it is so obtained, it shall be entered on the books of the next year, along with the list of the next year, and there shall be added to the tax omitted at the rate of twenty per centum per annum, on the amount thereof for one or more years, as the case may be.

Feb. 23, 1874. 30. All assessments of value, or taxes, made by the commissioner under any provision of this chapter, shall be subject to review by the committee on finance. Any party feeling aggrieved may appeal to the committee for redress.

31. If the commissioner shall fail to enter correctly and fully all of his own property, and all taxes with which he shall be chargeable, he shall be subject to a double tax, and a fine of not less than fifty nor more than five hundred dollars.

32. The commissioner, after completing his land-book and book of personal property, shall make two fair copies thereof, appending to the originals, and each copy, the following oath: "I, A. B., commissioner of the revenue for the city of Richmond, do swear, that in making out the foregoing book, I have, to the best of my skill and judgment, faithfully pursued the ordinances of the city in the execution of the duties of my office;" with the certificate of some officer authorized to administer an oath, that it has been taken and subscribed before him.

33. Each book shall be retained in the commissioner's office. The copies shall, on or before the first day of June, be delivered to the auditor. Such copies shall be examined by or

under the direction of the committtee on finance, who shall cause all errors therein to be corrected. The auditor shall keep one in his office, and deliver the other to the city collector. Feb. 23, 1874.

34. No payment shall be made the commissioner on account of his services until certified by the finance committee to have been satisfactorily performed. After such certificate, the auditor shall, on the order of the chairman of the committee, pay to the commissioner three-fourths of one per centum upon the amount of tax levied upon the property assessed and returned upon his real and personal property books, and upon licenses assessed on merchants, manufacturers, and so forth. He shall forfeit, unless specially excused by the committee on finance, ten dollars per day for each day beyond the first day of June, during which he may fail to deliver the copies of the books to the auditor, and the auditor shall deduct the same from his compensation.

35. In addition to the duties prescribed by this ordinance, the commissioner shall perform such other services as the city council or committee on finance may require of him, pertaining to the assessment of taxes. Ordinances 1869 ch. 12, §§ 35, 36.

36. The commissioner, in person or by one of his deputies, shall attend at his office each day, except Sundays, from eight till nine o'clock, A. M., for the transaction of business.

CHAPTER XIII.

CONCERNING THE LEVYING OF TAXES.

Estate and Persons.

March 9, 1874. 1. There shall be levied and collected for each fiscal year, the taxes following, to wit:

2. On all real estate not exempt from taxation, one and one-half per centum of the value.

3. On all personal property (including money and credits, stock and capital invested,) not exempt from taxation or employed in any business, for which a license tax is paid to the city, one and one-half per centum of the value, and herein shall be included the capital stock and assets of all savings banks and insurance companies; and all shares of stock in any bank or other corporation doing business in the city, upon the capital stock of which no tax is imposed, the taxes upon such shares to be paid by the cashier or principal officer of the company.

4. On each male resident of the city a poll tax of fifty cents, to be applied only to the support of public schools; and no child shall be entered in any such school whose father, if resident in the city, shall not have paid his poll tax.

Licenses.

5.* All persons desiring to prosecute in the city any business, as auctioneers, agents for the sale or renting of real estate, as commission merchants, traders, brokers, keepers of ordinaries, houses of private entertainment, private boarding houses, eating houses, or cook shops, city scavengers, or any other business which cannot be reached by the ad valorem system, shall pay a license tax for the privilege of prosecuting such business. Such persons shall be divided into eight classes, and the tax to be paid by them shall be, if of class first, eight hundred dollars; second, four hundred dollars; third, two hundred and fifty dollars; fourth, two hundred dollars; fifth, one hundred dollars; sixth, fifty dollars; seventh, thirty-five dollars; eighth, ten dollars. March 23, 1874.

6. The tax imposed by the preceding section, shall not include the privilege of selling by wholesale or retail any wines or spirituous liquors, or a mixture thereof, except to apothecaries furnishing such as medicines upon the prescription of a physician. For any such privilege an additional tax shall be imposed, and all persons desiring such privilege shall be divided into five classes, and obtain a special license, for which they shall pay, if of class first, two hundred and fifty dollars; second, one hundred and fifty dollars; third, one hundred dollars; fourth, fifty dollars; fifth, thirty-five dollars.

7. Junk dealers and pawn brokers shall be divided into classes, and pay a license tax, if in class first, of one hundred and fifty dollars; second, one hundred dollars; third, seventy-five dollars; fourth, twenty-five dollars.

8. Physicians, lawyers, dentists, artists, veterinary surgeons, and measurers or inspectors of lumber, shall be divided into six classes, and pay as a license tax, if in class first, one hundred dollars; second, seventy-five dollars; third, fifty dollars; fourth, thirty dollars; fifth, twenty dollars; sixth, ten dollars.

9. No person other than a salaried officer, acting in behalf of an insurance company whose principal office is situate in the city, and taxed upon its capital and assets, shall engage in the business of soliciting or receiving applications for in-

* Sections 5 to 26 were passed as sections 1 to 22 of separate chapter, March 10 and 23, 1874. Some of the sections afterwards amended at date noted in margin.

March 23, 1874. surance in any insurance company, or receiving and forwarding, directly or indirectly, through any agent thereof, payments of premiums on policies already issued by any insurance company, without obtaining a license. Every person engaged in such business, and communicating directly or indirectly through any other than its licensed resident agent, with an insurance company whose principal office is not situate in the city, shall be deemed an agent of such company. All other persons engaged in such business shall be deemed sub-agents.

10. Agents of insurance companies shall be divided into five classes, and pay a license tax, if in class first, of five hundred dollars; second, four hundred dollars; third, three hundred dollars; fourth, two hundred dollars; fifth one hundred dollars.

11. Sub-agents of insurance companies shall be divided into four classes, and pay a license tax, if in class first, of one hundred dollars; second, fifty dollars; third, twenty-five dollars; fourth, ten dollars.

12. Keepers of livery stables shall pay a license tax of one dollar per each stall.

13. Public theatres, and rooms used for public exhibitions, shall be divided into three classes, and shall pay a license tax, if of class first, of two hundred dollars; second, one hundred dollars; third, fifty dollars.

14. Express companies and telegraph companies, having a place of business in the city, shall be divided into four classes, and pay a license tax, if of class first, of five hundred dollars; second, two hundred dollars; third, one hundred and twenty-five dollars; fourth, fifty dollars.

15. The committee on finance shall classify all persons prosecuting, or proposing to prosecute, any business assessed with a class tax, in performing which duty they may require the attendance and advice of the commissioner of the revenue, the collector, or any city officer. They shall return such classification to the auditor on or before the first day of April. He shall promptly give notice, by due advertisement, in two or more of the city newspapers, that such classification is lying in his office, open to public inspection, and that at times and places therein to be specified, within the next ensuing ten days, the committee will meet to hear all persons complaining of the assignment made of themselves. After

such modifications as the committee may direct, a copy of such classification shall be immediately furnished to the commissioner of the revenue and to the city collector. No change in such classification shall afterwards be made except upon the order of the city council. Any person aggrieved by the action of the committee, may appeal to the city council at its next regular meeting; but hereafter no application for any change shall be entertained, except upon the recommendation of the committee on finance. March 23, 1874.

16. Annual licenses shall expire with the last day of the fiscal year. If the business for which the license tax is required, be commenced after the beginning of the fiscal year, application shall be made to the commissioner of the revenue, who shall, if such business be liable to a class tax, report to the committee on finance, who shall assign the applicant to his proper class. The tax upon the license shall be abated proportionally to the period of the year which has elapsed: provided, however, that in no case shall it be less than one-fourth of the annual tax.

17. Upon the surrender of any license with an assignment on the back thereof, a new license may be issued without charge for the unexpired term to the assignee: provided, that he shall comply with all the conditions upon which such license had been orginally issued.

18. The receipt of the collector, acknowledging payment of the license tax and reciting the character of the business authorized, shall be a sufficient license for prosecuting such business.

19. The collector shall, upon the fifteenth day of April, proceed to collect all license taxes not previously paid; and any person liable to such taxes who shall prosecute his business after the first day of May, without having paid such tax, shall be liable to a fine of not less than one dollar nor more than five dollars for every day of default.

20. Licenses for carts, hacks and other vehicles, or for the privilege of keeping dogs, goats or other animals, shall be issued by the auditor, upon the receipt of the treasurer, showing that the tax has been paid. For every such license, the following tax shall be paid: For every cart, dray or wagon, drawn by one horse or mule, seven dollars; if drawn by two animals, ten dollars; if drawn by three, fifteen dollars; if drawn by four, twenty dollars, unless the body of the vehi- April 27, 1874.

April 27, 1874. cle be on elliptic springs, or on wheels with tires not less than four inches wide, in which case the tax shall be seventeen dollars and fifty cents; for a buggy kept for hire, ten dollars; for a hack or any other wheeled carriage kept for hire, fifteen dollars; for a dog, one dollar and fifty cents, for a bitch, five dollars; for a goat, one dollar and fifty cents.

21. All theatrical performances, save at a licensed theatre or room for public exhibition, shall be liable to a tax of ten dollars per week; nor shall any such license be issued for a period less than one week; every circus exhibition, or exhibition of animals or jugglers, to a tax of thirty dollars per day; and every other public show, exhibition or performance, except in a licensed theatre or room for public exhibitions, to a tax of ten dollars per day; but no tax shall be required on a performance consisting only of vocal or instrumental music, or from a lecturer on any subject of literature, science or art, or from a mechanic or artist exhibiting a work, the product of his own invention, labor or skill, or a model illustrating such work, or from a farmer or stock raiser exhibiting productions or stock of his own raising; and that the mayor may, in his discretion, dispense with the tax in the case of any performance, exhibition or show, for a religious or charitable purpose exclusively.

March 23, 1874. 22. Hawkers and pedlers shall pay a tax of twenty dollars per year; keepers of billiard saloons, of fifty dollars per year for the first table in each saloon, and twenty-five dollars for each additional table; bowling alleys, of twenty dollars per year on each alley; and of pistol galleries, of twenty-five dollars per year.

April 27, 1874. 23. Licenses to exercise any privilege mentioned in the two preceding sections, shall, on the permit of the mayor, be issued by the auditor, upon the receipt of the treasurer showing that the tax has been paid. If the mayor refuse his permission, the city council, upon appeal of the applicant, may, nevertheless, direct the auditor to issue the license, on the treasurer's receipt aforesaid.

March 23, 1874. 24. In any case, the mayor may suspend a license for any performance, exhibition or show, until the house or room shall have been examined by the inspector of public buildings, or three citizens appointed for the purpose by his warrant, and until he is satisfied by their report, in writing, that such house or room has doors and openings of such number and so arranged as, in the case of fire, to afford facilities for escape, and that the same is sufficiently strong and safe. Every such report shall be filed by the mayor in the auditor's office. March 23, 1874.

25. If any person shall attempt to exercise any privilege mentioned in sections twenty and twenty-one of this chapter, without a license, or contrary to the orders of the mayor, he shall be subject to a penalty of not less than ten dollars nor more than twenty dollars for each offence, and shall also be liable for the license tax.

26. Whenever the city seal is to be affixed to any paper, not exempt by law from tax, the treasurer shall affix it, on the warrant of the auditor, and shall not deliver such paper, without obliterating the seal, until a tax of two dollars is paid.* April 27, 1874.

CHAPTER XIV.

CONCERNING THE COLLECTION OF THE ASSESSED TAXES.

1. The person elected to the office of collector of the city taxes, shall give bond, with sureties, in an amount not less April 8, 1872.

---

* The concluding section of the ordinance of March 23, 1874, added April 27, 1874, is not given above, but it may be as well to note here that it repealed "the ordinance passed June 23d, 1873, concerning sample merchants."

April 8, 1872. than fifty thousand dollars, to be approved by the city council, and entered upon their records.*

2. The collector may, with the consent of the city council, appoint one or more deputies, who may be removed from office by said collector, by the mayor, or by the city council. During the collector's continuance in office, his deputy may discharge any of the duties of the office of collector; but the collector and his sureties shall be liable therefor.

3. The collector shall, annually, give notice in at least three of the daily newspapers of the city, for fifteen days prior to the fifteenth day of June, that he will attend at his office daily, between the hours of nine o'clock A. M. and six o'clock P. M., from the fifteenth to the thirtieth of June, inclusive, for the purpose of receiving from any person charged with city taxes, the whole or one-half of the amount of tax charged; and that ten per centum will be added to the amount of tax charged in every case where the party assessed shall fail to pay the whole or one-half, within the time so limited. The collector shall in like manner give notice, for fifteen days prior to the fifteenth of December, that he will attend at his office daily, between the abovementioned hours, from the fifteenth to the thirty-first of December, inclusive, for the purpose of receiving from any person who has already paid one-half only of the city taxes charged to him, the remaining half; and that ten per centum will be added to the amount of said remaining half of the tax charged, in every case where the party assessed shall fail to pay said remaining half within the time so limited. But in case any person having failed to pay in the month of June one-half of the city taxes due from such person, shall fail to pay the whole amount thereof on or before the thirty-first day of December, there shall be added twenty per centum upon the amount of the tax so remaining due.

4. The collector shall, daily, from the fifteenth to the thirtieth of June, inclusive, and from the fifteenth to the thirty-first of December, inclusive, pay into the city treasury the amount received by him for city taxes during the said periods, retaining a commission of one per centum thereon. The amount of taxes received by the collector between the thirtieth of June and the fifteenth of December, and between the thirty-first of December and the fifteenth day of June

* See note on chapter IV, § 2.

following, he shall pay into the city treasury, on Wednesday of every week, retaining a commission of one per centum thereon. April 8, 1872.

5. The collector shall make out lists of the taxes received by him from the fifteenth to the thirtieth of June, inclusive, and from the fifteenth to the thirty-first of December, inclusive, showing the date of receipts, the names of the persons charged with tax, the amount charged, and the amount paid the collector. And the collector shall, as soon as practicable, after the expiration of the abovementioned periods of payments, prepare an alphabetical arrangement of the said lists for more convenient reference thereto.

6. The collector shall proceed to collect all of the taxes assessed on the books of the commissioner of the revenue, and all taxes of which an account or statement is delivered by the commissioner to the collector, under any ordinance of the city.

7. If all taxes with which any person or any estate of a decedent is assessed, be not paid before the first day of September, the collector shall distrain, except where one-half thereof has been paid under the third section, or except the same be suspended by order of the committee on finance, who shall report the reason therefor to the next meeting of the city council.

8. Any goods or chattels in the city belonging to the person or estate assessed with taxes, may be distrained therefor.

9. The goods and chattels of the tenant or other person in possession, claiming under the party or estate assessed with taxes on land, may be distrained, if found on the premises. But when taxes are assessed wholly to one person on a lot, part of which has become the freehold of another by a title recorded before the commencement of the year for which such taxes are assessed, the property belonging to the owner of that part shall not be distrained for more than a due proportion of such taxes.

10. No deed of trust or mortgage upon goods or chattels shall prevent the same from being distrained and sold for taxes assessed against the grantor in such deed, whilst such goods and chattels remain in the grantor's possession; nor shall any such deed prevent the goods and chattels conveyed from being distrained and sold for taxes assessed thereon, no matter in whose possession they may be found.

April 8, 1872. 11. Where the collector cannot find sufficient goods or chattels to distrain for taxes, any person indebted to, or having in his hands estate of the party assessed with such taxes, may be applied to for payment thereof out of such debt or estate, and a payment by such person of the said taxes, either in whole or in part, shall entitle him to a charge or credit for so much on account of such debt or estate against the party so assessed. If the person applied to do not pay so much as it may seem to the officer ought to be recovered on account of the debt or estate in his hands, the officer shall, if the sum due for such taxes exceed not one hundred dollars, procure from the police justice a summons directing such person to appear before him, at such time as may seem reasonable; and if the sum due exceed one hundred dollars, shall procure from the clerk of the court of hustings for the city, a summons directing such person to appear before said court on the first day of the next term thereof. And from the time of the service of any such summons the said taxes shall constitute a lien on the debt so due from such person, or on the said estate in his hands.

12. If such summons be returned executed, and the person so summoned do not appear, judgment shall be entered against him for the sum due for such taxes, and for the fees of the clerk and the officer who may execute the summons.

13. If the person so summoned appear, he shall be interrogated on oath, and such evidence may be heard as shall be adduced, and such judgment shall be rendered as upon the whole case shall seem proper.

14. A tenant from whom payment shall be obtained by distress or otherwise, of taxes due from a person under whom he holds, shall have credit for the same against such person out of the rents he may owe him, except where such tenant is bound to pay such tax by an express contract with such person.

15. Any officer who shall return real estate as delinquent for the non-payment of taxes, when such taxes, or any part thereof, have been received by him, shall forfeit, if the return was made by design, ten times the amount of taxes so actually received, and if the return was by mistake, twice the amount, one-half of which forfeiture shall, in each case, be to the city, and the other half to the person charged with such taxes. And if the collector shall return any real estate

as delinquent, when he had either found, or by using due diligence might have found, sufficient property within the city liable to distress for the taxes for which such real estate is returned delinquent, he shall forfeit to the city a sum equal to five times the amount of the said taxes. April 8, 1872.

16. For horses or any live stock distrained or levied upon, the collector shall provide sufficient sustenance whilst they remain in his possession. Nothing distrained or levied upon shall be removed by him out of the city, unless where it is otherwise specially provided. A distress or levy shall be reasonable.

17. In any case of goods and chattels which the collector shall distrain or levy upon for taxes, and which he may be directed to sell by an order of the court or police justice, (unless such order prescribe a different course,) he shall fix upon a time and place for the sale thereof, and publish notice of the same at least ten days before the day of sale, at the door of the courthouse of the city, and on a court day. The collector shall, at the time and place so appointed, sell to the highest bidder, for cash, the said goods and chattels, or so much thereof as may be necessary.

18. If such goods and chattels be mules, work oxen or horses, they shall be sold at the courthouse, between the hours of ten in the morning and four in the afternoon. The sale shall be on some day of a term of the court, except where the parties shall, at or before the time for advertising the same, in writing, authorize the collector to dispense with the provisions of this section, in which case the sale shall be according to the preceding section.

19. When there is not time on the day appointed for any such sale to complete the same, the sale may be adjourned from day to day, until it shall be completed.

20. If there be good cause to believe that a person assessed with taxes, not on real estate, intends to remove his property out of the city, or to sell out or close his business therein, the collector may, unless such taxes be paid on demand, distrain therefor, although the first day of September may not have arrived, and although one-half thereof may have been paid. To enable the collector to ascertain the amount of taxes charged to any such person, the commissioner, if his books have not been returned, shall, on the application of the collector, deliver him a statement of such taxes. Whenever

April 8, 1872. taxes are received under this section by the collector, before the fifteenth day of June, the collector shall, within one week thereafter, pay the same into the city treasury. Annually, on or before the first day of February, the collector shall render to the auditor an account of all taxes which shall have been in his hands within the year ending on that day, except such taxes as he may be entitled to credit for on account of real estate purchased for the city under the ordinance concerning the sale of land for taxes, and except taxes embraced in the lists hereinafter mentioned in the twenty-first and twenty-second sections.

21. The collector, annually, shall make out after the last day of December, and deliver before the first day of February, to the auditor, verified on oath, a list of property on the commissioner's book improperly placed thereon, or not ascertainable, stating in such list the names, alphabetically, of the persons charged with the taxes of such property, and the amount of such taxes; subjoined to which list, the collector shall make a memorandum of any persons or property which he thinks have been omitted on the books, and of any other errors which he has reason to believe exist therein.

22. The collector shall annually make out a list of the taxes, other than on real estate, which remain uncollected, with the names of the persons charged with such taxes placed alphabetically; which list shall be verified by his oath, and delivered by him to the auditor on or before the first day of February, and a copy thereof shall be posted at the front door of the city hall during the February term of the hustings court.

23. The lists mentioned in the two preceding sections shall be examined by the auditor and laid before the city council. The auditor shall credit the collector on account of the taxes mentioned in said lists with such amount as the city council may direct; and of that mentioned in the twenty-first section he shall, as soon as practicable, deliver a copy to the commissioner, who shall correct his books as may appear proper. After such credit is directed on account of any list, the collector shall not receive any of the taxes mentioned therein, but the list mentioned in the twenty-second section shall be placed by the auditor for collection in the hands of said collector, on such commission as the city council may direct.

24. If, after the collector receives such credit on account of real estate purchased for the city as is mentioned in the twentieth section, and such credit as the city council may direct under the preceding section, any of the taxes which shall have been in his hands remain unpaid, he or his representative shall, on being notified thereof by the auditor, pay into the city treasury the amount of such taxes, deducting therefrom a commission of one per centum thereon. If there be a failure to make such payment for three days after such notice, the collector shall have no commission on said amount, and the auditor shall deliver a copy of the collector's bond to the attorney for the city, who shall proceed thereon. April 8, 1872.

CHAPTER XV.

CONCERNING THE SALE OF LAND FOR TAXES.

1. The year for which taxes on real estate are assessed shall be deemed to commence on the first day of January, and there shall from that day be a lien on real estate for the taxes assessed thereon within the year so commenced. April 10, 1872.

2. The collector of city taxes shall, annually, after the first day of January, and before the March term of the hustings court of this city, prepare a list of the real estate in this city on which taxes remain unpaid for the last or any preceding year, stating the amount due for taxes on each lot, or part of a lot, and the name of the party assessed therewith, and describing such lot or part of a lot as it is entered on the commissioner's book; and he shall post a copy thereof on one of the doors of the city hall, on the first day of the March term of the said hustings court. He shall also, under the direc-

April 10, 1872. tion of the city council, cause to be published in all the daily newspapers of the city, at least ten days previous to the day of sale, a notice of the time and place of sale of the real estate listed as aforesaid; and on some day, not more than twenty nor less than ten days previous to such sale, he shall cause to be published in one or more of said daily papers, to be designated by the committee on finance, the list prepared as above stated of the several parcels of real estate so to be sold.

3. To the list and copy so published and posted he shall subjoin a notice that each lot or part of a lot therein mentioned, or so much thereof as shall be sufficient, will be sold at public auction, between the hours of twelve noon and four in the afternoon, at the city hall, on the first day of the May term of the court of hustings, unless there be previously paid the taxes on the same with the penalty thereon.

4. If the said taxes and such per centum be not previously paid, the collector shall proceed to make sale accordingly; and the sale may be adjourned from day to day, and proceed between the hours aforesaid, until it shall be completed. If, however, the sale be not completed on the last day of the court, it shall be adjourned to the first day of the next court. It may then proceed, and be adjourned in like manner, as at the previous term. Whenever there is an adjournment to the next court, notice thereof shall be given by advertisement in one of the city papers twice a week for two weeks.

5. The collector shall sell separately so much af each lot or part of a lot as shall be sufficient to satisfy the taxes, with the prescribed penalty and charges thereon, with the commission of one per centum on the amount of taxes due.

6. The collector shall not, directly or indirectly, purchase any real estate sold. If he does, he shall forfeit to the city twenty dollars for every such purchase, and the same shall moreover be void.

7. The collector shall make out for each purchaser a receipt to the following effect:

"*Memorandum of Real Estate* within the city of Richmond, sold this —— day of ———, eighteen hundred and ———, for the non-payment of taxes thereon for the year ———: April 10, 1872.

Name of party charged with the taxes.	Description of land charged.	Amount of taxes due.	Quantity of land sold.	Name of purchaser.	Amount of purchase money.

Received of ——— ———, ——— dollars and —— cents, the amount of purchase money for the land mentioned in the above memorandum."

Which receipt shall be delivered by the collector to the purchaser, on the purchaser's paying him the said purchase money.

8. The collector shall make out a list of the sales, with the following caption thereto: "List of real estate within the city of Richmond, sold in the month (or months) of ———, eighteen hundred and ———, for the non-payment of taxes thereon for the year (or years, if more than one year) eighteen hundred and ———." Underneath shall be the several columns mentioned in the seventh section, with a like caption to each column. And there shall be an additional column, showing the date of each sale, unless the sales were all on one day, in which case the day may be mentioned in the caption.

9. The collector shall subscribe and take, before a justice, the following oath: "I, A. B., collector of the taxes of the city of Richmond, do swear that I used due diligence to find property within this city liable to distress for the taxes mentioned in the foregoing list, but could find none; that I have received no part of the said taxes in any other way than by means of the sales mentioned in the said list; that the said list is, I verily believe, correct and just; and that I am not directly or indirectly interested in the purchase of any of the real estate therein mentioned."

10. The said list, with a certificate of the said oath subjoined or attached thereto, shall be returned to the auditor

April 10, 1872. on or before the last day of May, or when the sales are continued to the June court, the last day of June.

11. The owner of any real estate so sold, his heirs or assigns, or any person having a right to charge such real estate for a debt, may redeem the same by paying to the purchaser, his heirs or assigns, within two years from the sale thereof, the amount for which the same was so sold, and such additional taxes thereon as may have been paid by the purchaser, his heirs or assigns, with interest on the said purchase money and taxes, at the rate of twelve per centum per annum from the times that the same may have been so paid; or the same may be paid within the said two years to the treasurer of the city, in any case in which the purchaser, his heirs or assigns, may refuse to receive the same, or he or they shall not reside, or cannot be found in the city of Richmond.

12. The purchaser of any real estate sold for taxes, and not redeemed, shall, after the expiration of two years from the sale, obtain from the auditor a deed conveying the same, wherein shall be set forth what appears in his office in relation to the sale. If the sale be not of the whole lot or part of a lot that is delinquent, the purchaser shall have the part sold surveyed and laid off, at his expense, by the surveyor of the city, so as not to include the improvements on the same, if it can be avoided. A plat and certificate of every such survey shall be delivered to the auditor, and referred to in his deed, and annexed by him thereto.

13. When the purchaser has assigned the benefit of his purchase, the deed may, with his assent, evidenced by his joining therein, or by a writing annexed thereto, be executed to his assignee. If the purchaser shall have died, his heirs or assigns may move the chancery court of this city to order the auditor to execute a deed to such heirs or assigns.

14. If no such deed or order of court be made under this chapter within one year after the expiration of the said two years, the former owner, his heirs or assigns, may, after such year, and before such deed or order is made, redeem the land by paying such amount, with such additional taxes and such interest as is mentioned in the eleventh section, together with the costs of the survey or report, (and interest thereon,)

if any shall have been returned to the treasurer. The payment under this section may be to the treasurer. April 10, 1872.

15. When the purchaser of any real estate sold for taxes, his heirs or assigns, shall have obtained a deed therefor under this ordinance, and within sixty days from the date of such deed, shall have caused the same to be recorded in the clerk's office of the chancery court of this city, such estate shall stand vested in the grantee in such deed as was vested in the party assessed with the taxes (on account whereof the sale was made) at the commencement of the year for which the said taxes were assessed, notwithstanding any irregularity in the proceedings under which the said grantee claims title, unless such irregularity appear on the face of the proceedings. And if it be alleged that the taxes, for the nonpayment of which the sale was made, were not in arrear, the party making such allegation must establish the truth thereof, by proving that the taxes were paid.

16. Any infant, married woman, insane person, or person imprisoned, whose real estate may have been so sold, or his heirs, may redeem the same by paying to the purchaser, his heirs or assigns, within two years after the removal of the disability, the amount for which the same was so sold, with the necessary charges incurred by the purchaser, his heirs or assigns, in obtaining the title under the sale, and such additional taxes on the estate as may have been paid by the purchaser, his heirs or assigns, and interest on the said items, at the rate of ten per centum per annum from the time the same may have been paid. Upon such payment within two years after the removal of such disability, the purchaser, his heirs or assigns, shall, at the cost of the original owner, his heirs or assigns, convey to him or them, by deed, with special warranty, the real estate so sold.

17. When a parcel of real estate is offered for sale as aforesaid, by the collector, and no person present bids such sum as is required by the fifth section, the collector shall purchase the same on behalf of the city for the taxes, penalty and charges thereon. A list of the real estate so purchased by the city shall be made out by the collector, and after being verified by him, on oath, shall, on or before the last day of May or June, if the sale is made in June, be delivered by him to the auditor, who shall make out a

April 10, 1872. copy thereof and deliver it to the commissioner, and credit the collector with the amount for which the said real estate may have been so purchased, but not with any commission thereon. There shall be no right to such credit unless the said list be so delivered on or before the said last day of May, or of June, if the sale is made in June. And, on receipt by the commissioner of such certified list of sales, he shall forthwith transfer upon his books the several lots or parts of lots so sold to the purchasers thereof respectively, whether the same be purchased by the city, or by persons other than the city. And thereafter the taxes accruing thereon, shall be regularly assessed in the names of the parties so purchasing, who shall pay the same.

18. The previous owner of any real estate so purchased for the city, his heirs or assigns, or any person having a right to charge such real estate for a debt, may, within two years, and until a further sale thereof by authority of the city council, redeem the same by paying to the treasurer the amount for which such real estate was so purchased, with such additional sums as have accrued for taxes thereon, and interest at the rate of twelve per centum per annum on the former amount from the date of the purchase, and on the additional sums from the fifteenth day of December, in the year in which the same shall have accrued. When real estate so purchased is redeemed, the treasurer shall certify the fact to the commissioner of the revenue, who shall thereupon re-transfer the same accordingly.

CHAPTER XVI.

CONCERNING THE SALE OR PLEDGE OF SECOND-HAND ARTICLES.*

Sec.
1. Dealers in second-hand articles to obtain license, and pay tax thereon.
2. License to be placed conspicuously in shop; to whom and for what shop to be open; license necessary and not transferrable; penalty for doing such business without license.

May 30, 1870. 1. Hereafter the keeper or keepers of every shop within the limits of the city of Richmond, where any kind of arti-

* These junk dealers are classed in the general license ordinance, chapter XIII, and subjected to its lighter penalties for carrying on business without license, and perhaps that later provision may be considered as so far repealing this; but there appears to be nothing which can be construed as a repeal of the rest of this chapter.

cles, such as watches, jewelry, junk, old metals, or other like commodities, and all kinds of second-hand articles are purchased, sold, bartered, exchanged or pledged, shall obtain from the city collector a license to do so; and shall pay for said license the amount with which such person or persons may have been assessed. May 30, 1870.

2. Every person receiving such license shall place the same in some prominent place in his shop, where it may be seen by every one. Such shop shall be open at all times to the inspection of the mayor, the police, or any citizen of the city, county or state, and such mayor, police, citizen, or their agents, shall have power to take and carry away any and every article of such citizen, which may have been stolen, and bought by such dealer or dealers. No such business shall be carried on until the license tax shall have been paid; and the said license shall not be transferable; and the person or persons attempting to do the said business without first obtaining a license therefor, shall be subject to a fine of not less than two hundred dollars, or imprisonment not less than thirty nor more than sixty days.

Title 3.

OF THE CITY DEBT.

CHAPTER XVII.*

CONCERNING THE DEBT OF THE CITY.

Sept. 4, 1871. 1. In order to preserve in the office of the treasurer a duplicate record of the accounts of the debt of the city, and the transaction of all business connected therewith, it is hereby provided that the existing certificates of debts and bonds of the city, registered in the office of the auditor, and amounting, on the first day of July, eighteen hundred and seventy-one, to the sum of two millions eight hundred and eighty-four thousand six hundred and seventy-eight dollars and five cents, and all certificates or bonds hereafter issued, be registered also in the office of the treasurer; and the semiannual interest accruing thereon, shall be paid by the treasurer, on the warrant of the auditor, until the said certificates or bonds shall be redeemed.

2. The certificates of debt or bonds now registered in the auditor's office, shall continue registered therein, and all cer-

* This chapter corresponds in subject with chapter XVIII, of 1869. Chapter XVII of that revisal, was "Concerning Licenses granted by the Mayor," the provisions of which have been superseded by later provisions in chapter XIII of this collection, concerning the levying of taxes.

tificates or bonds hereafter issued under the authority of the city council, shall be registered in the same office, as well as in that of the treasurer. In the books containing such registry in both offices, reference shall be made to the special act of the city council authorizing their issue. Sept. 4, 1871.

3. Every such certificate or bond shall be signed by the treasurer, and be under the seal of the city, and countersigned by the auditor.

4. All bonds payable to bearer, shall be signed and countersigned as herein provided for the issue of certificates of debt, and coupons of interest transferable by delivery, shall be attached to said bonds, signed by the treasurer; and the said bonds and coupons attached thereto, shall be payable upon the warrants of the auditor at the office of the treasurer.

5. All certificates or bonds hereafter issued for the permanent debt of the city, shall only be in sums of one hundred dollars, or some multiple thereof.

6. Certificates of debt may, at the option of the holder, be exchanged for coupon bonds of the denomination of one thousand dollars, due July first, nineteen hundred and four, or coupon bonds may be exchanged for registered certificates, due thirty-four years after the first of January or July preceding their issue; and on like option several certificates and bonds held by the same owner, maturing at different dates, may be consolidated into one certificate in a sum of one hundred dollars, or any multiple thereof; if consolidated into coupon bonds they must be in sums of one thousand dollars; both certificates and bonds redeemable as herein stated. Any certificate must be cancelled upon its surrender, and new certificates of the multiple of one hundred dollars issued in lieu thereof, not exceeding together the amount of the former. Nov. 3, 1871.

7. The person appearing on the books of the office in which any certificate is registered as the owner thereof, shall be deemed the owner as it regards the city, so as to make valid all payments by the city of Richmond on account thereof, to such person, or his personal representative, made before a transfer of the certificate on the books of the said office. Sept. 4, 1871.

8. But if the person so appearing on the books as owner shall, bona fide and for valuable consideration, sell, pledge, or otherwise dispose of such certificate to another, and deliver to him the certificate, with the power of attorney, authorizing the transfer thereof to him on the books of the

Sept. 4, 1871. proper office, the title of the former in the said certificate (both at law and equity) shall vest in the latter for the whole amount of the certificate, or so much thereof as may be necessary to effect the purpose of the sale, pledge, or other disposition, and it shall so vest not only as between the parties themselves, but also as against the creditors of, and subsequent purchasers from the former, subject to the preceding section.

9. Upon the delivery of the said certificate a transfer may be made on the books of the city, either of the whole amount or any part thereof, by the person appearing on the said books as the owner, or by another having a power of attorney from him, duly authenticated, authorizing such transfer. Upon a transfer the former certificate shall be cancelled, and one or more new certificates shall be issued (according to the provisions of the first section,) not exceeding together the amount of that cancelled. But no transfer shall be made on the said books within ten days next preceding the first day of January and the first day of July.

10. Every cancelled certificate shall remain filed in the treasurer's office.

11. When any certificate shall be lost by the holder thereof, he may produce to the auditor proof of his having advertised the same once a week for three months in a newspaper published in the city of Richmond, file in the office of the auditor an affidavit setting forth the time, place and circumstances of the loss, and execute a bond to the city, with one or more sureties, approved by the committee on finance, conditioned to indemnify all persons against any loss in consequence of issuing any new certificate in place of the one so lost, and thereupon a new certificate may be issued and registered.

12. Notes for a temporary debt of the city shall be signed by the auditor and the treasurer, and recorded in both offices.

CHAPTER XVIII.*

CONCERNING THE SINKING FUND.

1. For the purpose of managing, preserving and applying the sinking fund, required by the charter of the city to be created, the mayor, the treasurer and the chairman of the committee on finance, for the time being, shall constitute a board, to be called "the commissioners of the sinking fund." March 9, 1874.

2. The city treasurer shall keep an account in one or more of the banks, designated as depositories of the city funds, in the name of the said board, and all sums deposited to the credit of the said account, shall be sacredly appropriated to the payment of the interest of the city debt and the principal of such part as may be redeemable, and to no other purpose whatever, unless in time of war, insurrection or invasion, the general assembly of the state of Virginia may authorize other disposition thereof.

3. Any two of the commissioners may form a board for the transaction of business. The mayor, or in his absence, the chairman of the committee on finance, shall be the president of the board. The auditor shall be the secretary, and shall keep a full and correct journal of the proceedings of every meeting, to be signed by himself and the president, and shall preserve all the books and papers and securities of the board in his office. The meetings of the board, unless otherwise ordered, shall be held in his office.

* Corresponds in subject with chapter XIX of 1869.

March 9, 1874. 4. The board shall meet at least twice a year—as soon as practicable after the fifteenth day of June and December, and as much oftener as the public interest may require. At each semi-annual meeting, the auditor shall present a full statement, showing the amount of the outstanding public debt, and the interest already due or to become due thereon, within the ensuing half-year; and the amount with which the board is chargeable on account of advancements previously made to satisfy any portion of the interest then overdue and unpaid. The board, after examination of the said statement, shall direct the auditor to have deposited to their credit such sum, specifying the amount, as in addition to advancements already made, shall appear to be necessary to enable them to satisfy and pay off all claims for interest then due, or to become due within the ensuing half-year, and in addition thereto, one-half of one per cent. of the principal of the outstanding debt of the city. The auditor shall forthwith issue his warrant to the treasurer, in accordance with such order, and the treasurer shall thereupon deposit such amount to the credit of the board out of any funds in the treasury, to the exclusion of any and all other claims upon the city.

5. Upon the first day of every fiscal year, the auditor shall issue his warrants directing the treasurer to deposit to the credit of the board the unexpended balance of every ordinary appropriation of the previous year, specifying in each warrant the amount so ordered to be deposited and the account from which the balance is derived. By similar warrant, when payment is to be made of any bond or note owned by the city, or of the proceeds of sale of any real estate owned by the city he shall direct the treasurer to receive the same and deposit it to the credit of the board.

6. After providing for the payment of the interest, the board shall apply any residue of funds to their credit to the redemption of such part of the principal of the city debt, as may be redeemable. If no part be redeemable, such residue shall be devoted to the purchase, at market value, of any outstanding certificates of debt or coupon bonds of the city. Any coupon bonds, or other evidences of city debt, purchased or redeemed, shall be immediately canceled in the presence of the president of the board,* and certificates of debt to the

* In the ordinance as passed immediately after the direction to cancel in the presence of the president of the board, there followed the words "in the manner prescribed in

said board, corresponding in amount, rate of interest and date of maturity, be issued in lieu of any such bonds purchased. If no bonds or certificates of debt of the city can be purchased, investment may be made in registered bonds of the state of Virginia, or of the United States, the accruing interest whereon shall, when due, be collected by the treasurer, on the order of the auditor, and deposited to the credit of the board. All such bonds or certificates, whether of the city or state of Virginia, or of the United States, shall be held by the board until some part of the city debt shall become due, when, so far as may become necessary, they shall be sold, and the proceeds applied to the redemption of the city debt. For the purposes contemplated by this section, the board may apply any funds to their credit; provided that there be always retained a sum at least equal to ninety per centum of any interest upon the city debt due or to become due prior to their next semi-annual demand upon the city treasury. March 9, 1874.

7. Payment out of any funds to the credit of the board shall only be made upon checks signed by the city treasurer, upon the face of which shall be printed in conspicuous characters, the words: "Sinking Fund." Such checks shall only be issued by the treasurer, upon the back of warrants signed by the auditor, as auditor and as secretary of the board, and specifying upon their face that the same is payable on account of interest due, or principal of the city debt, or investment ordered by the board; and unless the warrant specify that the amount to be paid is due on account of interest, the same shall be also signed by the president of the board.

8. The auditor shall issue his warrant for any interest due, upon application in person or by attorney of any party, appearing upon his books to be the owner of any certificate of debt, or upon the presentation of any matured coupons, every such coupon to be canceled in the presence of the party presenting it, before delivery of the warrant, unless there be some reason to doubt the holder's title, in which event he may call a meeting of the board and require their instructions.

---

section 5, chapter XX, of the City Ordinances." The compiler could find no such provision anywhere, as to the manner of canceling. Chapter XX, of the Ordinances of 1869, has no fifth section, and is on an entirely different subject from this of the sinking fund. Canceling is prescribed in certain cases by the fifth section of chapter XIX, but no directions are there given as to the manner of canceling. The words mentioned have therefore been omitted.

March 9, 1874. 9. The auditor and treasurer shall each keep books specially labeled, and reserved for accounts of the board, in which they shall retain receipts for all warrants or checks issued, upon account of the board.

April 27, 1874. 10. As soon as practicable after the first day of January, the treasurer shall render to the board a full account of the amount standing to their credit in the several depositories of the city, showing, in detail, the several items of credit during the previous year: and the auditor shall furnish a full statement of the outstanding city debt, setting out the amount of interest due and unpaid, or to become due during the ensuing year, and of the principal thereof maturing for payment during such year.

March 9, 1874. 11. The auditor, with his January report, as required in the fourth section of this chapter,* shall return a full statement of all disbursements ordered by him as secretary of the board, during the previous year, distributing the same between the three several heads of Interest, Redemption and Investment. The interest account shall show how much has been paid on account of the registered debt, and how much on acconnt of matured coupons.

12. After the receipt of the January reports of the auditor and treasurer, the board shall carefully examine the same and require the auditor to produce before them all coupon bonds and coupons canceled, and all matured coupon bonds, paid during the preceding year. Upon careful review of such accounts, the board shall cause all such coupon bonds and coupons to be burnt and destroyed in their presence, preserving a full record thereof.

13. On or before the first regular meeting of the city council in February of each year, the board shall make a report to the city council of their proceedings during the previous year, forwarding therewith copies of all reports made to them during such year by the auditor and the treasurer.

---

*This report of the auditor is required by the fourth section to be made to the semi-annual meeting of the board, to be held as soon as practicable after the 15th day of December.

Title 4.

OF THE CITY PROPERTY.

CHAPTER XIX.*

CONCERNING STOCK IN JOINT-STOCK COMPANIES.

1. There shall be annually appointed by the city council in the month of October, or as soon thereafter as practicable, three proxies in each company wherein stock is owned by the city, whose term of office shall continue until their successors are appointed, unless they be sooner removed.† Ordinances 1869

2. In a meeting of stockholders in a company the vote of the city on its stock may be given by such of the proxies appointed to such company as may be present, or by a majority of those present. If it be apprehended that any proxy will not be in attendance, the city council, or if it be not sitting, and the meeting of stockholders is sitting, or to sit within two days, three members of the city council (of whom the president shall be one) may, without removing such proxy, make a temporary appointment in his stead, to be in force during his absence.

---

* Corresponds with chapter XX of 1869.

† Though term of office is here referred to, it is doubtful whether these can be considered officers appointed by the council, and, consequently, whether the case can properly come under the rule of chapter IV, § 2. The time of appointment and the term of office are therefore left as they were.

Ordinances 1869 3. The proxies of the city in any company shall, from time to time, make report to the city council of matters affecting the interest of the city in such company, and lay before it copies of the report of the president and directors of such company, the proceedings of the stockholders thereof, and other documents relating to the company's works.

4. When a meeting of stockholders in a company in which the city owns stock is held out of this city, each proxy of the city attending such meeting shall be paid four dollars per day for every day of such attendance, and at the rate of four dollars for every twenty miles of necessary travel in going to and returning from such meeting.

CHAPTER XX.*

CONCERNING THE GROUNDS AND BUILDINGS OF THE CITY.

1. The committee on public grounds and buildings shall be charged with, and have the care and management of, all the grounds and other real property of the city, both within and without the city, except as hereinafter mentioned, so far as relates to the improvement and repairs thereof. No improvements or repairs shall be made or done to or upon any of the said property by the committee, at a cost exceeding one hundred dollars per month, in any one year, without authority from the city council.

2. The said committee shall report to the city council annually, or oftener, as they deem it proper, the state and condition of all the lands and buildings belonging to the city, and all such improvements and repairs as they may deem proper to have made or done to or upon any portion of the said property, or to the streets or other highways adjacent thereto, and at the same time render an account of all moneys received and expended by them; which said report shall be accompanied by an estimate of the costs of such improve-

* Chapter XXI of the Ordinances of 1869.

ments or repairs to be made by the superintendent of public grounds, as well as of all money expended by them or under their order in the improvements or repairs of the same. Ordinances 1869

3. The engineer of the city shall be the superintendent of all the grounds and buildings within and without the city, belonging to the city, except as hereinafter mentioned. He shall, once in every three months, or oftener, if he deem it necessary, report to the said committee the state and condition of the said property, the repairs done or necessary to be done upon or to the same, and the cost thereof, and make such suggestions as he may deem proper for the improvement of the said property, or any part thereof. Under the control and direction of the said committee, he shall, as far as practicable, keep all said property in good order, and prevent injury to any part or portion thereof, and for that purpose he is hereby given and vested with the powers and authority of a police officer of the city, and shall report promptly to the police justice* all violations of any ordinance of the city or of the law of the state, committed in, to or upon said property. It shall moreover be his duty to purchase, under the control, direction and approval of said committee, all fuel necessary for the use of the city, and have the same properly stored.

4. The said superintendent may, under the direction of the committee, make and sign any contract for the execution of work ordered by them under this ordinance, or under authority from the city council; and whatever work is so ordered, when executed, shall be paid for by a draft upon the auditor, stating the amount to be paid and for what; which draft shall be signed by the chairman of the committee, after examining and approving the same.

5. If the city council shall at any time authorize any buildings or other real estate owned by the city, to be rented out;

* In many places in the subsequent ordinances of this collection, especially in chapters of titles 6 and 11, it was found necessary to substitute "police justice" for "mayor," as has been done in this section. The compiler has made these substitutions with care, and he believes correctly; but as a remedy for possible error he would call attention to such changes; which in fact have been made by him in almost all of the cases where the title "police justice" now occurs, the chief exceptions being of the chapter defining the judicial powers of the office, and a few of the more recent ordinances concerning police matters, &c., in which the proper adaptations to the new system were made in the ordinances as passed. If any further corrections should be found necessary, they will probably be of some few provisions in which the change referred to has not been made, because of some uncertainty as to the extent of the powers of the new office. Possibly the council will have to pass an ordinance defining more exactly the powers of the police justice out of court.

Ordinances 1869 the superintendent shall, under the control and direction of the committee, rent out the same, and shall report to the auditor of the city all such contracts, stating the property rented, and to whom, what rent is to be received, when it commenced and when it is to terminate.

6. This chapter shall not apply to the alms house and the grounds attached to it, the water works, the gas works, or the burying grounds.

CHAPTER XXI.*

CONCERNING ST. JOHN'S BURYING GROUND.

Whereas the lots on Richmond Hill, on which the old church stands, and which are known in the plan of the city of Richmond by the numbers ninety-seven and ninety-eight, were for a long period of time used as a place of burial for the citizens generally; and in seventeen hundred and ninety-nine the council purchased from John Adams, lot number one hundred and eleven, and from Richard Adams, Jr., executor of Thomas B. Adams, lot number one hundred and twelve, and obtained deeds conveying the same to the city, which deeds were admitted to record in the county court of Henrico, on the eighth of April, eighteen hundred; and thereupon the council, by an arrangement with the vestry of the said church, caused the said four lots, comprising one entire square, to be enclosed by a brick wall; and the square has thenceforth been used as a place for the interment of the dead of every religious denomination, until the council obtained other cemeteries; and whereas, at the time of said arrangement, it was understood that the corporate authorities of the city should incur all the necessary expense attending the erection of gates and steps, and keeping the enclosure in good repair; and should at all times have power to establish such regulations as they might think proper as to the ground within said enclosure; therefore,

*Chapter XXII of 1869.

1. In the month of December of each year,* or as soon thereafter as practicable, the city council shall appoint three persons, who may be members of the city council or citizens, to act as a committee of the square in which the old church is situated. Any vacancy in said committee may, at any time, be filled by the city council. Ordinances 1869

2. The committee shall cause to be kept in good order the whole of said enclosure, with the gates and steps for passing through it, and every thing that is within the enclosure and outside the church. For these purposes the auditor shall pay, upon the order of the chairman of the committee, a sum not exceeding two hundred dollars in any year. Nothing in this section shall be construed to authorize the committee to prevent or interfere with the use of the church by the congregation thereof.

3. No body shall be buried in said square except by consent of the committee. Nor shall any body be buried in any place in the city other than at a burying ground owned by the city, except in the burying ground of the Society of Friends, on Cary, between Nineteenth and Twentieth streets, or that of the Hebrew congregation. Any person who shall bury or cause to be buried a dead body in a place in the city not allowed by this section, shall pay to the city a fine of five dollars for every day that said body shall remain in such place.

---

* See note on chapter XIX, § 1.

CHAPTER XXII.*

CONCERNING THE CITY CEMETERIES.

Ordinances 1869 1. The committee on cemeteries shall have the control and management of the Shockoe Hill and Oakwood cemeteries. So far as the same is not already done, or the ground is not already appropriated, the committee shall have authority to lay off the grounds into sections, half sections and quarter sections, and to fix the price of each section, half or quarter section, and to divide the grounds so as to appropriate a part for the burial of colored persons. But the burial of colored persons in Shockoe Hill cemetery shall not be authorized in any part thereof which is now reserved for the burial of white people. The committee shall also have a general control over the manner and arrangement of the interments in said cemeteries; of the preservation, improvement and embellishment of the grounds, and over the keepers and other persons employed about them; and they shall, from time to time, visit and inspect them.

June 21, 1870. 2. The committee shall, annually, in the month of July, appoint a keeper for Oakwood cemetery, who shall take charge of the same and keep it in order. The keeper shall act under the directions of the committee; and the committee shall take care that he performs his duties; and if he neglects the same; the committee may remove him and appoint another in his place, and shall report to the city council the cause of

* Chapter XXIII of 1869.

the removal. If at any time the said office is vacant, the committee may fill the vacancy; and the keeper so appointed shall hold his office until the next July unless sooner removed. The said keeper shall receive in full compensation for his services, a salary of five hundred dollars per annum, and be entitled to live, free of rent, in the house on the premises: provided, however, that no payments on account of salary shall be made to him until he shall have made all reports or returns that may be required of him by this ordinance or by the committee on cemeteries. The superintendent of the almshouse, having been also made keeper of the Shockoe Hill cemetery, shall, as such keeper, be under the direction of the committee thereon, who shall see that the said keeper performs his duties, and if he neglects the same, the committee shall report him to the city council. He shall perform all the duties imposed upon him by this chapter, and shall keep an account of all moneys received by him for burials, and of all expended by him in the hire of hands and other necessary expenses of the said cemetery, and shall make monthly reports thereof to the committee; which monthly reports shall be consolidated quarterly and returned to the auditor. And at the time of returning the said consolidated quarterly report, he shall pay to the treasurer such sum as shall have been received by him for burials during the preceding quarter, after deducting the amount paid by him for the hire of hands and other necessary expenses of the cemetery. June 21, 1870.

3. Any white person, a resident of the city of Richmond or county of Henrico for one year, may select in the said cemeteries any section, half-section or quarter-section, to which no other person has acquired title, and obtain from the keeper a certificate of his location. But no location of any person in his own right, or on his own account, shall be of more than a section or less than a quarter-section, unless some military company or some society shall, with the consent of the committee, purchase one or more sections; and they shall be required to conform to the ordinances. Ordinances 1869

4. Upon such certificate being presented to the treasurer, and upon payment being made to him of such price as may be fixed by the committee for the section, half-section or quarter-section, as the case may be, the treasurer shall issue and deliver to the person making the location and payment,

Ordinances 1869 a certificate describing the number of the range and the number of the section; and if the location be of less than a whole section, the number of each half or quarter-section, and setting forth that the person is entitled to the section, half-section or quarter-section so paid for.

5. The person to whom the treasurer issues such certificate shall thenceforth be entitled to the section, half-section or quarter-section so paid for, as a burying-place for himself or for any white person who is a member of his family, or one of his descendants or friends. But there shall be no enclosure erected in the cemetery of greater height than four feet. And when a section, half-section or quarter-section shall remain without any interment therein for twenty years, and the purchaser shall have died or removed from the city, and no relative of his is known to the committee to reside in the city, they shall give notice thereof once a week for four weeks in a newspaper published in the city; and if no relative of the purchaser appear within thirty days from the last day of said publication, then the said section, or half-section, or quarter-section, as the case may be, shall revert to the city. And whether there be such reverter or not, the city council may at any and all times, regulate the interments in said cemetery, or any part thereof, as may seem to it proper.

6. A citizen of this city, or a citizen of Henrico, or any stranger or person visiting the city or county, may be buried in that part of the cemetery appropriated for promiscuous interments, and called the "public portion," on payment of two dollars and fifty cents to the treasurer, whose receipt therefor shall be produced to the keeper of the cemetery before the interment is made.

7. Notwithstanding the provisions hereinbefore contained, a person convicted of an offence, for which an infamous punishment is denounced, shall not be interred within the enclosure of the cemetery, unless a majority of the committee assent thereto.

8. The keepers, when informed that a grave is required for the body of any person, if such person is to be buried in a section which has been purchased, shall have the grave dug in the section, in the spot designated by the friend of the deceased who applies to him; and in other cases the grave shall be dug in a proper place; and in either case he shall have the

body properly interred therein: for which he may charge, except for a pauper, a price as follows: For a grave for a person over fourteen years of age, if the coffin be in a box, three and a half dollars; if not in a box, two dollars; and for all other persons, two dollars, whether in a box or not. Ordinances 1869

9. Every grave which the keeper has dug, whether for the body of a white or colored person, shall be at least six feet deep, unless the committee shall authorize a less depth in the "public portion;" and in no case shall it be of less depth than five feet. And no interment shall be made in said "public portion," which shall disturb the remains of a dead body, or which shall displace or injure any monument, stone or slab erected over a grave.

10. Under the direction of the committee, the keepers shall plant trees and other plants in and through the grounds, and shall improve and keep in order the walks and grounds.

11. Whenever any person shall die in the city of Richmond, it shall be the duty of the physician who attended during his or her last sickness, or of the coroner when the case comes under his notice, to furnish, within twenty four hours after the death, to the undertaker, or other person superintending the burial, a certificate setting forth, as far as the same can be ascertained, the full name, sex, color, age, residence, place of nativity, occupation and condition (whether married or single) of the person deceased, and the cause and date of death.

12. No person having charge, as sexton or otherwise, of any vault, burying ground or cemetery within the city or its sanitary jurisdiction, shall be allowed to bury any dead person in any grave, vault or tomb, until he has been furnished with a certificate as aforesaid from a licensed physician or the coroner.

13. No undertaker or other person shall move the dead body of any person who has died in the city, and has not been buried, to any place beyond the limits of the city, or of its sanitary jurisdiction, without procuring a permit from a member of the board of health, upon the aforesaid certificate from the attending physician or coroner. Nor shall any master, agent or person having charge of or attached to any steamboat, sailing or other vessel, car, stage, or any other public or private conveyance, move, convey, or allow to be conveyed, the dead body of any person who has died in the June 21, 1870.

June 21, 1870. city, to any place beyond the limits of the city, or of its sanitary jurisdiction, without a permit as aforesaid.

Ordinances 1869 14. In case any person shall die without the attendance of a physician, or if the physician who did attend at the time of the death, refuses or neglects to furnish a certificate as aforesaid, it shall be the duty of the undertaker, or of any person acquainted with the facts, to report the same to the health officer, or any member of the board of health, who shall be authorized to give a certificate as aforesaid, provided it be not a case requiring the attendance of the coroner.

15. Every sexton or other person having charge of any burying ground, cemetery or vault, within the city or its sanitary jurisdiction, shall, before twelve o'clock of Monday of each week, make return to the board of health, of the bodies of persons buried since the last return thereof, with the certificate required in section eleven, and in such form and specifying such particulars as the special regulations of the board of health shall require.

June 21, 1870. 16. In case any physician or coroner shall refuse or neglect to furnish such certificate as aforesaid, he shall forfeit and pay the sum of five dollars for each offence; and every undertaker, sexton or other person, removing the dead body of any person, or who, having charge of any vault, burying ground or cemetery, steamboat, vessel, car, stage, or any other public or private conveyance, refuses or neglects to perform any of the duties required by this ordinance, shall forfeit and pay for every such offence the sum of twenty-five dollars.

April 10, 1872. 17. Any person who shall shoot, hunt or range over the grounds of a city cemetery shall, upon conviction of such offence, be liable to a fine of not less than five nor more than twenty dollars. And the keepers of city cemeteries are hereby invested with police jurisdiction and authority to arrest any and all persons so offending, and carry him or them before the proper officer, to be dealt with according to this ordinance. And said keepers are directed to post at conspicuous points of the cemeteries, under their charges respectively, due and full notice of this ordinance.

CHAPTER XXIII.*

CONCERNING THE GAS WORKS.

1. There shall be elected by the city council a superintendent of the gas works, who shall continue in office for two years, and until his successor is appointed and qualifies, unless sooner removed.† And the committee on light, as soon as practicable after its appointment, shall appoint an inspector of gas, and report his name to the city council. Ordinances 1869

2. The committee shall meet in the afternoon, on the first Thursday in every month, and also meet at such other times as they may see fit. They shall have the superintendence and general government of the gas works. And the superintendent of the gas works and the inspector of gas shall, so far as may be consistent with the duties prescribed by this chapter, act according to the directions of the said committee.

* Chapter XXIV of 1869.

† See note on chapter IV, § 2.

Ordinances 1869 3. Each of the officers before mentioned, to wit, the superintendent and inspector, shall, before acting in his office, give bond with sureties in the following penalty, to wit, the superintendent in five thousand dollars, and the inspector in two thousand dollars. There shall also be signed by each of them, at the time of his receiving his official books and papers, a writing specifying, so far as can be conveniently done, what are received by him; and the said writing shall be recorded among the committee's proceedings. When an officer's term of office expires, his official books and papers shall be delivered by him to his successor, or in such other manner as the committee may direct.

4. Each of said officers shall use for an office such room as the city council may prescribe. The whole time of each shall be devoted to the performance of his official duties. Each of them shall attend in his office certain hours every day, except Sunday, the fourth day of July, and Christmas day, unless such attendance be prevented by sickness, or by absence from the city with leave of the committee; and each of them shall, on any of the said excepted days, or at night, perform any service for which there is a necessity, without its being extra service.

5. The hours for each of said officers to attend in his office, as required by the preceding section, shall be as follows: 1. The hours for the superintendent so to attend shall be from nine to eleven o'clock A. M., unless his presence be then required at some portion of the works; and he shall be present at all regular meetings of the committee. 2. The hours for the inspector so to attend shall, except on the days in which he is engaged in taking the state of the metres, be from seven to nine A. M., between the first day of April and the first day of October, and from eight to ten A. M., during the rest of the year; and shall also be, on the days for turning off the gas, from the time he has finished so turning it off until two hours after sunset; and shall likewise be until sunset of every other day, unless he be at the time engaged elsewhere in the duties of his office.

6. The superintendent, subject to the control of the committee, shall have a general charge of all the buildings, fixtures and pipes erected or laid down for the gas works, and of the lands on which the said buildings are erected. He shall have the works kept in proper operation, and the gas

furnished as pure as practicable, with promptness and regularity, at the city lamps and buildings, and to all persons entitled to its use under the provisions hereinafter contained. Ordinances 1869

7. Under the direction of the committee, the superintendent shall have street mains laid down, lamp posts erected, and the public lamps set and kept clean and in good order. He shall preserve a map of the location of the main pipes, showing the course, distance and size of each of them. When there is any extension of the main pipes, the place of such extension and size of the pipe used in making it shall, as soon as possible, be marked by him on the map. He shall enter in a book, to be kept in his office, the quantity, description and cost of the materials used in making such extension, or in erecting any fixtures authorized by the committee, and report the same to the committee at its next regular meeting after such extension is made.

8. The superintendent, subject to the committee's control, may employ such men as he may deem suitable to perform the necessary work under his supervision, over which, and the subordinate officers in the department, he shall exercise a controlling influence.

9. He shall, at each monthly meeting, lay before the committee a list of articles and materials which will probably be required during the month, together with the cost thereof, and the probable amount necessary to pay the hands employed, and report what, if any, materials are no longer serviceable. He shall have an account kept of the names of the men employed, their kind of work, and the days of the week or month they work. This account shall be so made out as to show what is chargeable to current expenses, and what to construction in its several branches. At the end of every month he shall enter the substance thereof on roll-books, showing opposite each person's name his rate per day and the sum payable to him for the month. The aggregate of what is payable to the men for each period of a month shall be paid out of the city treasury on the draft of the chairman of the committee in favor of the superintendent, who shall, within three days thereafter, go to his office at the gas works, between the hours of four and seven P. M., and pay to each of the men his part thereof. To each pay-roll the superintendent shall subjoin a synopsis, showing the amount chargeable to each branch of construction or current expenses; and

Ordinances 1869 the said pay-roll and synopsis shall be laid before the committee at their next meeting.

10. Subject to such restrictions as may be imposed by the committee, the superintendent may purchase materials, tools and other articles proper for carrying on the operations of the works. What may be so purchased shall be taken care of by him and used as required. All bills for the same shall be laid before the committee by the superintendent at the next regular meeting after they shall have been presented. And what the committee may allow for such purchases, or for any necessary current expenses of the works, shall be paid out of the city treasury by the draft of the chairman of the committee, attested by the superintendent. Such draft, and every order under the preceding section, shall always state whether it is for construction or current expenses; if the amount be partly for one and partly for the other, the portion of each shall be stated.

11. In a book kept for the purpose, the superintendent shall, at six A. M. and six P. M. of each day, have entered the state of the station metre, the height of gasometers, the gas made, and the gas used. In the said book entries shall be made in separate columns, to show the gas made per day, gas made per night, gas used per night, coal used per day, rosin used per day, the bushels of lime used per day, and the number of retorts in use. From said book the superintendent shall, at the end of every month, make in a book kept by him, called the retort house journal, concise entries, showing on each day of the month the state of the station metre, the gas made, gas used, coal used, rosin used, and the number of retorts in use, and showing the contents of the gasholders, the bushels of lime used each day, and whatever else the superintendent may deem proper to secure a faithful record of the operations of the works; and the same shall be submitted monthly to the committee.

12. As soon as practicable after the last day of every January, the superintendent shall return to the committee an inventory of materials, tools and other articles, stating the quantity, description and cost of those on hand, and make a report showing what were on hand at the time of his previous return, what have been obtained since, what have been used since, and what remain on hand; showing also how much coal, coke, rosin and lime was used during the year

ending the last day of January, and how much gas was made during the year, and what was the largest quantity of gas made, and the largest quantity of gas used in any one twenty-four hours; showing farther the length and size of the street mains laid during the year, and the length and size of the same laid since the commencement of the works; and showing likewise the number of public lamps, number of private consumers, a list of the officers and number of hands, with their duties and pay during the said year, and any other matters which the committee may direct. Ordinances 1869

13. The clerk in the auditor's office shall attend all meetings of the committee, and act as clerk, and make and keep a true record of its proceedings.

14. A book shall be kept in the auditor's office, with a caption importing that the owners of property, whose names are undersigned, request that the gas may be introduced into the premises mentioned opposite their respective names, upon the terms prescribed by the ordinances of the city. When the owner of any property within the range of the pipes applies for the introduction of gas into his premises, he shall write his name in said book under said caption, and write opposite thereto the date and number of his application, the number of burners that he will probably require, and the location of his premises. All applications for gas involving an extension of any street main, shall be accompanied by a pledge, in writing, of each party making such application, that he will use and employ on his premises the number of burners stated in the application to be requisite; and if he shall fail to take and use the gas, in accordance with such pledge, for thirty days after the street main shall have been extended to a point accessible or opposite to his premises, then the inspector shall assume such consumption of gas as shall be in average proportion to the number of burners pledged, bills for which shall be made out and collected as in the case of the gas actually consumed. Sept. 23, 1873.

15. As soon as practicable after every such application, there shall be furnished by the auditor to the superintendent a copy thereof; and there shall be furnished to the inspector by the applicant a plan of the tubing and fittings, with the size and length of each piece of tubing, and the position of each burner plainly marked thereon. Such plan shall be furnished, and the tubings and fittings for conveying gas within Ordinances 1869

Ordinances 1869 the applicant's premises, after it has passed the metre, may be put up by some competent person employed by the applicant. But the tubing, and the screws used in putting up, must be such as the superintendent allows, and must be consistent with the following section:

16. The relative sizes and lengths of tubing, and proportions of metres introduced for consumers, shall be according to the following table:

Size of Tubing.	Greatest length allowed.	Greatest number of burners.	Size of Metres.	Greatest Number of Burners.
$\frac{1}{4}$ inch.	6 feet.	1 burner.	2 lights.	4 burners.
$\frac{3}{8}$ "	20 "	3 "	3 "	5 "
$\frac{1}{2}$ "	30 "	6 "	5 "	10 "
$\frac{5}{8}$ "	40 "	12 "	10 "	20 "
$\frac{3}{4}$ "	50 "	20 "	20 "	40 "
1 "	70 "	35 "	30 "	60 "
$1\frac{1}{4}$ "	100 "	60 "	45 "	100 "
$1\frac{1}{2}$ "	150 "	100 "	100 "	250 "
2 "	200 "	200 "		

17. All tubings, fittings and fixtures must, after they are put up, be examined and approved by the inspector, before gas is supplied. He shall make such examination as soon as practicable after he is notified of the purpose, and always within three days after such notification. On such examination, he must compare the work done with the plan, and must, before the gas is supplied, see that the work does in all respects correspond with the plan already furnished, or see that there is furnished another plan corresponding with the work; and must subject the whole of the tubing, fittings and fixtures to trial, with an air pump, under a pressure of a column of mercury ten inches high, and see that they are tight under this pressure, and put up in a workmanlike manner, as well as in their proper places. When in respect to the work done the inspector has ascertained all that is here required, he shall introduce gas into the premises, unless the superintendent order otherwise.

18. The plans shall be legibly marked with the name of the applicant, the location of his premises, and the date of his receiving the gas, and then delivered to the auditor, who shall number them in the order the applications stand upon his book, and file them in his office. He may allow them to be

copied in his presence; but they shall not be removed from his office unless by the committee's orders, or unless it shall be necessary for their safety. Ordinances 1869.

19. The superintendent shall have laid down street mains and pipes, erect lamp posts, and have the public lamps set and kept clean and in good order. The inspector shall have made and put on all metre connections, place proper metres on the premises of the respective consumers, and perform properly all duties pertaining to these portions of the business. Especially shall he endeavor to render the metres easy of access, to avoid any injury or inconvenience to the building or its occupants, and to avoid exposing the metres to extremes of heat or cold. For digging the trenches and doing other work requiring no mechanical skill, there may be employed such laborers as the superintendent may think necessary.

20. The service pipe laid down in a street, from the main to the edge of a street, shall be provided or paid for by the person for whom the work is done. For all the service pipe, turns, cocks and other fittings, from the edge of the street to the metre, the applicant shall pay such prices as the committee shall, by resolution, determine will afford a fair remuneration for the articles furnished and the labor done.

21. The inspector shall keep a book, called the service pipe book, wherein he shall keep an account of all the pipes and materials used, from the mains to or about the public lamps, and to or about the premises of private consumers, distinguishing between what is chargeable under the preceding section, and what is not, so that the superintendent, in his annual inventory, may state correctly the amount used, and so that what any person is chargeable with may be collected from him. At the end of every month the inspector shall make out and deliver to the auditor a report of the name of each person so chargeable, the location of his premises, and the several items for which he is chargeable, with the sum due for each item, and the aggregate amount. Of all his reports, the inspector shall, in a book used for this purpose keep copies. And when a report of the inspector is received by the auditor, the latter shall endorse thereon the date of his receiving it, and sign his name to such endorsement.

22. When the tenant of premises using gas is about to remove, he shall give the inspector at least three days' notice

Ordinances 1869 thereof, that the gas may be stopped, or he will be chargeable for any gas that may pass through the metre before gas is stopped off. Any person leaving a house without paying for the gas consumed by him therein up to that time, shall not have the use of gas in the house to which he may remove until the amount so due from him shall have been paid. A consumer, discovering any defect in a metre or service pipe, or any escape of gas or deficiency of light on his premises, shall give immediate notice thereof at the inspector's office, that the defect may be remedied; and it shall be remedied by the inspector as soon as possible after receiving such notice. Should the tenant omit to give at least three days' notice of his intention to remove, or to report immediately to the inspector any defect in a metre or service pipe, any escape of gas or deficiency of light on his premises, he shall be fined not less than five nor more than ten dollars.

23. The inspector shall keep a register, showing the date of proving, date of lighting, number of the metre, state of the metre at lighting, number of lights, number of burners, and number of additional burners introduced afterwards. He shall also keep a book, called the metre book, showing the name and location of each consumer, the number of the application, and number of the metre. He shall take the register of all weekly metres once a week, and of all other metres once a month, and he shall inspect every metre once a month, and oftener, if necessary, to ascertain whether the metre is in good working condition. If it be not, and the defect can be remedied without removing it, he shall remedy it before leaving the premises; if this cannot be done, he shall report the defect to the superintendent, who shall have the metre repaired, or a good one put in its place.

Nov. 4, 1874. 24. For the purposes of convenient inspection of metres and collection of bills for gas consumed, the city is hereby divided into three districts, as follows: That portion of the city eastward of the centre line of Fourteenth street, continued to corporation line, shall constitute the First District; that portion between the said centre line of Fourteenth street and the centre line of Fourth street, continued to the corporation line, shall constitute the Second District; and that portion westward of the said centre line of Fourth street continued to the corporation line, shall constitute the Third District. On the first day of each month, the inspector shall return to the auditor the metre book, with the state of all the metres in the First District; on the tenth day of each month, he shall in like manner return the state of all the metres in the Second District; and on the twentieth day of each month, the state of all the metres in the Third District. The book shall show the quantity of gas consumed by each person during the month for which payment is to be made, to be ascertained from the state of the register. When the inspector requires a metre to be covered or filled with alcohol to prevent it from freezing, if such covering or such alcohol is not furnished by the consumer, the inspector shall furnish such cover or alcohol, and the cost thereof shall be charged to the consumer, and the amount collected of him in the same mode that gas bills are collected. The committee may employ such person or persons to assist the inspector as may be necessary, at such price as they may fix, to be reported to the city council; and when, from sickness or any other cause, the inspector may be unable to perform the duties required of him, he shall report the same to the superintendent, who shall furnish the necessary aid. Nov. 4, 1874.

25. With the exception of what is used in the street lamps, or in a building or upon land belonging to and used by the city, gas shall never be furnished without charge therefor. It may be furnished at the rate of two dollars and fifty cents per thousand feet to any such association or benevolent institution as the city council may, by resolution, declare entitled to receive it at that rate in consideration of the public benefits conferred by such association or institution. The supply of gas to every other person shall be upon the condition of his paying therefor at the rate of three dollars for every thousand feet, to be ascertained as prescribed by the preceding section. The committee or the superintendent, in any case wherein he or they deem such precaution proper to secure the city against loss, may require the deposit of a sum in advance, or other security, to insure payment of what will become due for gas. Payment for gas shall be made monthly, by all persons, except those who, by the superintendent, may be required to pay oftener. Ordinances 1869

26. From the metre book so returned to the auditor, he shall promptly note in a book, to be kept by him, called the bill book, the name and location of each consumer, the number of the metre, its state as so entered, its state at the pre-

Ordinances 1869 vious settlement, and the amount chargeable to said consumer. The auditor shall also enter in his bill book the name of each person reported to him under the twenty-first section, the sum to be paid by him, and for what.

27. For the respective sums payable by the several persons so reported by the inspector, or appearing by the metre book to be so chargeable, the auditor shall promptly make out bills, showing what amount is due without any abatement, and also, what will be due after allowing the deduction provided for in the next section, and have the same presented by the inspector to the persons who are to pay them (or at their place of business or residence), and shall note within three days after sending said bills the day of the delivery of each.

28. From the amount of the bill for gas of a consumer, there shall be a deduction of five per cent., provided the residue of the bill paid to the treasurer at his office, within five days next after its presentment, and before three o'clock P. M. If a bill for gas, or anything else which is furnished by the city in connection with the supply of gas, shall remain unpaid for ten days next after that on which it is presented, the auditor shall notify the superintendent, who shall cause the gas to be stopped from the premises in respect to which the default exists, and not allow it to be used on those premises again until such bill is paid.

20. The superintendent shall make such sales of coke and other articles as the committee may authorize. Upon any such sale, the price required by the committee shall be paid to the superintendent, who shall give to the purchaser a receipt for the sum paid, bearing date the day of the payment, and stating the name of the purchaser, the article sold, and its quantity.

30. The superintendent shall, on the first day of every month, pay to the treasurer the moneys received by him under the previous section; and shall report to the committee at each regular meeting an account of the coke or other articles sold in the previous month, and the quantity. And if the superintendent shall fail to pay over the money so received by him, or to make the report hereby required, in the first case the auditor, and in the other the committee, shall report such failure to the city council. And in all cases

where the superintendent fails to make a report required of him, his salary shall not be paid until it is made. Ordinances 1869

31. During the first five days of every month, the following returns shall be made to the auditor by the superintendent and inspector, severally, of the respective sums payable since their previous several returns on the following accounts, that is to say: there shall be a return, by the superintendent, of the money received by him for coke and other articles sold; a return, by the inspector, of the persons from whom money has become payable for the consumption of gas, and of the persons from whom money has become payable for other articles chargeable under the twentieth and twenty-first sections.

32. The auditor shall keep a ledger, wherein, for every month, he shall enter from his bill book the name and location of each consumer (whose bill is made out in or for that month), the date to which his bill comes, the state of his metre, the feet of gas chargeable, amount of discount, amount paid, and when paid. If any bill remains unpaid for fifteen days after its presentment, the auditor shall make out another bill for the amount due, with the addition of ten per centum thereon, and shall deliver the same to the collector of the city taxes, taking his receipt therefor, who shall collect the same as if it were due for city taxes; and shall, after deducting five per centum for his compensation, pay the balance to the treasurer within thirty days after the bill is put into his hands; and the official bond of said collector shall extend to secure the faithful collection and payment of the said money: provided, however, that if the amount of any such bill be due from a tenant, or one who was tenant of the premises when it became due, the owner of the premises or a tenant under him, other than the person from whom such gas bill is due, may pay the same to the treasurer without the addition of any per centage thereon. It shall be the duty of the auditor to demand from the collector monthly settlements of such bills as are placed in his hands; and for failure to make such settlement the collector shall forfeit the per centage which he is hereby authorized to deduct.

33. Annually, as soon as practicable after the last day of January, the auditor shall make out accounts to ascertain the following results, to wit: First. The amount expended for

Ordinances 1869 the construction of the gas works from their commencement to the beginning of the preceding fiscal year. Second. The amount expended for construction during said year. Third. The amount paid to the treasurer for income during said year. Fourth. The amount disbursed during said year for current expenses. Fifth. The net balance of the year's income remaining after paying current expenses, and after paying the interest on all moneys expended for the construction and extension of the works. Sixth. An account charging the gas works with all expenditures on account of them, including interest, and crediting them with all receipts, including a charge for gas used in the street lamps and in the city buildings which is not paid for, and the money received for coke and other articles sold, and the price of said coke or other articles applied to the use of the city, so made out as to show for what the charge is made or credit given. The committee shall examine said accounts, and return the same to the city council with the superintendent's inventory, a report from him of the condition of the works, and any plans of the committee for extending the works, or adding to the buildings or machinery. The plans for such extensions or additions, and the contracts therefor, must always be submitted to and approved by the city council, before said plans are executed, and before said contracts shall be binding on the city.

34. The treasurer shall keep on his books accounts of the money expended about and received from the gas works, so as to ascertain the results contemplated from the accounts required by the preceding section, and as soon as practicable after the accounts so required are returned, shall examine the said accounts, and compare the same with those on his books, and if he find any variance in the results, shall inform the city council thereof.

35. At the end of every week the inspector shall make to the superintendent of streets a report designating the location, and quantity and kind of paving needed in the streets in which street mains and service pipes have been laid; and the superintendent of streets shall have it replaced as soon as possible. These reports shall be entered and signed as required by the twenty-first section.

36. It shall be the duty of the superintendent, the inspector, and such other men engaged about the works as the su-

perintendent shall from time to time designate, to attend at places, where, from fire or other cause, there is danger of a loss of gas by burning or waste, with a stop-cock key, and pliers, to shut off the gas, remove metres, or do anything else proper for the safety of property belonging to the city connected with the gas works. Ordinances 1869.

37. If any person shall deface or injure any house, wall, lamp, metre, or other fixture connected with or pertaining to the gas works, or shall tie to a lamp post, or any fixture connected therewith, any horse or other animal, or any boat, batteau or other vessel, or shall, without authority from the superintendent, or other authorized agent of the committee, climb a lamp post, or light a lamp, or open a communication into, or remove any of the pipes, or shall put up any pipe or burner, in addition to what may have been put up by authority and approved, or introduce the gas into such additional pipe or burner, or leave the end of a pipe or other opening without being secured with a blind cap, secured so as to prevent a leak, or in any manner consume or waste the gas, without paying for the same, every person so offending shall pay the whole cost of restoring the property injured, (if any,) the amount to be assessed by the superintendent or inspector, and also pay a fine of not less than two nor more than twenty dollars for each offence. The whole of the amount received to be paid to the treasurer. If, however, any person shall accidentally injure a street lamp, or other property of the city gas works, and shall voluntarily pay to the treasurer, before he has been summoned to appear before a magistrate, the amount of the damage done, he shall be exempt from any further penalty under this section.

38. After gas has been introduced into any premises, no gas fitter or other person than the inspector, shall disconnect or interfere with any metre without a written permit from the superintendent. Nor shall any person disconnect any of the tubings or fittings, or open the same for extension, alteration or repair, without obtaining from the inspector or one of the other officers, a written permit, whereof there shall be forms in a permit book, on the margin of which there shall be a copy or sufficient memorandum of every permit that is given. Such permit may be had whenever the office is open. When such permit is given, or when there is a leak in or injury to the metre or pipes within the premises, the inspector may

Ordinances 1869 stop the flow of gas at the cock outside said premises. After gas has, for any purpose, been stopped by the inspector or authorized agent of the committee, it shall not be let on until it is authorized by said inspector or such agent. Any person violating this section in any respect, shall pay a fine of not less than five nor more than twenty dollars.

39. Every person occupying any lot or tenement into which gas is conveyed under this chapter, shall permit the superintendent or inspector, or any authorized agent of the committee, to enter such lot or tenement, at seasonable hours, to examine the service pipe, metre, and other gas apparatus, or take up, repair or remove the same, or to see if this ordinance has been violated. Any person refusing so to do shall, for each refusal, pay a fine of five dollars.

40. The committee, or the superintendent, subject to their approval, may at any time have the communication of any service pipe cut off, if they deem it necessary to protect the works against abuse or fraud. And they, or the superintendent, with their assent, may make from time to time such further rules and regulations, not inconsistent with this ordinance, as may be found necessary or deemed advisable to ensure the proper management of the works, and the faithful performance, by the officers and workmen, of their duties.

41. Every officer of the gas works shall report to the superintendent every violation that shall come to his knowledge of this or any subsequent ordinance relating to the gas works, and the superintendent shall prosecute all who may be guilty of any such violation, reporting the same to the committee at its next monthly meeting, and shall diligently enforce this ordinance.

Dec. 9, 1872. 42. The agent or clerk receiving coal and delivering coke at the gas works, the several deputies in the inspector's office, and the bill clerk in the auditor's office, shall give bonds with sufficient surety, to be approved by the city council, each in the sum of one thousand dollars, conditioned for the faithful performance of their respective duties, and each shall take the oath of office prescribed by law.*

* This section, as passed, had the additional words "within thirty days from the passage of this ordinance, which bonds and certificatos of the oath of office shall be filed in the office of the city clerk." These words are omitted above as unnecessary, being partly applicable only to the then incumbents, and as to after appointments the disposition of the bonds and evidences of the oath being fully provided for by chapter V.

43. In taking the state of the metres, it shall be the duty of each deputy to note and report in writing to the inspector of gas all metres failing to register, or otherwise out of order, and the inspector of gas shall make a report in writing concerning such to the committee on light, at their first regular meeting in each month. All entries, including figures, upon the metre books, shall invariably be written in ink, under penalty of dismissal of the party offending therein. Dec. 9, 1872.

44. The inspector of gas, or any deputy, who shall be guilty of any discourtesy or rudeness, or other disorderly conduct towards any person in the transaction or execution of any official business, shall be therefor reprimanded by the committee, or dismissed from office, if the aggravation or repetition of such offence shall seem to the committee to make a dismissal proper or necessary.

45. The inspector of gas and his deputies, and the bill clerk in the auditor's office, are strictly prohibited, under penalty of the forfeiture of their office or employment, from collecting any bill for gas consumed, or paying or assuming to pay such bill for any consumer other than themselves.

46. No person shall have the use of any gas at any house or other place who is delinquent for gas consumed by him at any other place or house.

CHAPTER XXIV.*

CONCERNING THE MARKETS.

Ordinances 1869 1. Of the markets in this city, that formerly known as the Old Market, shall, with the vegetable market attached thereto, be called the First Market, and that formerly known as the New or Shockoe Hill Market, shall, with the vegetable market attached thereto, be called the Second Market.

2. There shall be appointed by the city council a clerk for each of said markets; each of which clerks shall, before acting in his office, give bond in the pealty of two thousand dollars.†

3. Over each market a general supervision shall be exercised by its committee, and whenever a market is held, the clerk thereof shall attend it. No market shall be held on Sunday. On all other days the market shall be held as follows: From the first day of May until the first day of September following, on Monday, Tuesday, Wednesday, Thursday, Friday and Saturday, from daylight until ten o'clock A. M., and on Saturday, from five to nine o'clock P. M.; from the first day of September until the first day of May following, on Monday, Tuesday, Wednesday, Thursday and Friday,

* Chapter XXV of 1869.

† See note on chapter IV, § 2.

from daylight until twelve o'clock M., and on Saturday, from daylight until eight o'clock P. M. If after the time prescribed for holding any market, a person be found thereat with anything for sale, he shall forfeit such thing to the city, and shall pay a fine of not less than two nor more than twenty dollars. Ordinances 1869

4. As soon as practicable after the market is closed on any day, and always before it is next held, the clerk shall have his market house, with the streets and alleys adjoining, watered, swept and cleaned. The whole market premises, including such ground as may be used with or pertain to the market, shall be kept by him clean and neat. And twice a year he shall have his meat market house whitewashed inside. And the work herein specified shall, for the second market, be given out by contract.

5. Meat, fish and vegetable stalls, benches and stands at the several markets, shall be assessed annually on the last Monday in December, by the committees on the markets, respectively. But no person shall occupy a meat stall or bench until he obtains a license from the city council, first having satisfied the council as to his character and capacity. And such license may be revoked, at the pleasure of the city council, for a violation of any of the criminal laws of the state, or of the ordinances of the city, or for any other cause which the city council may deem sufficient: provided, that whenever the current price of meat shall exceed twenty cents a pound in the markets, such meats may be sold by any person or persons at any place or places in the city, without obtaining a license therefor. And such sales without a license may be continued for six months, though the current price of meats in the markets may be reduced to less than twenty cents per pound.

6. The rent of a bench, stall or stand at a market, shall be paid to the clerk of the market in advance for such time, not exceeding three months, as the committee may direct. Not more than one stall, bench or stand shall be rented to or occupied by the same person at the same time; and a renting shall always be for a year at a time, except in cases provided for in the following section.

7. If the rent of a stall, bench or stand be in arrear more than ten days, or if by reason of death or other cause, there be a failure for ten days to supply the same with wholesome

Ordinances 1869 meat or vegetables, as it has been rented for the one or the other, the committee may declare such stall or bench to be vacant. In every such case, and in every case in which the license of a renter of a stall or bench is revoked, the clerk of the market, after posting at the front of the market house, notice, for at least twenty-four hours, shall rent the stall, bench or stand for the balance of the year to the highest bidder. If from such renting there cannot be satisfied all that the previous occupant became bound for, the clerk, on behalf of the city, shall proceed, by warrant or otherwise, against the party liable for the residue, to recover the same as soon as may be after said residue becomes payable.

8. At or near the end of a year for which a stall, bench or stand of the meat or vegetable market is rented, if there be more than one applicant for it, or if the committee see cause so to direct, the clerk of the market, after posting notice as aforesaid, shall rent such stall, bench or stand at auction for the highest premium that may be bid in cash beyond and in addition to the rent assessed by the committee. The aggregate of said rent and premium shall thenceforth be the rent per annum for said stall, bench or stand, until the same is again rented at auction. And no renter of a stall, bench or stand, shall be permitted to re-rent the same; but if any such person shall not desire to use it, it shall be surrendered to the city, and shall be rented out by the clerk of the market, as prescribed in the seventh section of this chapter.

9. If any of the following things be sold by any person not a butcher, at a market, there shall at the time of such sale be paid by such person to the clerk of the market, as follows: For each slaughtered beef, twenty-five cents; for each slaughtered veal, mutton, hog or shoat, ten cents; for each sturgeon, ten cents; and for each pig, five cents. Any person violating this section shall, for every offence, pay a fine of not less than one nor more than twenty dollars.

Nov. 13, 1871. 10. If any person shall sell or offer for sale any fish, fowls, butter, eggs, or other things not hereby enumerated, he shall pay to the clerk of the market the sum of not less than ten nor more than twenty cents per day.*

Ordinances 1869 11. No fish shall be sold or offered for sale in either of the market houses, or anywhere within the police jurisdiction of

* Section 10, was wholly repealed October 9, 1871, and what is given above re-ordained November 13, 1871.

the market houses, except under the sheds called the fish markets, or at such other place as may be designated by the committee on markets. Any person violating this section shall pay a fine of not less than ten nor more than twenty dollars.* Ordinances 1869.

12. Every butcher shall keep over his stall a sign with his name thereon, painted in letters which can be easily read. He shall be in person neat and cleanly, shall keep clean the benches, and all parts of his stall and the pavement thereof, and shall whitewash the interior twice a year. No butcher shall extend any of the blocks, benches or other fixtures of his stall, beyond the distance of nine feet out from the side wall. No person shall occupy a stand more than eight feet along the line of the curbstone. And no butcher at a meat market, nor any seller at a fish or vegetable market, shall leave about the market house, after market hours, any loose barrel, box, bench or plank.

13. No butcher shall erect or have at a market house any box in which to lock up meats, unless such box be elevated on legs at least two feet above the floor or pavement of the market house, and be constructed according to a plan furnished by the committee of such market. And every butcher having at a market house a box, shall have it thoroughly cleansed at least once a week. No article shall be kept therein for a longer period than one week, unless it be smoked or salt meat. If at any time any article therein become offensive, or if brine or anything else be found dripping from any such box on the floor or pavement of the market house, the article thus offensive, or producing such dripping, shall, by order of the clerk, be immediately removed from the market house. A person violating this or the preceding section, in any respect, shall, for every such violation, pay a fine of not less than one dollar nor more than five dollars; and every day that any such violation continues, shall be deemed a distinct offence.

14. Every butcher shall each day bring to the market house the hides with the ears of every animal brought by him that day to the market for sale, and shall keep the same exposed to public view for at least two hours. No butcher shall bring any dog within or to the market during market hours. Nor

* The section which followed this as section 12, in the Ordinances of 1869, designed in restraint of forestalling, regrating, &c., was repealed October 9, 1871.

Ordinances 1869 shall he bring to the market after the first of May and before the first of November following, any beef tallow, except such as may be necessarily attached to the hind-quarters of beef. Nor shall he leave in a market house, or any adjacent street, alley or ground, the head or a foot or other part of an animal. Nor shall any person deposit any filth, offensive matter, dirt or rubbish in or about either market house or any such street, alley or ground. Any person violating this section in any respect shall, for each offence, pay a fine of not less than two nor more than ten dollars.

15. If any person shall, at either market, or within two hundred yards thereof, keep tied later than an hour after sunrise any live calf, sheep, lamb, hog or shoat, he shall, for every such offence, pay a fine of five dollars, unless such animal arrive at the market at a later hour, in which case it may remain about the market house for a time not exceeding one hour, and during that time may be offered for sale.

16. Any butcher or other person who shall sell or offer for sale, at a market, any sturgeon not previously skinned, or any unsound meat, fish, flesh, fowl, eggs, or other unsound article, or any meat which is distempered or blown, raised or stuffed, or which is dressed or garnished falsely, or in any way calculated to deceive, shall pay a fine of not less than five nor more than twenty dollars, and forfeit what is so sold or offered for sale.

17. The clerk of each market shall examine all meats, fish and fowls offered at such market for sale, and take possession of such as by the preceding section are prohibited from being so offered, and unless, on an appeal by the person offering the same to the committee of the market, the decision of the clerk be reversed, the said clerk shall cause what he so takes possession of to be buried in a suitable place.

18. No person selling fruits or vegetables at market, by measure, shall sell the same in any other than dry measure; and the said measure shall be of the same size at bottom and top. No person shall buy or sell at market any beef, pork, mutton, veal, shoat, lamb or butter, in any other manner than by weight. And no article sold or offered for sale at a market shall be weighed with steelyards. Every butcher shall keep, in a conspicuous part of his stall, his patent platform balances and weights, or his scales and weights, the scales well balanced and in good order, and the weights correct.

Any person violating this section shall pay a fine of not less than one dollar nor more than five dollars. No person shall sell on commission for the owner articles brought to the market for sale, or buy articles at the market house for sale again in the city or elsewhere; and for the violation of this provision the articles shall be forfeited to the city, and there shall be a fine of not less than two nor more than twenty dollars. Ordinances 1869

19. The clerk of each market shall, from time to time, examine the scales, balances, weights and measures used by persons at such market, to see whether they are sealed according to law, and conform to the preceding section; and also examine butter and other articles sold or offered for sale by weight, to see that they are not deficient. Persons having at market illegal scales, balances, weights or measures, shall forfeit the same to the city. Articles offered for sale by weight, and found deficient, shall likewise be forfeited to the city; or if sold, the value thereof shall be forfeited. In every case in which the clerk of a market shall have good cause to believe that anything is forfeited under this section, or under any other section of this chapter, he shall seize the same, and summon the person in possession thereof at the time of the seizure, to appear before the police justice at some other time within twelve hours, to show cause why the said thing should not be adjudged forfeited. Any person convicted under this section shall be excluded from the market either as principal or agent.

20. No person shall sell from any stand, cart or wagon, on Sixth, Marshall or Broad street, adjacent to the Second market, until all the benches within the vegetable market and the square on the eastern side thereof are fully occupied, and then only at such places as the clerk of said market may, under the instructions of the committee, direct. A person violating this section shall, for every such violation, pay a fine of one dollar.

21. The clerk of a market may order any butcher or other person having at his market a cart, wagon, dray or other vehicle, or a horse or beast of burden, to remove the same; and if such butcher or other person fail to obey the order, he may be fined one dollar for every fifteen minutes such failure may continue.

Sept. 8, 1873. 22. If a person at a market use obscene, profane or threatening language, or shall fight thereat, or lie, sit or stand upon any bench or stall, or in any way deface the same, or cause it to be defaced, abused or misused, or shall place or cause to be placed any nuisance thereon, the said person or persons so offending, shall upon conviction be fined not less than two nor more than ten dollars, one-half of which fine so recovered shall go to the informer, or failing to pay said fine the offender shall be imprisoned in the city jail not less than one nor more than thirty days.

Ordinances 1869 23. The clerk of a market shall prosecute all offenders against this ordinance. To enable him the better to execute his office and preserve order about the market, he shall have the powers of a police officer, within two hundred yards around the market in every direction.

24. There shall be appointed by the clerk of each market a deputy, to be approved by the committee of said market, which deputy shall, in case of the clerk's sickness or temporary absence, perform the duties of clerk, and for this purpose shall have the like powers. The deputy's pay shall be at the rate of two dollars per day for such time as he may actually perform the duties of clerk. The same shall be paid out of the clerk's salary, unless, upon the recommendation of the committee, the city council shall otherwise direct.

25. The clerk of each market shall, on the first day of every January, April, July and October, render to the auditor an account, verified on oath, of all moneys which he may within the preceding three months have received by virtue of his office, stating when and from whom the same was received, and pay to the treasurer the amount thereof. If he fail for twenty days to render such account or to make such payment, the auditor shall report such default to the city council at its first meeting afterwards, and shall suspend the payment of his salary until the report is made. It shall be the duty of the said clerks to keep regular accounts of their daily receipts, and submit the same to the inspection of the committees on the markets whenever required by any member of either committee. It shall not be lawful for the clerk of either market to buy articles of any kind offered for sale therein, or within two hundred yards thereof, for any person or persons other than for his own use or family consumption. For any violation of this section, the clerk so offending shall be fined not less than fifty nor more than one hundred dollars.

CHAPTER XXV.*

CONCERNING THE WATER WORKS.

1. There shall be elected by the city council a superintendent of the water works, who, before acting in his office, shall give bond, with sureties, in the penalty of five thousand dollars, which shall be approved by the city council.† When his term of office expires, his official books and papers shall be delivered by him to his successor, or disposed of in such other manner as the committee on water may direct. Ordinances 1869

2. The committee on water, as soon as practicable after its appointment, shall appoint an assistant superintendent of the water works, a superintendent of the pump house and an assistant superintendent of the pump house, who may be removed at any time by the committee. Upon every appointment to either of these offices the committee shall report to the city council the name of the person so appointed.

3. The committee shall have the superintendence and general government of the water works. The superintendent of the water works, and the officers mentioned in the preceding section, shall, except as otherwise prescribed by this chapter, act according to the directions of said committee. The clerk in the auditor's office shall attend all meetings of

* Chapter XXVI of 1869.

† See note on chapter IV, § 2.

Ordinances 1869 the committee, and act as its clerk, and make and keep a true record of its proceedings.

4. The superintendent, subject to the control of the committee, shall have a general charge of the reservoirs, pump house, and all the buildings, fire plugs, fixtures and pipes erected or laid down for the water works, and of the lands on which the said reservoirs, pump house and buildings are. He shall carefully inspect all parts of the works, and have the same kept in good order and in proper operation, and the water furnished as pure and clear as practicable, with promptness and regularity, at the city buildings, and to all persons entitled to its use under the provisions hereinafter contained.

5. The superintendent of the pump house and his assistant shall remain in or at the pump house, and it shall be their special duty to take good care of the buildings and machinery. But they shall be at all times subject to the control of the superintendent of the water works.

6. Subject to the control of the committee, the superintendent may employ in and about the works such men as he may deem suitable and necessary. He shall keep an account of their names, the kind of work done by them, and the days of the week or month they work. He shall quarterly present to the committee a statement of the materials, tools, and other articles necessary for carrying on the works for the following quarter, and an estimate of their cost. And, subject to such restrictions as may be imposed by the committee, the superintendent may purchase such materials, tools and other articles. What may be so purchased shall be taken care of by him and used as required. All bills for the same shall within three months be laid by the superintendent before the committee. What the committee may allow for such purchases, or for any necessary current expenses of the works, shall be paid by a draft drawn on the auditor, signed by the chairman of the committee, and attested by the superintendent.

7. The superintendent shall preserve a map of the location of the main pipes, showing the course, distance and size of each of them, and when there is any extension of the main pipes, shall, as soon as possible, mark on the map the place of such extension, and the size of the pipe used in making it. He shall enter in a book, to be kept in his office, and shall report to the auditor, the quantity, description and

cost of the materials used, and the cost of labor employed in making such extensions; and the auditor, in books to be kept in his office, shall keep accounts thereof. Ordinances 1869

8. In a book, kept in his office, the superintendent shall make an entry of all branch pipes, hydrants and other fixtures, from the main in the streets. The entry shall state the quantity, description and cost of the materials used in laying down and fixing the pipes and fixtures; and it shall designate the point of junction of each branch pipe with the main pipe, and the course and distance of the pipe to the premises supplied thereby, so as, in after time, to avoid difficulty in ascertaining the position of any part of the pipe.

9. A book shall be kept in the superintendent's office, with a caption importing that the owners of property whose names are undersigned, request that water may be introduced upon the premises mentioned opposite their respective names, upon the terms prescribed by the ordinances of the city. When the owner of any property within the range of the pipes applies for the introduction of water into his premises, he or his agent shall write his name in said book, under said caption, and write opposite thereto the date and number of his application, the location of his premises, and the purpose for which the water is to be used. The city water shall not be introduced into the premises of any applicant until there is written what is here required.

10. After there is written what is so required, water from the main pipe in the public street or alley shall without delay be conducted by the superintendent to the applicant's premises, by means of suitable service pipe and fixtures, with a separate attachment for his particular house or tenement. No hydrant or cock shall be allowed to be on a sidewalk, or in an exposed situation, from which water may be taken without detection; and there shall be placed on the service pipe, near the curbstone, a stop-cock, (with an iron cover marked "city water works,") so that the supply of water may be stopped at any time when it is proper to do so. The said applicant may have the water introduced into his premises, from the service pipe laid down by the superintendent as above directed, by means of suitable service pipe, hydrant and fixtures: provided such work be conducted by practical and competent plumbers, and the materials used in the construction thereof be of the best quality, and of such weight

Ordinances 1869 and description as the committee may prescribe in the particular case, or may prescribe for such work in the part of the city where the same is located: and provided, that on the completion of the work, and before the water is turned into it, notice thereof shall be given to the superintendent or his agent, and the work be by him inspected and approved.

11. The supply of water to any person shall be on condition of his paying a water rent at certain rates: which shall be fifty per centum upon the rates prescribed in the next section.

12. If for the purpose of building: For each table used for brick making, twenty-five dollars per annum. When in a building bricks are laid or stone work or plastering done, five cents for each thousand bricks; two cents for each cubic yard of stone work, and twenty cents for each hundred yards of plastering. But if the water be conveyed by hose, barrels or buckets, and not along the gutters, the charge shall be two and a half cents for each thousand bricks; for each cubic yard of stone work, one cent; and ten cents for each hundred yards of plastering. A license shall be obtained from the superintendent for each building for which the city water is wanted for any of these purposes.

If for a public building, at the following rate per annum, to wit: For the capitol, seventy-five dollars; state armory, fifty dollars; medical college, fifty dollars; state courthouse, twenty-five dollars; a theatre, twenty dollars; a church, ten dollars; a public hall, ten dollars, in addition to other charges on same building; Henrico county courthouse, sixty dollars.

For schools, at the following rate per annum, to wit: For a boarding school, ten dollars, and three per centum on the actual or estimated rent of the premises used for the purpose. For a private school, six dollars.

For depots, manufactories, workshops and warehouses, at the following rate per annum, to wit: For a railroad depot, seventy dollars, for every locomotive in which the city water is used making six trips in the week, and in the same proportion for every such locomotive making fewer than six trips in a week. This shall pay for all the uses of water at such depot, except for stationary steam engines, water closets and baths. For each stationary steam engine, four dollars for each estimated horse power. But no steam engine shall be supplied except where the water is taken in the building where the engine is used, for the usual purposes for which water is used in such building. For a rolling mill, or a foundry and machine shop, or a barrel factory, or stemmery, ten dollars, if not more than fifteen persons be employed therein; for each additional person, twenty cents; for each spike machine, thirty dollars; for each manufacturing mill, thirty dollars; for a tobacco manufactory, sixty cents for each hand employed therein, but no charge to be less than ten dollars; for a tobacco warehouse, or a currier shop, twenty-five dollars; for a rectifying establishment, thirty dollars; for a dyeing establishment, fifteen dollars, exclusive of use of steam boiler; for a lager beer, porter, soda or bottling establishment, thirty dollars; for a blacksmith's shop, or a printing office, or a barber's shop, ten dollars; for a carpenter's shop, seven dollars. Ordinances 1869.

Bakeries, restoratives, taverns, stables, billiard saloons, &c., at the following rate per annum, to wit: For a bakery, fifteen dollars, if the tenement be used exclusively as such; if, besides being used as a bakery, the bakery be also occupied as a dwelling for a family, then only eight dollars for the bakery; for a house of private entertainment, twelve dollars, and one per centum on the rent of the buildings used for such purpose; for an ordinary, or house of public entertainment, or restorative, twenty dollars, and three per centum on the actual or estimated rent of the premises used for such purpose; for each bar, whether kept in a hotel or elsewhere, ten dollars, in addition to other charges on the same premises; for a livery stable, fifty cents for each stall, whether used or not; for a packet boat office, ten dollars; for a private stable, one dollar for one horse or mule, and all over one, fifty cents for each horse, and one dollar for a private carriage; for a stable where hacks or carriages are kept for hire, one dollar for each horse and three dollars for each carriage or hack, and one dollar for each buggy or wagon; for each mule or wagon lot, twenty-five dollars; for each stable where wagons, drays or carts are kept for hire, one dollar for each horse or mule, and no stable shall be charged less than five dollars; for a billiard saloon, ten dollars.

Stores and offices, at the following rate per annum, to wit: If a tenement be used exclusively as a grocery store, hat store or shoe store, ten dollars for such tenement; if, besides being used as a store, the house be also used as a dwelling

Ordinances 1869 for a family, then only five dollars for the store. If a tenement be used exclusively as a dry goods store or book store, seven dollars for such tenement; if, besides being used as a store, the house be also occupied as a dwelling for a family, then only five dollars for the store; for each apothecary store, ten dollars, unless soda water be there manufactured, in which case the same shall be paid as for a soda water manufactory; for each confectionery store, ten dollars; if, besides being used as a store, the house be also occupied as a dwelling, then only five dollars for the store, and when candy is made, ten dollars additional; for each auction store, or other store not mentioned above, ten dollars; for each office not otherwise provided for, three dollars.

Dwelling houses, when valued at one thousand dollars or less, five dollars; for each additional family occupying the same house, five dollars each: when valued at more than one thousand dollars and not over two thousand dollars, six dollars; when the house is occupied by more than one family, five dollars each: when valued at two thousand dollars and not over five thousand dollars, eight dollars; when the house is occupied by more than one family, six dollars each: when valued at five thousand dollars and not over eight thousand dollars, ten dollars; when occupied by more than one family, seven dollars each: when valued at eight thousand dollars and not over twelve thousand dollars, twelve dollars; when the house is occupied by more than one family, eight dollars each: when valued over twelve thousand dollars and under fifteen thousand dollars, fifteen dollars; when occupied by more than one family, nine dollars each: when valued over fifteen thousand dollars, twenty dollars.

Baths, water closets, fountains and hose, at the following rate per annum, to wit: For each public bath tub, six dollars; for each private bath tub, three dollars; in the case of a water closet in a public house, for each seat, six dollars; in the case of water closets in a private boarding house, or in a private house, three dollars if there is but one seat, and two dollars each if there be more than one. But no bath or water closet shall be supplied except when the water is taken in the building where such bath or water closet is, for the usual purposes for which water is used in such a building; for a fountain in a yard, fifty dollars, to be used at the discretion of the committee; and for a fountain in a store, five dollars.

In such cases as the superintendent, under the regulations of the committee, may allow the use of small hose, one-eighth nozzle, ten dollars, if such use be for sprinkling the carriage way of streets, and three dollars if it be for sprinkling a side-walk, yard or garden. There shall be a fine of ten dollars on any person who shall for any such purpose use the hose between eight o'clock in the morning and five o'clock in the afternoon, or who shall at any time use hose for washing a carriage or other vehicle with the city water. Ordinances 1869

13. In any case not hereinbefore provided for, the water rent shall be at such rate as may be fixed by the superintendent, subject to the committee's control. And in cases that are hereinbefore provided for, it shall be lawful for the city council, at any time hereafter, to add to or increase the rates for water to be thereafter supplied.

14. For convenience in the preparation of bills and collection of water rents, the city is hereby divided into three districts, as follows: That portion of the city eastward of the centre line of Fourteenth street continued to the corparation line, shall constitute the first district; that portion between the said centre line of Fourteenth street and the centre line of Fourth street continued to the corporation line, shall constitute the second district; and that portion westward of the said centre line of Fourth street continued to the corporation line, shall constitute the third district. Water rents shall be payable half-yearly in advance: In the first district, on the first day of May and the first day of November; in the second district, on the first day of March and the first day of September; in the third district, on the first day of January and the first day of July; except that when the supply of water is commenced in a district between the days above fixed for payment of rents in that district, the person supplied shall, at the time of such commencement, pay at the rate before mentioned up to the next day fixed for payment of water rent in that district; and rents for water used in brick or stone work, or plastering, shall be payable on the first ensuing day fixed for payment of water rents in the district in which such water is used. Nov. 4, 1874.

15. When, upon such application as is before mentioned, a hydrant is erected on any premises, and water commenced to be supplied at such hydrant, rent for such water shall continue to be payable for at least one year, whether the party Ordinances 1869

Ordinances 1869 desires the supply for that length of time or not. In other cases, a person supplied with water may discontinue the use thereof by giving to the superintendent notice, in writing, for one month prior to the expiration of the time for which he has paid; otherwise, he shall be chargeable for six months next following such expiration. Though said month's notice be not given, yet when there are two houses or tenements, and payment for water supplied at the hydrant of each has been made for not less than a year, a water taker, removing from the one to the other, shall give notice of such removal to the superintendent, who shall thereupon stop the supply of water at the one and furnish it at the other, and payment shall be made accordingly. And if any person who is taking water at a house removes therefrom, he shall give notice thereof on or before the day of his removal; and if he shall fail to do it, he shall pay a fine of not less than five nor more than ten dollars.

16. Fifteen days before the water rents shall be payable, as provided in section fourteen, the superintendent shall furnish the auditor with a correct list of all persons to whom water is supplied, and the sum payable by each for water rent. The auditor shall keep an account thereof in his office, and shall have bills made out for the same, showing the amount due, and the amount which will be due after deducting five per centum therefrom; and he shall place said bills in the hands of the superintendent, who shall have every bill presented to the person who is to pay it, (or at his residence or place of business,) stating, at the foot of the bill, the day of its presentment; and shall, within ten days after receiving any bill from the auditor, return to him a memorandum, stating the day it was presented.

17. From the amount of the bill for water there shall be a deduction of five per centum, provided that the residue of the bill be paid to the treasurer, at his office, within five days next after its presentment, and before three o'clock P. M. If a bill for water shall remain unpaid for ten days after that on which it is presented, the auditor shall notify the superintendent, who shall cause the water to be stopped from the premises in respect to which the default exists, (if the same can be done without stopping the water from the premises of others who have paid;) and he shall not allow it to be used on those premises again until said bill is paid. If any

bill remains unpaid for fifteen days, the auditor shall make out a bill for the amount due, with the addition of ten per centum thereon, and deliver the same to the collector of the city taxes, taking his receipt therefor, who is hereby authorized and required to collect the same as if it was due for city taxes, and after deducting five per centum for his compensation, pay the balance to the treasurer within thirty days after the bill is put into his hands; and the official bond of the said collector shall extend to secure the faithful discharge of his duties under this ordinance. But any bill may at any time be paid to the treasurer, with the addition of five per centum: provided, however, that if the amount of said bill is due from a tenant, or one who was a tenant of the premises when it became due, the owner of the premises or a tenant under him, other than the person from whom the water rent referred to in said bill is due, may pay the same to the treasurer without the addition of any per centage thereon. It shall be the duty of the auditor to demand from the collector monthly settlements of such bills as are placed in his hands, and for failure to make such settlement the collector shall forfeit the per centage which he is authorized by this section to deduct. Ordinances 1869

18. If any person, other than the superintendent or his agents, shall introduce into any lot or tenement water from the city pipes, or introduce any ferule or other fixture into any of said pipes, or construct or lay down, or have constructed or laid down, any pipes or other works, for the purpose of introducing water into a lot or tenement, or break up any street, lane, alley or road for the purpose of constructing or laying down any such pipes or works, every person so offending shall pay a fine of not less than ten nor more than fifty dollars; and every twenty-four hours during which such work or fixture shall continue, shall be a distinct offence. But after water has been introduced into a lot or tenement, as provided in section ten of this ordinance, the fine shall not be incurred by the owner or occupier of such lot or tenement, when he, by permission in writing of the superintendent, or (if he refuse) by permission of the committee, causes to be attached to the said pipes, fixtures for water closets, boilers, baths, wash basins, or other things for which water is required, provided such fixtures be constructed by practical and competent plumbers, and the mate-

Ordinances 1869 rials used in their construction be of the best quality, and sufficiently strong to withstand double the required pressure, and provided that on the completion of the work notice thereof be forthwith given to the superintendent or his agent, and the work be by him inspected and approved.

19. No plumber shall make any addition to, or alteration of, any fixtures connected with the water works, without having first received a written permit from the superintendent or the committee to do so; nor shall any attachment be made for any purpose whatsoever from any pipe, except it be the pipe supplying the premises for which such work is to be done; and all pipes put in by plumbers shall have separate stop-cocks to each branch thereof, so that no difficulty may occur in shutting off the water when it is necessary to do so, under a penalty of ten dollars for each violation.

20. Every person occupying any lot or tenement into which water is conveyed under this ordinance, shall permit the superintendent or his agent, or any authorized agent of this city, to enter such lot or tenement, at seasonable hours, to inspect the works therein, or to see if this ordinance has been violated. Any person refusing so to do shall, for each refusal, pay a fine of five dollars.

21. If any person shall deface or injure any house, wall, cock, wheel, fire plug or other fixture connected with or pertaining to the water works, or shall bathe in the reservoir, basin or canal thereof, or deposit any offensive matter, or any stick, mud or rubbish in said reservoir, basin or canal, or shall, without lawful authority, climb over or get through the fence or enclosure of the reservoir, or place any building material, rubbish or other matter on the stop-cock of a street main or service pipe, or obstruct access to any fixture connected with the water works, or remove or injure any pipe, fire plug, hydrant or cock, or open any of them so as to waste the water, or if any person shall use the city water for a purpose for which he has neither paid nor obtained a license to use it, every such person shall, for each offence, pay a fine of not less than five nor more than twenty dollars.

22. When the occupier of a lot or a tenement, on which has been erected or placed a hydrant, cock or other fixture, to supply water, shall permit the water to run from the hydrant, cock or fixture, without proper care to prevent waste, or shall permit the water to be used, taken or received by

any person, other than said occupier, or a member or visitor of his family, there shall, in each case, be a fine on the said occupier of not less than five nor more than twenty dollars; and in the latter case there shall be a like fine also on the person so using, taking or receiving the water; and in every such case the superintendent shall stop the water from said lot or tenement, and not turn it on again uutil a satisfactory assurance is given him that the like case will not happen again. So, likewise, if any hydrant, cock or other fixture be found leaking, and the owner or occupier of the premises shall refuse or fail to have the necessary repairs made, the superintendent shall stop the water from said lot or tenement, and there shall be a fine of ten dollars on any person who shall turn on the water before such repairs are made. If any person not acting under the authority of the superintendent or the committee, shall turn the city water on any premises whatsoever, or if any person shall take, receive or use the city water before first having paid the charges for the same, he shall pay a fine of ten dollars for each offence. Ordinances 1869

23. Notwithstanding the preceding provisions, the committee may grant to any poor person, without charge therefor, license to use the water from a hydrant on another lot or tenement, with the permission of the occupier thereof. The superintendent shall keep a separate list of all licenses granted under this section.

24. Nothing in this chapter shall prevent the occupier of a lot or tenement, supplied with city water, from having, when his hydrant or pipe is out of order, the use of water from a hydrant on another lot or tenement, with the permission of the occupier thereof; nor prevent any person from taking city water to extinguish fire, nor prevent city water from being used by a fire company in examining, or practicing, or cleaning and putting in good condition their engines and hose.

25. The superintendent shall diligently enforce all ordinances relating to the water works, and prosecute all who may violate any of their provisions; and it shall be the especial duty of the police to report violations of this chapter which come within their knowledge.

Title 5.

HEALTH.

CHAPTER XXVI.*

CONCERNING HEALTH AND THE CITY HOSPITAL.

Ordinances 1869

1. The committee on health shall exercise a general supervision over the hospital, and recommend to the city council such improvements in or about the premises as they may deem advisable.

2. The physician of the almshouse shall be, ex-officio, physician of the hospital; and the superintendent of the almshouse shall be, ex-officio, superintendent of the hospital.

3. The committee may employ a person as housekeeper of the hospital, who shall reside therein and keep it and the furniture thereof in good order, and when necessary act as nurse; and who shall perform such other duties as the committee may require.. The committee may also, at and for such times as they may see occasion, employ other nurses and attendants, who shall respectively perform such duties and under such regulations as the committee may prescribe. The committee may pay the housekeeper, nurses and attendants, for their respective services, such compensation as said committee may deem reasonable.

---

* Ch. XXVII of 1869.

4. The committee may authorize such vehicles and horses to be purchased and kept for the removal of persons to the hospital, and snch other things to be obtained for the comfort or cure of persons in the hospital, or for use and consumption therein, as they may deem proper. The compensation mentioned in the preceding section, and the expenses incurred under this section, shall be paid by the auditor, upon the drafts of the chairman of said committee, provided what is so paid shall not exceed what may be appropriated by the city council for such compensation and expenses. Ordinances 1869

5. There shall be received into the said hospital all persons infected with any infectious disease dangerous to the public health. Negroes shall be in separate apartments from white persons, and females in separate apartments from males.

6. The board of health shall be the health officers of the city. They shall have all the powers and perform all the duties devolved upon health officers by the laws of the state. It shall be their special duty to remove to the hospital all persons in the city infected with any infectious disease dangerous to the public health of the city, unless such person be sick at his own residence, or cannot be removed without danger of life. May 12, 1873.

7. All expenses incurred for the removal of any person infected with a dangerous disease, and for maintaining, nursing and curing him, or incurred in entering any lot, house or vessel suspected of having persons or things infected with a dangerous infectious disease therein, and removing them to the hospital, shall be paid to the superintendent of the hospital (who shall account therefor quarterly to the auditor) by such infected person, or by the owner of such lot, house or vessel, as the case may be: or if such person or owner be a married woman, by her husband; or if an infant, by his parent or guardian. An account of all such expenses not paid to the superintendent shall, by him, be filed with the auditor, who shall, unless the amount thereof be paid, or the committee on finance otherwise direct, cause the same to be recovered from the person liable therefor, by suit or warrant, as the case may be. Ordinances 1869

8. Every physician practicing in the city of Richmond, who shall be in attendance upon a patient affected with small-pox or varioloid, shall report the name and location of the patient to the board of health, in writing, within twenty-

Ordinances 1869 four hours after he is satisfied of the existence of the disease; and he shall also report the recovery or death of every such patient under his charge; and for his failure to comply with either of these requirements, the physician so offending thall be fined ten dollars for every twenty-four hours he so fails to report such patient.

Jan. 13, 1873. 9. The head of every household in the city of Richmond, is hereby required, whenever any case of small-pox or varioloid shall occur upon his or her premises, to at once hang out on a staff or pole projecting at least three feet from the front of the dwelling, a white flag at least one foot square. In case of a failure to put out said flag, he, she or they shall be fined not less than five nor more than ten dollars for each day of the omission to do so, to be collected on complaint before the police justice.

CHAPTER XXVII.*

CONCERNING THE BOARD OF HEALTH.

Constitution and powers of board.

Modified from Ordinances 1869 1. The city council shall appoint three physicians,† one from Monroe or Clay ward, one from Madison or Jackson ward, and one from Jefferson or Marshall ward; who shall constitute a board of health. They shall, at their first regular meeting after their appointment, choose a president, who shall continue in office until his successor is appointed. The board shall have the services, when required, of the clerk in

---

* Chapter XXVIII of 1869.

† The ordinance of 1869 directs these appointments to be made annually in the month of May; but as the members of the board are salaried officers they now fall under the rule of chapter IV, § 2.

the treasurer's office, and shall keep a journal of their proceedings, which may be at all times examined by the city council. Ordinances 1869

2. The president of the board of health shall receive annually, for his services, one thousand dollars; and the other members of the said board shall receive annually, for their services, one hundred dollars each. Dec. 8, 1873, § 7.

3. The members of the board shall inspect the wards of the city carefully, twice a month, from April to September, and once a month for the balance of the year, visiting all localities suspected of being unhealthy or exposed to disease. They shall suggest to the council such measures as they think fit to preserve the health of the city, and especially to prevent the introduction and spread of contagious and infectious diseases, and to prevent or regulate the pursuit of callings prejudicial to the public health or comfort. They shall also consider and report upon all such matters as may be referred to them by the city council, and make monthly reports of their proceedings. Ordinances 1869

4. The members of the board are hereby invested with police authority in the performance of their duties. They may require deleterious matter, wherever found, to be removed by the occupant of the premises (or by the owner, if the premises are unoccupied), and conveyed beyond the limits of the city; and they may require yards and premises and the street gutters in front of any premises, when they think it important to the health of the neighborhood, to be cleansed and limed by the occupant or owner of such premises. They shall report to the police justice all offences against the health regulations of the city, and all persons who fail, after five days' notice, to remove deleterious matter, or to cleanse and lime their premises and the gutters in front as aforesaid; and thereupon such person shall be fined, in the discretion of the police justice, not less than five nor more than twenty dollars, unless he is satisfied of their inability to comply with the orders of the board of health.

5. No person shall deposit, or cause to be deposited, in any street or public or private alley, any filth, garbage, ashes, rubbish or other such thing, under penalty of being fined not less than five nor more than twenty dollars for every such deposit; and each day such deposit remains shall be a distinct offence.

Ordinances 1869 6. Whenever, in the opinion of the board, it shall become necessary, the board may require the services of the city hands and carts, under their direction, in cleansing particular localities, and may order lime from the city gas works or elsewhere, to be distributed in such localities.

7. The occupant of any house or lot shall cause all refuse matter, except garbage,* to be put in boxes or barrels, and in the most convenient place on such lot for removal, under penalty of a fine of not less than one nor more than ten dollars.

Sanitary Inspectors.

Nov. 13, 1871. 8. The chief of police shall detail three of the police force to report to the president of the board of health, to act as sanitary inspectors.

9. The said inspectors shall, from the time of their detail, be under the control of the board of health, and receive instructions from said board, and perform such services as said board may require, to carry out the health ordinances of the city.

10. The said inspectors are also charged with the duty of compiling quarterly or semi-annually, statements of the births within the city, as said board may determine, and for its proper performance the said board is hereby instructed to have suitable forms printed at the expense of the city.

14. In the event of the inefficiency of any of said inspectors, the board of health is empowered to report the fact to the chief of police, and demand a new inspector.

12. The said inspectors, while detailed, shall be kept on the roll of the police force, and shall be entitled to the same pay as other members of the force. In case of any sudden or anticipated disturbance within the city, the chief of police shall have power to demand the services of said inspectors until such disturbance is quelled.

---

* The ordinance in chapter LXX, passed November 12th, 1874, contains more special and in some things essentially different provisions as to the deposit of *garbage*, which is there defined to be *refuse animal and vegetable matter.* It also prescribes by what authority the business of collecting and transporting garbage may be engaged in. The above section is therefore modified to accord with these later provisions.

CHAPTER XXVIII.*

CONCERNING SINKS, CESS-POOLS AND PRIVIES.

1. From and after the first day of February, eighteen hundred and seventy-five, no part of the contents of any privies, privy vaults, boxes and sinks, (except substances not soluble in water,) shall be removed therefrom, or shall be transported through any street, avenue, alley, or other public place, except as the same shall be removed and transported by means of some air-tight apparatus, pneumatic, or other process, so as to prevent the contents of said privy, vault, and so forth, being agitated or exposed in the open air during said process of removal and transportation. Nov. 26, 1874.

2. That the president of the board of health be and he is hereby instructed to contract for the term of one year for the removal of the night soil of this city by the process authorized by the preceding section: provided, that in no case shall the charge for such service exceed the price of one dollar-and-a-half for six-and-a-half cubic feet or fifty gallons, and eighteen cents for each cubic foot in the same receptacle in excess of said six-and-a-half cubic feet, or two-and-a-half cents per gallon for each gallon in excess of said fifty gallons, the measurement to be made as the president of the board of health may elect. The charges for said work shall be paid by the occupant of each lot on which said service is rendered, and may be collected by distress and sale, as taxes for the benefit of the city are authorized to be collected; and if paid by the owner, he shall have like remedy for the collection of the same against the tenant or occupant.

* Chapter XXIX of 1869.

Nov. 26, 1874. 3. Each party or company who contracts with the president of the board of health for the removal of night soil shall, upon the order of the board of health, perform his duty in cleansing any privy, vault, box, and so forth, upon premises occupied or unoccupied, of which complaint has been made, and the rates of compensation shall be the same as in the preceding section; and the order of the board of health shall create a lien upon said property for the expense of said service.

4. No person shall remove from any premises in the city the night soil contained in the privies, vaults, sinks, boxes, and so forth, of such premises, except the parties, or their agents, with whom the president of the board of health may contract, as is provided for in section second of this ordinance; nor shall the owner or occupant of any such premises employ any person to remove said night soil except the parties aforesaid; nor shall any person bury or cover up any night soil on any lot, street, or alley of this city. Any person violating this section, or any of its provisions, shall be fined not less than five nor more than fifty dollars for each offence.

5. Each party who contracts with the said president of the board of health for the removal of the night soil shall, in each case, immediately after its removal, deodorize and disinfect the premises from which the said night soil is removed, using such disinfectants as the board of health shall direct; and they shall select places of deposit, to be approved by the board of health; the said places of deposit to be kept deodorized and disinfected at all times, and open to the inspection and approval of the health authorities of the city. If the said parties, in removing the night soil or other filth, shall spill any of it in the streets or alleys of the city, or shall fail to disinfect and deodorize the premises from which it has been taken, or shall fail to deposit it at the places indicated by the board of health, or to keep such places in an inoffensive condition, they shall be liable to a fine of not less than ten nor more than twenty dollars for each separate offence.

6. Nothing in this ordinance shall be construed as applying to the removal of the contents of what are known as "earth closets."

7. Each party or company who contracts to perform this service, shall give bond in the sum of fifteen hundred dol-

lars, with security, to be approved by the committee on health, with condition for the faithful performance of his duties, and shall pay to the city a license tax of fifty dollars per annum. Nov. 26, 1874.

CHAPTER XXIX.*

CONCERNING DEAD ANIMALS.

1. Hereafter if any person not authorized so to do by contract with the city of Richmond, shall remove from the city any dead horse, mule, cow or other cattle, or the carcass thereof, he shall be fined, for the removal of every such animal or carcass, not less than five nor more than thirty dollars. Ordinances 1869

2. It shall be the duty of the owner of every such dead animal as is mentioned in the preceding section, and of the owner or occupier of the lot and premises wherein such dead animal or the carcass thereof may be, to give notice of the death of such animal, or of its being on his lot or premises, to the person contracting with the city for the removal of such animals from the corporate limits thereof. And if the owner of such animal, or the owner or occupier of the lot whereon the body of any such animal may be, shall fail to give such notice to such contractor for six hours after he shall know or be informed of the death of such animal, or that it is on his lot, he shall be fined not less than five nor more than ten dollars.

3. The contractor for the removal of dead animals from the city shall fix at least one place in each ward of the city where the notice required in the preceding section may be given, and shall publish the same in three of the daily papers of the city every day for two weeks, and shall keep a sign at the said places to indicate the same; and he shall have some person, or a book or slate, at each of said places, to whom the notice may be delivered, or in which it may be written.

---

*Chapter XXX of 1869.

Ordinances 1869

4. If the said contractor shall fail to remove any dead animal or carcass within six hours after notice thereof has been left at the place designated by him, or has been given to him in person, he shall be fined not less than five nor more than twenty dollars: provided, that the hours of the night shall not be computed in either this or the preceding section.

5. It shall be the duty of every policeman who shall know of a dead animal or carcass lying in a street or alley or lot in the city, to give notice thereof to said contractor in the mode prescribed in the preceding section; and for the failure to remove such dead animal within six hours from the time when the notice is so given, the said contractor shall be liable as hereinbefore provided.

6. If the said contractor shall fail to comply with his contract in removing dead animals a proper distance from the city, so that the same shall become offensive to the people in any part of the city or of the suburbs, he shall be fined not less than ten nor more than thirty dollars for each offence; and shall, moreover, be liable to an action on his bond for a breach of the condition thereof.

CHAPTER XXX.*

CONCERNING QUARANTINE.

1. There shall be established, by and with the concurrence of the county court of Henrico, a quarantine ground for the city of Richmond, between a line drawn across James river, from a point at high water mark on the Henrico side and a point at high water mark on the Chesterfield side of said

---

* Chapter XXXI of 1869.

river, so as to touch the lower end of Hancock's island, and a line drawn from the Henrico side, at a point at high water mark, opposite Warwick, to a point at high water mark on the Chesterfield side; which points shall be designated and marked by the superintendent of quarantine. Ordinances 1869

2. Quarantine shall be performed on the said ground by vessels, persons and merchandize, coming or brought from any port or place whence the city council, by resolution, published in one or more of the newspapers published in the city of Richmond, shall declare it probable that any plague or other infectious disease may be brought, during such time, and in such manner, as shall be directed by the council, by resolution published as aforesaid; and until they are discharged from such quarantine, no such person or merchandize shall be brought on shore, or go, or be put on board any other vessel, but in such case and in such manner as shall be permitted by the orders of the city council; and the vessels and persons receiving goods out of such vessels shall be subject to the orders concerning quarantine, and for preventing infection, which shall be made by the city council.

3. The president of the board of health shall be the superintendent of quarantine, who, during the time of actual quarantine performed on said grounds, shall receive five dollars per diem for his services; and the other members of the board shall be his assistants; and he may have such other assistants as the city council may appoint.

4.* The quarantine herein provided, and all persons, vessels and goods subject thereto, shall, in all things, be governed and regulated by the twentieth, twenty-first, twenty-second, twenty-third, twenty-fourth, twenty-fifth, twenty-sixth, twenty-seventh and twenty-eighth sections of chapter eighty-four of the Code of Virginia, edition of eighteen hundred and seventy-three, and any acts amending the same, and such regulations consistent therewith as the city council may ordain.

5. The superintendent of quarantine shall, under the direction and approval of the city council, provide, by contract, sufficient buildings and shelters for the safe keeping of the goods or merchandize which it may be necessary to land from on board of any vessel performing quarantine in obe-

* This section changed to adapt it to the last edition of the Code. The reference to sections in the Ordinance of 1869, in fact did not agree with either of the last two editions. Possibly it was there taken from some old ordinance existing before 1860, and meant the Code of 1849.

Ordinances 1869 dience to this ordinance, as well as for the accommodation of the persons superintending or performing quarantine.

6. All vessels subject to quarantine shall, immediately on their arrival, anchor within quarantine anchorage ground, and there remain with all persons arriving in them, subject to the examinations and regulations imposed by law.

7. The mayor, whenever in his judgment the public health shall require it, may order any vessel at the wharves of the city, or in their vicinity, into quarantine or other place of safety; and may require all persons, articles and things introduced into the city from such vessels, to be seized, returned on board, or removed to the quarantine ground. In case the master, owner or consignee of the vessel cannot be found, or shall neglect or refuse to obey the order of removal, the mayor shall have power to cause such removal at the expense of such master, owner or consignee; and such vessel or persons shall not return to the city without the written permission of the mayor. Such vessel, when removed to the quarantine ground, shall, in all respects, be subject to the regulations of quarantine.

8. It shall be the duty of the superintendent of quarantine to board every vessel subject to quarantine, or to visitation (if, in the opinion of the superintendent, such visit be necessary), immediately on her arrival; to inquire as to the health of all persons on board, and the condition of the vessel and cargo, by inspection of the bill of health, manifest, log-book or otherwise; to examine, on oath, as many and such persons on board of vessels suspected of coming from a sickly port, or having had during the voyage, sickness on board, as he may judge expedient, and to report the facts and his conclusions to the mayor. Vessels subject to quarantine shall, under the authority and direction of the superintendent, remain at quarantine at least thirty days after their arrival, and at least twenty days after their cargoes shall have been discharged, and shall perform such further quarantine as the superintendent shall prescribe, unless sooner discharged by his written permission. But nothing in this ordinance contained shall prevent any vessel arriving at quarantine from again going to sea, or returning to the port of departure before breaking bulk.

9. The superintendent shall have power to direct the location, within the quarantine anchorage ground, of any vessels

subject to quarantine regulations; to cause any vessel under quarantine, when he shall judge it necessary for the purification of the vessel or her cargo, to discharge the cargo at the quarantine ground, or some other suitable place out of the city; to cause any such vessel, her cargo, bedding and the clothing of persons on board, to be ventilated, cleansed and purified, in such manner and during such time as he may direct; and if he shall judge it necessary to prevent infection or contagion, to destroy any portion of such cargo, bedding or clothing which he may deem incapable of purification; to prohibit and prevent all persons arriving in vessels subject to quarantine, from leaving quarantine until fifteen days after the sailing of their vessels from their ports of departure, and fifteen days after the last case of pestilential or infectious disease that shall have occurred on board shall have terminated, and ten days after their arrival at quarantine, unless sooner discharged by his written permission; to permit the cargo of any vessel under quarantine, or any portion thereof, when he shall judge the same free from infection, to be conveyed to the city of Richmond, or to such place as may be designated by the mayor, after having reported in writing to the mayor the condition of said cargo and his intention to grant such permission, but such permission shall be inoperative without the written approval of the mayor; to permit the cargo of any vessel under quarantine, or any part thereof, if in his opinion it will not be dangerous to the public health, tc be shipped for exportation by sea; but the vessel receiving the same shall not approach nearer than the lower edge of Rocketts bar, without the written permission of the mayor. Ordinances 1869.

10. Every vessel performing quarantine shall be designated by colors fixed in a conspicuous part of her main shrouds.

11. No lighters shall be employed to load or unload vessels at quarantine, without permission of the superintendent, and subject to such restrictions as he shall impose.

12. All passengers under quarantine who shall be unable to maintain themselves, shall be provided for by the master of the vessel in which they shall have arrived; and if the master shall omit to provide for them, they shall be maintained on shore at the expense of such vessel; and such vessel shall not be permitted to leave quarantine until such expense shall have been repaid.

Ordinances 1869 13. The master of any vessel released from quarantine and arriving at the city of Richmond, shall, immediately after such arrival, deliver the permit of the superintendent to the mayor, or to such person as he shall direct; but such vessel shall not approach nearer than the lower edge of Rocketts bar, without the written permission of the mayor.

14. No person, without the permission of the superintendent, shall enter within the enclosure of the quarantine ground, or go on board of, or have any communication or intercourse or dealing with, any vessel under quarantine. Any person going on board a vessel under quarantine, without license from the superintendent, may be compelled to remain there, in the same manner as he might have been if he had been one of the crew of the vessel.*

*By the statute (Code of 1873, ch. 84, § 22, p. 733,) any person violating quarantine regulations shall forfeit not less than five nor more than five hundred dollars.

Title 6.

POLICE.

CHAPTER XXXI.*

CONCERNING THE POLICE DEPARTMENT OF THE CITY.

* Chapter XXXII of 1869.

Charter, § 84. 1. The police department of the city of Richmond, shall be under the general control and management of police commissioners thereof, who shall consist of the mayor, the president of the city council, and the police justice, and shall constitute a board of police commissioners for said city; of which board the mayor shall be president, and shall have a casting vote; and any two of said board shall form a quorum for the transaction of any business.*

2. The board of commissioners may adopt rules and by-laws for the government thereof, and also may establish, promulgate and enforce proper rules, regulations and orders for the good government and discipline of the police force; but such rules, regulations and orders shall not in any way conflict with any ordinance of the city council, nor with the provisions of the charter of the city, or the constitution and laws of this state, or of the United States.

Charter, § 85. 3. The police commissioners, after taking the oath of office as such commissioners, shall meet at the office of the mayor, or other suitable place, at such time as may be expedient, and as they shall from time to time designate, and on special occasions, as the mayor may, in writing, appoint. They shall

*By chapter VIII, § 2, the clerk to the police justice is required to act as clerk or secretary to the board of police commissioners.

perform the duties of said office without any compensation, reward or salary therefor from the city, except that nothing herein shall in any way conflict with the payment of the salary elsewhere provided to be paid to the said mayor and police justice for their services in their respective offices. Charter, § 85.

4. It shall be the duty of the police commissioners to select from among the electors of the city, and appoint by warrant of appointment, bearing the signatures of all three of said commissioners, to be immediately filed with the city clerk, so many permanent policemen, officers and patrolmen as may be authorized by the city council; and said board shall also appoint, with the approval of the city council, one chief of police, who shall hold office for the term of two years, through whom said board may promulgate all rules, regulations and orders of said board, and to the orders of the mayor: provided, that the orders of such single commissioner do not conflict with the rules, regulations or orders of said board then in force; and said chief, and each policeman of said police force appointed in manner as aforesaid, may hold his respective office during the term of good behavior,* or until said board, by unanimous vote, shall remove him; but in case of misconduct on the part of such chief or any member of said police force, then he may be removed by the decision of a majority of said board, as hereinafter provided, or by the city council. Charter, § 86.

5. In times of exigency, the commissioners, or a majority of them, or any one of them, if the others should be absent from the city or unable to act, may appoint temporarily, without authority from the city council, a suitable number of additional policemen for such time as shall appear necessary; not, however, to extend beyond the time of the next meeting of the city council. Charter, § 87.

6. The chief of police and every policeman duly appointed as aforesaid, shall have issued to him a warrant of appoint- Charter, § 90.

* This term of good behavior is, so far as the chief of police is concerned, inconsistent with the previous provision of the section, making his term of office two years. But as this whole section is an exact transcript of section 86 of the charter, the inconsistency cannot be gotten rid of except by an amendment of that instrument. If the proviso inserted about the middle of the section included the clause allowing the chief and each policeman to hold during good behaviour, it is believed that this clause would, by the law of statutory construction, prevail over the preceding provision relative to the term of the chief of police; but there is nothing in the language or arrangement of the section to show this with any certainty; and indeed the most probable reading seems to be that which confines the proviso to the one clause relative to the orders of the mayor, with which it commences.

Charter, § 90. ment, signed by the president of the board and countersigned by the city clerk, stating the date of his appointment, which shall be his commission; and he shall take such oath as the ordinances of the city council require, and subscribe the same in a book to be kept for that purpose by the said city clerk.

Charter, § 88. 7. The mayor, at any time, upon charges being preferred, or upon finding said chief of police, or any other member of the force, guilty of misconduct, shall have power to suspend such member from service until the board of commissioners shall convene and take action in the matter; but such member shall not remain so suspended for a longer period than thirty days, without an opportunity of being heard in his defence. Upon hearing the proofs, a majority of said commissioners may discharge or restore such member, in accordance with their judgment and decision upon the case; and the pay or salary of such member shall cease from the time of suspension to the time of restoration to service, unless otherwise ordered by said board of commissioners in their written decision, which shall be filed with the city clerk. Any violation of the rules, regulations or orders of the board, or orders of any superior, shall be good cause for dismissal.

Jan. 10, 1870. 8. The police force shall consist of the chief of police, three captains, who shall be designated as first, second and third captains, and shall rank in the order of their numbers, beginning at the first, who shall be first in rank; and eighty policemen, from whom there shall be appointed ten sergeants. The said captains and sergeants of the police shall, in criminal cases, have the same powers, perform the same duties, receive the same fees, and be subject to the same penalties as are prescribed by law for constables;* and one of said captains shall reside in each police district.

Charter, § 89. Ordinances 1869 ch. 32, § 16. 9. The salary or pay of the chief of police and policemen shall be as determined by the city council, and shall be payable monthly; and any policeman prevented by sickness from doing service shall receive the same pay, upon his producing the certificate of the surgeon of the police that he was sick. All bills of expense on account of the police department shall be audited by at least two of the police commissioners.

---

* Under section 91 of the charter the police board may, if they think fit, change this designation of members of the force who shall have powers, &c., of constables.

10. The city shall be divided into three police districts by the limits of the wards of the city; but these districts may be altered from time to time by the chief of police, under the control of the board of commissioners. The present watch-houses at the first and second markets shall continue to be so, and that at the first market shall be designated as the first, and that at the second market shall be designated as the second watch-house; and there shall be a place designated as "police head-quarters." Under like control the chief of police shall divide the districts into beats, and may alter their limits.

Ordinances 1869 ch. 32, § 3. Charter, § 84.

11. Subject to the control of the board of police commissioners, and the orders of the mayor, the chief of police shall be the chief executive officer of police, and shall have control of it and of its officers and members, and of all persons at any time employed in it; he shall, when instructed by the board of commissioners, promulgate all rules, regulations and orders adopted by the board for the government of the police force; he shall report to the mayor every day all that he is bound to notice in discharge of his duty, the members of police he may have suspended, and the men unfit for duty, and make to him a report upon the reports of the officers of police; he shall have the general charge of the peace and good order of the city, and see to the observance of the ordinances of the city and acts of assembly relating to it, and in any emergency he may direct the whole police force, or any part thereof, to any place in the city he may deem proper.

Charter, §§ 84,86. Ordinances 1869 ch. 32, § 4.

12. The chief of police shall daily assign one captain of police and three sergeants to duty in each police district; and he shall distribute the policemen in such proportions as may seem proper among said districts; and shall make such regulations for a proper system of relief, (other than dividing the police into two portions, one for the day, and one for the night,) that at all times during the day-watches one-fourth of the force shall be on duty, and at all times during the night-watches three-fourths of the force shall be on duty. The chief of police shall also divide the force, so that one-fourth of the policemen assigned to each district shall be required to sleep at the station houses when off duty, in order to provide for any sudden emergency. The captain of each police district shall have charge of the entire district to which he is assigned, subject to the orders and responsible to the

Jan. 10, 1870.

Jan. 10, 1870. chief of police, and shall be relieved by the sergeant first assigned to said district, whom he shall hold responsible for the command during his absence from duty.

Ordinances 1869 ch. 32, § 6. 13. If the chief of police is, for any cause, unable to attend to the duty of assigning the officers of police and policemen to their districts, the first police officer or the captain highest in grade present shall perform the duty. And if an officer of police is unable to attend to his duties or is absent, the chief of police may appoint one of the sergeants to perform the duties.

Jan. 10, 1870, 14. Each captain of the police shall keep a muster roll of the police of his district, and call it at the hours of relief, and shall deliver it to the chief of police; he shall also report in writing to the chief of police any delinquency on the part of any policemen that shall come to his knowledge, and any excuses made by any policemen for absence from duty, or the unfitness of any member for his office, and any charge that may be made against a member. With the assistance of his sergeant he shall keep a book in which shall be entered all arrests made, the disposal of prisoners, all nuisances reported, ordinances enforced, complaints and applications of citizens, and other police matters; and shall deliver daily with the muster roll a copy of such entries made during the preceding twenty-four hours.

Ordinances 1869 ch. 32, § 8. 15. When necessary, the policemen shall, by means of rattles or otherwise, summon to their assistance other policemen from adjacent districts. When a person is apprehended by policemen in a district in which there is no watch-house, they shall proceed with him to the next district in the direction of a watch-house, and by means of rattles or otherwise summon the policemen of that district, and transfer him to such policemen, who shall in like manner convey and transfer him till delivered at the watch-house.

Ordinances 1869 ch. 32, § 9. 16. Each officer of police shall report to the chief of police every nuisance or obstruction that he may find in any drain, gutter or other part of a street or alley, or that he has reason to believe or is informed is in any house, or upon any land in the city; and shall execute the orders of the police justice or of the mayor in regard to any such nuisances or obstructions. Each of them shall, when in his opinion repairs are required, without delay report the same, if they be required to a street or public alley, to the superintendent of streets; and if to a pipe, hydrant or other fixtures of the water works, or any fixture of the gas works, in a street or public alley, to the respective superintendents of such works. Each of them shall report to the chief of police every violation of any ordinance of the city that he has reason to believe or is informed has been committed, and make such reports and give such other notices and information as may be prescribed by any ordinance, or be useful in the enforcement thereof. Ordinances 1869 ch. 32, § 9.

17. The whole of the police force shall endeavor to prevent the commission of offences in the city, and to preserve the good order and peace thereof, and secure its inhabitants from personal violence, and their property from loss and injury; and shall generally have power to do whatever may be necessary to these ends. Every member of the force shall earnestly endeavor, when any offence is committed in the city, to detect and arrest the offender, and strive to enforce all ordinances prescribing any fine or punishment for, and all acts of assembly relating to, offences in the city or the police thereof. Although an officer or policeman be applied to when it is not his time for regular duty, he shall, upon application, whether in the day or night, do all that the emergency requires. No member of the police force shall absent himself from the city without having obtained the written consent of the mayor. Nor shall any member of the police force go out of the corporate limits to perform the duties of police officer or detective, or to assist in performing any such duty, unless a formal requisition has been made on the mayor, by the mayor or other presiding officer of the city, town or county requiring his services, and then only to act in strict accordance with the written instructions given by the mayor of this city, prescribing also the length of time he shall be absent. And any one acting in violation of this restriction shall have his pay stopped from the day he leaves the city, and be summarily dismissed from the service. Ordinances 1869 ch. 32, § 10. Charter, § 92. April 17, 1871.

18. It shall be the duty of the chief of police, at least twice in each week, to explore in person all of the streets and alleys of the city, and to give information and prosecute for the violation of the laws of the state and ordinances of the city concerning any matter of police regulation, and by all legal means to endeavor to enforce the same; and he shall Ordinances 1869 ch. 32, § 11.

Ordinances 1869 ch. 32, § 11. attend at the police headquarters at sunrise, where and when each of the officers of police shall report to him the condition of his district during the previous twenty-four hours, and especially shall report all offences therein committed, either against the laws of the state or the ordinances of the city, and the names, if known, of the persons committing the same; and whether said offenders were arrested; and the names of all persons whom he may deem to be material witnesses against such offenders. He shall also report to said chief of police all misconduct or neglect of duty by any policeman under his command.

Ordinances 1869 ch. 32, § 13. Charter, §§ 84, 86, 88. 19. The policemen and sergeants may be suspended from service by the chief of police when he sees cause for prompt action, subject to the approval of the mayor and of the board of police commissioners. Every such case of suspension shall at once be reported by the chief of police to the mayor; who, if he does not see fit to order the restoration of the suspended policeman or sergeant to service, shall, as soon as practicable, and within the limit of time prescribed in the seventh section of this chapter, bring the case before the board of commissioners; and by that board it shall then be proceeded with and disposed of as prescribed in the case of a suspension by the mayor. The policemen, as well as the officers of police, shall reside within the city; and no person shall be appointed a policeman who cannot read and write.

Ordinances 1869 ch. 32, § 14. Charter, § 84 &c. 20. The mayor shall from time to time make report to the city council of the state of the police, with such suggestions for its improvement as he may see fit, or as may be recommended by the board of police commissioners.

Ordinances 1869 ch. 32, § 15. Charter, § 84 &c. 21. The city attorney shall, when required by the board of police commissioners or the mayor, prepare forms in respect to any matter connected with the police of the city; of which the said board or the mayor may have blanks printed at the expense of the city, for the use of the police.

Ordinances 1869 ch. 32, § 17. 22. No officer appointed to any office under this ordinance shall receive from the city, for services in such or any other office, any other compensation than is herein mentioned. And every policeman shall upon oath account for and pay over daily to the officer under whose command he is at the time, all costs that he may receive, and all sums he may be entitled to as informer, with all money to which the city may be entitled; and the officers of police shall in like manner, with their daily reports to the chief of police, account for and pay over to him all such moneys, and all the moneys received by them to which the city is entitled. And the chief of police shall, in the first four days of every month, in like manner, account for and pay into the treasury of the city all such moneys. And no member of the police shall receive a gratuity from any person whatever. But he may receive any reward which may be advertised for the apprehension of criminals, or which may be offered by the executive of the state, or by the municipal authorities of the city.

Ordinances 1869 ch. 32, § 17.

23. The board of police commissioners shall fix on the uniform, badges and numbers for the captains of police, the sergeants and policemen, which shall always be worn by them when they appear in public, whether they are on duty or not; and the badges and numbers shall be furnished at the expense of the city. Every person applying at the watch-houses, shall be entitled to have the name of any person wearing the particular number that the applicant may name. Every policeman, unless it shall be otherwise ordered by the board, shall be armed ordinarily with a baton not less than twenty-two inches long and one and three-quarters inch thick, at the expense of the city, and, in cases of emergency, with revolvers and other suitable weapons; and the chief of police shall procure a suitable quantity of such weapons, with which he may arm the police, furnishing them also with badges; and each person shall give his receipt for such weapons and badges as he may receive, which shall remain the property of the city. The board of commissioners shall have authority, if they think proper, to provide a suitable number of muskets for each watch-house, wherewith to arm the police in cases of great emergency.

Ordinances 1869 ch. 32, § 18. Charter, § 92.

24. If any person except a policeman shall publicly wear any such uniform, badge or number, as may be worn by a policeman, he shall forfeit and pay for such offence not less than one nor more than twenty dollars.

§§ 24 to 31 from Ordinances 1869 ch. §§ 19 to 26.

25. It shall not be lawful for any officer or policeman to be employed to attend at any theatre or other place of public amusement or entertainment.

26. If any member of the police shall be found to frequent any of the public houses or bar rooms where spirituous or fermented liquors are vended, except in his official capacity, and if it shall be ascertained that any of them are in the

Ordinances 1869 habit of using intoxicating liquors to excess, it shall be sufficient cause for the immediate dismissal of such offending member.

27. The policeman on duty at night in a district shall light the street lamps and extinguish them at such times as he may be directed by the proper agent of the committee on light.

As amended Jan. 10, 1870. 28. If any person resist any captain of police or policeman in the discharge of his duty, he shalt pay a fine of not less than ten nor more than twenty dollars. And if any person shall fail or refuse to aid or assist a captain of police or policeman, when called upon so to do by such captain or policeman when in the discharge of his duty, he shall be fined not less than five nor more than twenty dollars.

Ordinances 1869 29. There shall be a police contingent fund of twenty-five hundred dollars, to be designated the secret service fund. The mayor may from time to time draw on the said fund for such sums as he may think necessary in detecting and arresting offenders, and rendering the police efficient; and shall keep a book specifying the sums drawn, and for what purpose used; which book, on request, he shall exhibit to the chairman of the committee on police.

30. To the committee on police, without any special order for that purpose, shall stand referred all matters and statements required by this ordinance to be made to the city council, or any other matter specially reported by the mayor or the board of police commissioners concerning the police.

31. There shall be two or more detective officers appointed by the council of the city of Richmond, to be styed "detectives for the city of Richmond," who shall have all the powers of a captain of police under the charter and ordinances of this city: provided, that before any officer so appointed enters upon the duties of his office, he shall give bond to the city in the penalty of two thousand dollars, for the faithful performance of his duty. Such detectives shall be entitled to receive any reward which may be offered for the detection of crimes, or arrest or punishment of criminals, or parties accused of crime, or the recovery of stolen property. The city shall not be liable for either salary or fees in the execution of the duties of said detectives.

Nov. 7, 1870. 32. There shall be appointed by the board of police commissioners, with the approval of the city council, a surgeon of police, who shall attend all policemen when sick or otherwise physically unable to perform the duties of their position; and shall report in writing, each day, to the chief of police, such men as may be unfit for duty, and when able to resume duty. Nov. 7, 1870.

33. He shall carefully examine all men appointed to the position of policemen, and shall pronounce them physically able to perform all the duties thereof prior to their confirmation.

34. He shall receive, in full compensation foi his services, the sum of eighty dollars per month, to be paid out of a police fund in the hands of the chief of police, said fund to be raised by levying a tax not exceeding one dollar per month upon the members of the police force; and in the event of such tax being insufficient to pay the monthly salary of said surgeon of police, the city shall not be bound, either in whole or in part, for the payment of said salary.

CHAPTER XXXII.*

CONCERNING THE FIRE DEPARTMENT OF THE CITY.

Ordinances 1869

1. All the powers and duties hereinafter vested in or imposed upon the fire department, or any officer or member thereof, shall be exercised and performed under the supervision and control of the committee on the fire department; and all engine-houses, engines, apparatus and other property connected with the fire department of the city, shall in like manner be under the supervision and control of the said committee.

June 19, 1871.

2. The fire department of the city of Richmond shall consist of a chief engineer, six commanders, six foremen, four enginemen, five helpers, five hostlers, and sixty-six firemen. The chief engineer and the commanders shall be appointed by the city council biennially, in the month of July. The commanders shall be numbered by the city council, and shall rank according to their numbers, the highest in rank being number one. They and the chief engineer shall hold office until their successors qualify, and before acting shall take the following oaths: The chief engineer shall make oath that he will discharge the duties of his office to the best of his

* Chapter XXXIII of 1869.

abilities; and each commander shall take the same oath, and also, that he will obey the lawful orders of his superior officers. The chief engineer and commanders shall constitute a "board of control," and shall, as soon as practicable after their qualification, appoint six foremen, four enginemen, five helpers and five hostlers, who shall hold their positions until their successors are appointed. The commanders, under such regulations as the board of control may prescribe, shall enlist sixty-six firemen, for general service in the fire department, for the term of two years, who shall sign articles of enlistment in the form prescribed by the board of control. Before acting, the foremen, enginemen, helpers, hostlers and firemen, shall take the oath prescribed for commanders; and certificates of all oaths under this chapter, taken before any person qualified to administer oaths, shall be deposited among the records of the board of control. The fire department shall be kept up to its full force by enlistments and appointments, made as aforesaid whenever vacancies occur. June 19, 1871.

3. All engine-houses, horses, engines, hose and apparatus, and all hooks and ladders, and all other instruments for the extinguishment of fires, for the use of the fire department, shall be provided by the city council. And it shall not be lawful for any persons to organize a company or association within the city for the purpose of acting as a fire company, or to keep within the limits of the city any fire engine or reel, with a view to act as such company or association. And every person appearing in any street of the city as a member of such company or association for the purpose of acting as a fire company, or bringing into any street of the city such fire engine or reel, shall, for every such offence, pay a fine not exceeding twenty dollars. Ordinances 1869

4. The board of control shall meet once a month, at which meeting the officer present highest in rank shall preside. Three members shall constitute a quorum; and all questions shall be determined by a majority of voices. They shall keep a journal, and submit it, when required, to the city council; and the clerk in the treasurer's office shall be the clerk of the board of control. They shall assign a commander, a foreman and a proper complement of men to each company, and station the companies in the several wards as they think best. They shall supply each company with the necessary engine, hose and apparatus; keep them in repair;

Ordinances 1869 prescribe a uniform, and make all needful rules and regulations for the fire department, consistent with the laws of the state and ordinances of the city, and perform all other duties imposed on them by ordinance. The system of fire alarms may be prescribed by the board of control.

5. The chief engineer, or, in his absence, the officer highest in rank, shall command the fire department. Each commander, or, in his absence, his foreman, shall command his own company. The officer in command of the department shall have the control of the engine-houses, engines, apparatus and all other property of the fire department. He shall inspect the same once in every week, order indispensable repairs, and report them to the board of control, and see that everything is kept in a condition for efficient service. He shall have semi-annual inspections of the apparatus and the whole department. During fires and inspections he shall control all fire plugs, maintain order among the firemen and bystanders, preserve property, command both city and fire police, note and report to the police justice all violations of law or of the city ordinances, and do all things proper for the efficient operation of the department. He shall report annually to the city council, in the month of July,* the names and ages of the firemen, the number and localities of the fires which have occurred during the year, the causes thereof, if they can be ascertained, the names of the owners of the property destroyed or injured, the amount of such destruction or injury, the amount of insurance, the name of the insurance companies, and such other matters touching its operations and organization as he shall think proper.

6. Each commander shall, under such regulations as the board of control may prescribe, report monthly to the chief engineer the names and residences of his firemen, the condition of his engine-house, engine, hose and apparatus, specifying such repairs as he thinks necessary or desirable. He shall inspect the engine-house, engine and apparatus at least once in every day, and cause the same to be kept clean and in good condition. He shall report to the police justice all persons loitering in or about the engine-house. He shall report to the chief engineer all misconduct among his men,

*In the ordinance of 1869 this report was required to be made in May, but the organization of the department by appointment of officers, &c., was then fixed for that month, and so the fireman's year commenced in that month. Now the council appointments, under provisions of chapter IV, must be made in July, if practicable.

and shall prevent minors from running with the engine, taking hold of any part of the apparatus, or meddling with the same in any way. He shall report all such persons to the police justice, and if he knowingly permit such meddling, he shall be fined by the police justice five dollars for every offence. Ordinances 1869

7. The commander of each company, or, if he be absent, the foreman, or, if he be absent, the policeman of the company shall report to the chief engineer, immediately after a fire, every officer or fireman who shall not be on duty in a reasonable time after an alarm of fire is first given. The chief engineer shall return monthly to the board of control a list of such reports, and the board of control shall impose the following fines, unless sufficient excuses are rendered: Two dollars on each commander, one dollar and a half on each foreman, three dollars on each engineman, two dollars on each helper or hostler, and one dollar on each fireman. They shall certify the same quarterly to the auditor, and he shall deduct such fines from the pay of the officers and men. If the chief engineer be absent from fires or inspections without excuse, the board of control shall report him to the council.

8. The chief engineer and commanders may be suspended by the committee until the next meeting of the city council, and may be removed by the city council; and the other members of the department may be discharged by the committee or by the board of control at any time.

9. If any officer or other member of the department be insubordinate, disorderly or negligent, he may be fined by the board of control not exceeding ten dollars; which fine shall be certified and deducted from his pay, as above prescribed.

10. If any person interfere with a fireman in the discharge of his duty, or loiter about the engine-houses, or if any minor or other person meddle with the engines, hose or apparatus, as hereinbefore mentioned, he shall be fined by the police justice not less than five nor more than twenty dollars.

11. The chief engineer shall cause each commander to detail annually one or more men for police duty, and shall assign one to the command of the squad. They shall constitute the fire police; and it shall be their special duty to main-

Ordinances 1869 tian order during fires; to keep the ground clear, by ropes across the streets or otherwise; to protect property from fire and pillage; to arrest and commit to the station-houses all persons who persist in interfering with the firemen after due admonition to desist therefrom; to report to the officer in command all violations of law or of the ordinances of the city, and to execute his orders. Each policeman, while on duty, shall wear a badge on his breast.

12. The police of the city in the neighborhood of a fire shall assist the fire police, and during fires obey the orders of the officer in command of the fire department. They shall carry the names and residences of the officers of the department in their district, and shall call them on an alarm of fire at night.

13. The enginemen, helpers and hostlers attached to the steam fire engines, shall not engage in any other occupation, except by the special permission of the board of control.

14. The officer in command of the department in time of riot or insurrection shall, on the requisition of the mayor, assemble his department and assist the police of the city in restoring order or quelling insurrection.

15. All accounts for work done shall be examined by the board of control, and certified to the committee on the fire department, who shall examine, and if they allow them, certify the same to the auditor; or if they think proper they may report such accounts to the city council, with a recommendation either that they be allowed or rejected.

16. The fire engines shall have no names but the letter of the company; and each company shall be designated by some letter of the alphabet, and by no other name.

17. The word "firemen," wherever used in this chapter, shall apply equally to the members of the hook and ladder company, and the phrase "engine-house," shall apply to the house in which their apparatus is kept.

18. Hereafter no person under twenty-one years of age, and who does not list for state or city taxes, shall be eligible to membership in the department; and hereafter no person shall be elected a member thereof unless he is a citizen of Richmond; nor shall any member be allowed to remove his residence beyond the corporate limits of the city.

19. Upon occasion of any alarm of fire, whenever any fire engine or hose or ladder carriage, or apparatus belonging

thereto, shall be passing along any of the streets of the city, it shall be the duty of the drivers of all vehicles to give the way nearest the middle of the street for the unobstructed passage thereof; and any driver of any vehicle failing so to do, shall be fined not less than ten nor more than twenty-five dollars. Ordinances 1869

20. The chief engineer or the officer in command of the fire department, whenever it is reported to him or comes to his knowledge that any building is in danger of being fired, either from carelessness of the owner or occupant, defective chimney, or other cause, shall, if he thinks there is good reason so to do, give notice to said owners or occupants, in writing, to correct the same within twelve hours thereafter; and if it is not done within the time specified, he shall report the case to the police justice.

21. Should any person knowingly give or cause to be given any false alarm of fire by means of the telegraph boxes connected with the fire-alarm telegraph, he, she or they shall be subjected to imprisonment for one month, and a fine of not less than one hundred nor more than two hundred dollars, at the option of the police justice, to be recovered as other fines are recoverable. Oct. 2, 1871.

22. Authority is hereby given to the mayor to offer a reward of one hundred dollars or less for the apprehension and conviction of any person or persons, who shall knowingly give or cause to be given any false alarm of fire by means of telegraph boxes connected with the fire-alarm telegraph.

CHAPTER XXXIII.*

CONCERNING STREETS.

* Chapter XXXIV of 1869.

Committee.

1. The committee on streets generally shall convene as soon as practicable after their appointment, and as often thereafter as they may deem proper. A majority of the committee shall constitute a quorum for the transaction of business. The chairman, or any three of the committee, may, at any time, call a meeting of the committee. Ordinances 1869.

Engineer of the City.

2. There shall be appointed by the city council* an engineer of the city, who shall be a citizen of Richmond, and shall hold his office until a successor is appointed, or he be removed. He shall give bond, with one or more sureties approved by the city council, in the sum of five thousand dollars, with condition that he shall faithfully perform all the duties of his office, and that he will not, directly or indirectly, for himself or others, or by others in trust for him or on his account, have any interest in any purchase, lease, contract or agreement made by the city.

3. The engineer of the city is authorized to appoint an assistant engineer, to act under his control and direction, who Jan. 12, 1874. Charter, § 63.

* See note on chapter IV, § 2.

Jan. 12, 1874. Charter, § 63. shall be approved by the city council, and receive such compensation as they may determine. The said assistant may be removed at any time by the engineer, the mayor or the city council. The engineer may also, with the assent of the committee on streets, employ a clerk in his office at a rate of compensation not exceeding twelve hundred dollars per annum; but such clerk shall only be employed when and as long as said committee shall think it necessary, and be compensated at said rate, for such part or parts of the year as he may be employed.

Ordinances 1869 4. The engineer of the city shall by himself, or by his assistant, for whom he shall be responsible, make all such surveys, plans and estimates as may be required of him by the city council, or either branch thereof, the committee on streets generally, or any committee of the city council. It shall be his duty, under the direction and control of the committee on streets generally, to superintend the general state of the streets and culverts, and the laying out or repairs of the same, and to report all encroachments, nuisances or obstructions thereon. He shall also be the architect and draftsman of the city, and in respect to buildings and other improvements, make such plans, specifications and estimates as the city council may require, and do, in relation thereto, whatever else it may direct.

5. The engineer shall personally attend at his office a portion of each day, except when leave of absence may be granted him by the committee on streets generally; and his office shall be open for the transaction of business from eight in the morning until three in the afternoon from the first day of April to the first day of October, and from nine in the morning until three in the afternoon during the rest of the year. He shall systematically arrange and keep in a fireproof safe in his office the papers of his office not otherwise provided for. He shall keep a record of all his proceedings, and a set of books in which shall be entered, under appropriate heads, the receipts and expenditures of his department. He shall also attend all meetings of the committee on streets generally, and have a record kept of their proceedings.

6. Annually, as soon as practicable after the last day of January, the engineer shall make a report to the committee

on streets generally, containing a general statement of the expenses of his department during the preceding fiscal year; the amount expended on the various streets or other improvements in each ward; the cost of maintaining the city carts and hands, and such other information and suggestions as he may consider desirable; which report the said committee shall examine and submit to the city council, with such remarks as they may deem proper. Ordinances 1869

7. The engineer shall make a survey and plan of the city, showing distinctly each lot, and the size and number thereof, according to the original plan, each public street and alley, and the width thereof, with such explanations as may be directed by the city council. And in laying down the lines of lots, streets and alleys, he shall have reference to the actual lines thereof, in all cases in which they have been built upon or laid out, as at present, for the last twenty years. And he shall also lay down on said plan the original lines of said lots, streets and alleys, where the same can be ascertained. The said survey and plan shall be returned by the engineer to the city council; and if approved by the city council, it shall be enrolled among their proceedings, and afterwards recorded in the clerk's office of the hustings court. But said survey and plan shall not be finally approved by the city council until the same shall have been returned, as herein directed, for twelve months, and examined and approved as directed by the charter of the city.

8. It shall be the duty of the respective superintendents of the water and gas works to report in writing at least once in two weeks to the engineer of the city, all pavements, whether of stone or brick, taken up by either of them for the purpose of laying or repairing water and gas pipes, or any fixture or other thing in connection therewith; and upon such report it shall be the duty of the engineer to proceed, as early as practicable, to cause the said pavements to be replaced, so that the replacing thereof shall be completed Oct. 14, 1871. within fifteen days after such report, and the cost of the same to be paid by the water or gas department, as the case may be, upon a bill properly certified by the city engineer; and further, before excavating or breaking open the paving of any street or sidewalk, it shall be the duty of these respective superintendents to report to the engineer in writing,

Oct. 14, 1874. their intention in regard to the same, who shall see that the whole is done in accordance with the requirements of the said street or sidewalk.*

City hands and carts.

August 21, 1871. 9. The engineer of the city, with the approval of the committee on streets generally, shall hire for the city such number of hands, and purchase such materials, horses, mules, carts and tools as they may deem proper. Any sum or sums of money payable for any such purpose or hiring shall be paid upon a draft on the auditor, stating the amount to be paid and for what given, certified by the engineer of the city, and signed by the chairman of the committee on streets generally.

Expenditures.

Ordinances 1869 10. The engineer of the city may, with the approval of the chairman of the committee on streets generally, order such repairs in the streets or culverts of the city as may, in his judgment, require immediate action or earlier attention than could be obtained by reference to the committee: provided, that the sum paid for such repairs shall not exceed the sum of one thousand dollars in any one year.

11. The committee on streets for each ward, or a majority of them, may order such repairs and improvements in the streets and public alleys in their respective wards as they shall think proper, and may instruct the engineer of the city to cause the same to be made under their direction: provided, that the sum paid for such repairs and improvements for each ward shall not exceed the sum of one thousand dollars in any one year.

12. The committee on streets generally may order such general repairs and improvements to streets, culverts or sewers of the city as they shall think proper, and may instruct the engineer of the city to cause the same to be made under their direction: provided, that the sum paid for such general repairs and improvements shall not exceed the sum of five thousand dollars in any one year. The said committee may also allow a reasonable compensation for such chain

* The two sections following this in the ordinances of 1869 (chapter XXXIV, §§ 10 and 11), provided for the appointment and prescribed the duties of an overseer of city carts and hands. They were repealed August 21st, 1871, and nothing definite seems to have been substituted for them. See notes on chapter XLII.

carriers, books, instruments and stationery as they may authorize to be employed or procured at the request of the engineer of the city. Ordinances 1869

13. The committee on streets generally shall, by report in writing, recommend from time to time to the city council to order such repairs and improvements to the streets, and the construction and repairs of such culverts or sewers of the city as the said committee may think should be ordered by the city council. No order for any such repairs, improvements or construction not so recommended by the committee on streets generally, shall be passed by either branch of the city council, unless by a vote of two-thirds of the members present.

14. All orders or contracts for work or material authorized by the city council or the committees on streets shall be signed on the part of the city by the engineer of the city. Every contract shall contain such provisions for security as the city council or said committee may direct.

15. Every order by the committee on streets of a ward for the execution of work shall be given to the engineer of the city in writing, and shall be signed by a majority of the committee.

16. So much as is payable for work done on any authorized contract or order shall be paid upon a draft on the auditor, stating the amount to be paid and for what; which draft shall be certified by the engineer of the city and signed by the chairman of the committee ordering the work.

Streets and Sidewalks.

17. Wherever the word "street" or "streets" is mentioned in this ordinance, it shall be understood as including alleys, lanes, courts, public squares and public places; and it shall also be understood as including the sidewalks, unless the contrary is expressed, or such construction would be manifestly inconsistent.

18. The engineer shall report to the committee on streets generally, and the said committee to the city council, such grade or grades of the streets and public alleys of the city as have been, or, in his opinion or in the opinion of said committee, ought to be established, with such profiles thereof as may be deemed proper by himself, or as he may be directed by said committee to make. The city council may act on

Ordinances 1869 the grade of such part of a street or alley as is reported by said committee, and may establish for such part whatever grade it may deem proper. No grade so established shall afterwards be altered, unless directed by the city council, after a previous report from the committee on streets generally in respect to its expediency. Any person intending hereafter to build or erect any house or other structure upon the line of any street or public alley, shall first obtain from the engineer of the city a certificate in writing of the line and adopted grade of such street at the place where such house or structure is to be erected; and it shall be the duty of the engineer to file in the auditor's office a duplicate of the said certificate. If any person shall hereafter build or erect, or attempt to build or erect, any house or other structure upon the line of any such street or alley, without having first obtained such certificate, he shall be fined not less than twenty nor more than one hundred dollars.

19. To designate the corners, widths, lines, and the established grades of streets, there shall be put or erected stones or posts at such place or places as the committee on streets generally may direct for that purpose.

20. The intersections of streets of which the sidewalks are paved with brick shall be paved with granite flagstone, or other material suitable for crossings, to connect with the brick pavement. Any person desiring to cross any sidewalk, to enter any private alley on his or her premises, shall first obtain permission so to do from the committee on streets of the ward in which said property lies, and shall pave the sidewalk with granite, and shall cause the curbing to be placed upon a level with the top of the gutter. No person shall be allowed to place a bridge or any other obstruction in or over any paved gutter.

21. Upon every street of thirty feet wide or more, where alleys are opened, or carriage-houses or stables erected in such manner as to make it necessary to cross the sidewalk with horses or vehicles, there shall be placed at such alley, or in front of the entrance to such lot, stable or carriage-house, by the owner or occupier of the property, suitable granite, or other pavement approved by the engineer of the city, of the width of the brick pavement on said street.

22. When such use is made of the sidewalk, and the owner or occupier of the lot or premises neglects to have such flag-

stone crossings so placed, the committee on streets for the ward in which such lot or premises is, may, in writing, direct the engineer of the city to cause the work to be executed; and unless the cost thereof be paid by the owner or occupier of the lot or premises, the engineer of the city shall, annually, between the first day of February and the first day of June of each year, report in writing the respective amounts wherewith the owners are respectively chargeable, to the commissioner of the revenue for the city, who shall, on the property in respect to which the owner is chargeable, assess (in addition to the other taxes thereon), for the year in which he receives such report, the amount with which such owner is reported chargeable. Ordinances 1869

23. Every person occupying a house or lot shall, as far as such lot extends, cause the paved gutter or drain in a street or any public alley opposite thereto to be constantly kept open and free from obstruction; and if he fail so to do, may be fined not less than one dollar nor more than ten dollars; and for each day after the first that such obstruction remains, shall be fined not less than two nor more than twenty dollars.

24. When a person, by reason of an office under or contract with the city, has to do work in a street or public alley, or on any property of the city, there may be put by him such things for such time and in so much of said street or alley, or of a street or alley convenient to said property, as may be authorized by the engineer of the city. And whenever any person shall be engaged in digging a ditch or sinking a pit in any street or public alley, he shall place barriers sufficient to prevent a person or animal from falling in such ditch or pit; and at night, unless the street or alley immediately adjacent thereto be lighted with gas lamps, shall place a light near such ditch or pit. If he fail so to place such barriers and light, he shall pay a fine of not less than five nor more than twenty dollars; and every night on which the failure continues shall be a distinct offence. And when a person, by reason of an office under or a contract with the city, has to do paving or other work directed or authorized by the city council, upon any public street, lane or alley in the city, he may erect, set up or place a rope, chain or bars across any of said streets, lanes or alleys which he is about to mend or repair, or in which he is about to execute such

Ordinances 1869 other work as may require this protection, to such an extent and for such.a length of time as may be authorized by the committee on streets generally. And if any person or persons shall throw down or remove such rope, chain or bars, or ride on, drive upon or otherwise injure the said work, or interrupt the workmen during its progress, every such person shall, for every such offence, pay a fine of not less than ten nor more than fifty dollars.

25. Any person engaged or about to be engaged in building, repairing, excavating, or making any improvements on a house or lot on which materials are to be used, or from which they are to be removed, may deposit materials in that part of the street or public alley opposite and next to his premises, on so much of the carriage way as does not exceed one-half the width thereof, so that the use of the gutter be not obstructed. But where two persons are building or making other improvements hereby authorized, opposite each other on the same street, each shall occupy but one-fourth of the street. And no such deposit of materials shall be made in a street so as to obstruct improvements which the city is making in said street. The committee on streets for the ward in which such premises are, may, on being satisfied of the necessity thereof, grant a special permit in writing, authorizing such materials to be deposited in a part of said street or alley opposite another's premises, on so much of the carriage way as aforesaid, or may authorize the deposit to commence earlier or continue longer than is hereinafter provided. But except by such permission, the deposit shall not be made in any case of small repairs more than one day, nor in other cases more than three days before the work is commenced; and the remains shall be cleanly removed, in case of small repairs, by the end of the first day, and in other cases by the end of the third day next after that on which the work is finished. And a person engaged in repairing a roof, wall or chimney of a house on a street or public alley, shall place barriers sufficient to warn a foot passenger against passing such roof, wall or chimney. If he fail to place the same he shall pay a fine of ten dollars; and every day on which the failure continues shall be a distinct offence. In no case shall a sidewalk or paved gutter be obstructed under this section, unless it be actually necessary for placing such brrriers, or for the execution of the work.

26. Any person may carry from his lot or put in a street or public alley, on any part of the carriage-way nearest to the gutter or drain, ashes, dirt or rubbish: provided the same be free from offensive matter, and be removed by him from said street or alley within twenty-four hours; or if one of the committee on streets for the ward in which the said lot is, shall, in writing, allow a longer time for the removal, then within such time as may be so allowed. Ordinances 1869

27. If any filth, rubbish, ashes, dirt or other things be carried from a lot or other place and put in a street or public alley, or if any nuisance or obstruction be put or caused to be put or remain therein, in any case in which it is not authorized by the ordinances of the city, the person who so puts or causes it to be so put, or is in fault in respect to its remaining, shall, for any such offence, be fined not less than one nor more than ten dollars; and for each day after the first that the same is upon the street or alley shall be fined not less than two nor more than twenty dollars. In construing this chapter, no article taken from or to be shipped on board of, or to be used in or about a vessel in the dock, and deposited in the street not more than thirty feet from the northern margin of the dock, shall be deemed a nuisance or obstruction, provided the same be removed within twenty-four hours from and after sunrise of the day next succeeding that on which it was deposited.*

28. Every person occupying a house or lot on a street or public alley upon which, on that half of the street or alley next to and opposite his house or lot, any filth, rubbish, ashes, dirt, stones or other thing, or any nuisance or obstruction is put or suffered to remain in any case not authorized by this ordinance, shall forthwith remove the same, or give information thereof to the engineer of the city, or to one of the officers or sergeants of police. And if twelve hours elapse without such removal or information, he may be fined not exceeding ten dollars; and each day that elapses without such removal or information shall be a distinct offence.

29. Neither the purchaser nor seller of any coal or fire-wood shall place or permit any such coal or fire-wood to remain in any street more than thirty minutes after sunset in the evening; nor shall any greater quantity than two loads

* The remainder of this section, as it was in the Ordinances of 1869, chapter XXXIV, § 30, is here omitted, as inconsistent with later ordinances of the council, particularly that intended to restrain the Richmond, Fredericksburg and Potomac railroad company, from leaving trains, cars, &c., in the street.

Ordinances 1869 of such wood or coal, in any case, be permitted either by the purchaser or seller, or other person having the charge thereof, to lie or continue in any street. Nor shall any purchaser or seller, or other person as aforesaid, permit any such wood or coal, at any time, by day or night, to remain in any street so as unnecessarily to obstruct the passage, nor more than two hours in any case. Whosoever shall be guilty of a breach of any of the provisions of this section, shall be liable to a penalty for each offence of not less than three dollars nor more than fifty dollars.

Nov. 7, 1870. 30. No person or persons shall break or dig up, or assist in breaking or digging up, any part of any street, or remove any gravel, dirt or manure therefrom, without having first obtained the written permission of the committee on streets generally, or the engineer of the city, nor shall any city officer, employee or contractor, or any other person, in laying gas or water piping, or in repairing the same, or in constructing or repairing culverts, or in making connections with city or private culverts, dig into or break up, or assist in digging into or breaking up any street or public alley, unless the earth removed by such digging or breaking up, be returned and thoroughly rammed or consolidated, so as to place the street or public alley in the same condition it was before such digging or breaking up. Any person failing to comply with this section shall be liable to a penalty of not less than ten nor more than fifty dollars, one-half to the informer; and, in case of such failure by any officer or employee of the city, such penalty to be deducted from the amount next payable to him for services.

Ordinances 1869 31. No person shall obstruct any street, or any part thereof, by placing therein any house, barn, shop or other building; and no person shall remove or draw, through or upon any street, any house, barn, shop or other building, without the permission of the committee on streets generally. Any person offending against either of the provisions of this section, and any person who shall aid and assist in so offending, shall be liable to a penalty of not less than ten nor more than fifty dollars, and of a like sum for every twelve hours that the said obstruction shall continue, or that the said house, barn, shop or other building shall remain in or upon any street.

32. If any engine, car or other vehicle be drawn or propelled upon a railroad or rail-track in a street, at a greater

rate than four miles an hour, the person who does it or causes it to be done, or assists in doing it or causing it to be done, shall pay a fine of ten dollars. Every locomotive engine put or placed upon any railroad or rail-track in this city shall have attached thereto a bell of thirty pounds weight at least, and such bell shall be rung whenever the said engine is about to pass the crossing of any two streets, and shall continue ringing until such engine shall have passed such crossing; and if any such engine shall pass across any street in this city without first ringing and continuing to ring said bell, in manner aforesaid, the owner of said engine, as well as the person then having the control, conduct and management thereof, shall each be fined not less than five nor more than twenty dollars. And if any person shall blow, sound or use, or cause to be blown, sounded or used, by means of or with steam, any whistle or other thing upon any public street or alley, he shall be fined not less than five nor more than twenty dollars. Ordinances 1869

33. If any owner or driver of a wagon, dray or cart, whether licensed or not, shall permit the horses, mules or other animals by which the same is drawn, to go in a street or public alley faster than a walk, or to be fed therein, except that any vehicle having springs may be drawn at a rate of speed not exceeding five miles per hour; or if any person run a horse race, or cause the same to be run, or shall ride or drive a horse or other animal at a greater speed than six miles per hour, in any public street or alley, he shall be fined not less than ten nor more than fifty dollars. March 23, 1874.

34. No person shall tie or fasten a horse or other animal to any tree or to any box or case around such tree in any street of the city, or upon any sidewalk, or lead or ride a horse or mule, or drive a wagon, dray, cart or other vehicle upon a sidewalk, unless across such part thereof as is or shall be at the time paved with stone or flagging. Any person violating this section shall, for each offence, be fined not less than two nor more than ten dollars. Ordinances 1869

35. If any owner or driver of a wagon, whether licensed or not, shall, in a street or public alley which is paved, drive such wagon with a wheel locked, or if any owner or driver of any wagon, hack, dray or cart, whether licensed or not, shall wantonly crack his whip, to the annoyance of others, or suffer his vehicle, when not receiving or discharging a

Ordinances 1869 load, to pass or stand upon a street or public alley without holding the reins in his hands, every such offender shall, for each offence, pay a fine of not less than two nor more than twenty dollars.

36. Any driver of a vehicle meeting any other vehicle in a street or public alley, shall seasonably drive to the right hand, so that each may pass the other without interference. And when in a street or public alley a vehicle is overtaken by any other vehicle, the driver of the former shall bear to the left, until the latter shall have passed. In no instance shall a driver of a carriage, wagon, dray or cart, stop the same in the middle of a street or public alley, or opposite to an intersecting street or alley, or upon any granite crossing, but he shall always stop the same as near to the sidewalk as he can without being on it. A driver violating this section in any respect shall, for each offence, pay a fine of not less than one nor more than ten dollars.

37. Any officer of the police of the city may order any vehicle standing in the streets to be removed as may seem to him most convenient for persons passing by. If a driver shall fail to obey such order, the owner of the vehicle shall pay a fine of five dollars.

38. For any offence against the thirty-third, thirty-fourth, thirty-fifth, thirty-sixth or thirty-seventh sections of this ordinance, committed in the presence of any police officer of the city, he may arrest the offender and take him forthwith before the police justice. Such officer may pay twenty-five cents for the safe-keeping of the vehicle or animal during the absence of the driver or owner, and what is so paid shall be included in the costs, if any, recovered against the offender.

39. If any person engaged in any military exercise shall fire or discharge, in any street or public alley of this city, any cannon, gun, pistol, or any other firearms, except on the fourth of July, the twenty-second of February and the nineteenth day of October, or at a military burial, or some extraordinary occasion allowed by the mayor (and by him notified through the newspapers, or by posting handbills or otherwise), or if any person shall, in any street or public alley in said city, play at bandy or throw snow balls, stones or other missiles, or discharge arrows from a bow or cross-bow, or blow a horn, he shall be fined not less than one nor more than ten dollars.

40. No person shall water any of the streets within the city by or with a watering cart (except under the direction and supervision of the committee on streets generally), nor without having first obtained written permission from the said committee. The perforations of the sprinklers of said watering carts shall be limited to one-twentieth of an inch in diameter; and the streets shall not be passed over by said watering carts oftener than three times each day, under a penalty of not less than five nor more than fifty dollars for each and every offence. No such permission shall be given for a longer period than one year at any one time, and the person or persons obtaining it shall pay the regular license tax imposed on carts, and such rates for the use of water as may be imposed by direction of the committee on water. **Sept. 5, 1870.** **Ordinances 1869**

41. The committee on streets generally are hereby empowered so to regulate the width and height of the sidewalks of any streets, as shall in their judgment be most conducive to the convenience and interest of the city.

42. Whenever any street in the city shall have been graded and curbed, in whole or in part, including the sidewalk, it shall be incumbent upon the owner or owners of the property fronting upon either side of the street, to have the whole of the sidewalk paved with brick, or such other material as the committee on streets generally may approve, and the guttering paved with stone the usual width, so far as such street has been graded and curbed, at their own proper costs: provided, that they shall have the privilege of having the work done under the supervision of the engineer, by such person or persons as they may think proper. All repairs to sidewalks, from and after the passage of this ordinance, shall be done at the cost of the owners of the property fronting upon the same. Where property corners, whenever the same shall be paved and guttered, it shall be done along the depth thereof, one-half of the expense of the same to be paid by the city. It is hereby further provided, that whenever a street shall have been graded and curbed, the engineer shall notify the owner or owners of the property fronting upon the same, that the paving and guttering must be immediately laid; and should the owners, from neglect or from the want of means, not comply with the said order for fifteen days, the engineer is hereby authorized to have the repairing and all necessary work done, and charge the cost of the same to the **April 14, 1873.**

April 14, 1873. owners thereof: provided, that the committee on streets may cause said work to be done and charged against the property, to be collected as other taxes, in three annual payments, with interest at eight per centum per annum.

Ordinances 1869 43. Doors to a cellar shall not extend on a sidewalk more than five feet; and whenever a cellar door is made or repaired (whether the cellar be old or new), the construction thereof shall be such that the door or doors when closed shall be level with the sidewalk. On a street less than fifty feet wide there shall not be used any part of the sidewalk as an entrance to a cellar, unless by resolution of the city council, and then the doors shall be so made and kept in such manner as the resolution may prescribe. And in all cases in which any person shall desire to occupy any portion of a street or public alley for the purpose of getting into a cellar or basement, or into a house, he shall apply to the city council by petition in writing, and file therewith a plan showing accurately how much of the walkway he proposes to occupy; and the petition and plan shall be referred to the committee on streets generally, who shall cause the engineer of the city to examine the premises and report fully to the city council everything which, in their opinion, should influence the judgment of the city council in their action upon the application.

44. Any person owning a house in the use of which any part of a street or public alley is occupied by the permission of the city council for a vault, entrance to a basement or cellar, or to the house, or for any other permanent purpose, shall pay annually therefor to the city, a rent of eight cents for each superficial foot. And the engineer of the city shall measure the same and make return thereof to the commissioner of the revenue, showing the name of the owner of the house or the party taxable therefor, and the commissioner shall charge the same to the owner as a part of the taxes on said house.

45. The committee on streets for the ward in which a vault is desired under a sidewalk, may, by writing, grant permission to a person to have the same made; and the person obtaining the permission shall file the same with the engineer of the city within ten days. Such person shall have it made with a substantial brick or stone arch, which shall extend from the front wall of the house before which the vault is, no nearer than two feet six inches to where the inner edge

of the curbstone is or will be when laid down. The openings to the vault shall not be more than eighteen inches in diameter, and shall be near the said line, unless, in the opinion of the engineer of the city, that is impracticable. It shall be level with the sidewalk, as it then is, but may afterwards be removed, if necessary, when the grade of the street is established or changed. It shall be secured with a cast-iron covering, fixed in a solid frame of stone or iron, so laid that the upper part of the frame shall be as nearly level with the pavement as it can be, consistently with the turning the water from the opening; and it shall be secured with such bolt or weight as the engineer of the city may direct; and the person obtaining permission to make a vault shall have the same completed, under the direction of the engineer of the city, within thirty days, unless further time is allowed by the committee for the ward. Ordinances 1869.

46. If any cellar or vault heretofore made conform neither with this ordinance nor with the ordinances in force at the time of the passage hereof, or if hereafter, when a cellar or vault is made or repaired, the same be not such as is required by this ordinance, the owner of the house to which the cellar or vault is attached, shall pay a fine of not less than ten nor more than twenty dollars; and every day that the cellar or vault shall not be as hereby required, shall be a distinct offence. And if the occupier of a house to which a vault is attached suffer the same to be open or unfastened at any time other than when it is opened for putting something therein, or shall then suffer it to be open or unfastened longer than is absolutely necessary for that purpose, or if the owner or occupier of a house to which a vault or cellar is attached, shall fail, in any respect, to keep in safe and proper order the opening to such vault, or the doors to such cellar (whether made heretofore or hereafter), he shall pay a like fine. The suffering a vault to be opened or unfastened as aforesaid, or the failure to keep in safe and proper order such opening or doors, shall be deemed a distinct offence for each day or night thereof.

47. No person shall construct or place, or cause to be constructed or placed, any portico, porch, door, window or step, which shall project into any street, or any gate which shall open outward over any sidewalk, under a penalty of not less than five nor more than fifty dollars for each offence, and a

Ordinances 1869 like penalty for every day that the said portico, porch, door, window, step or gate shall be continued as aforesaid after notice to remove the same.* Wherever, in that portion of the city annexed by act of the legislature, passed February thirteenth, eighteen hundred and sixty-seven, houses or porches which have been erected prior to that date project over or encroach on the public streets a distance not exceeding three feet, the same may be allowed to continue until the first day of January, eighteen hundred and seventy-five, and should the projection of any building or any portion thereof encroach more than three feet, the encroachment may continue or not at the discretion of the city council. And wherever in any part of said city a street has been or shall hereafter be encroached upon or obstructed by a fence or other enclosure, or by any building or any part thereof, except in the cases hereinbefore provided for, the owner or owners thereof shall remove the same to the proper line of said street when notified by the engineer of the city to do so; and if the same be not removed within twenty days after the said owner or owners shall have been notified as aforesaid, it shall be the duty of the engineer to cause the same to be removed, and to make out and render to the auditor of the city an account of all reasonable charges therefor, which account the auditor shall forthwith place in the hands of the city collector, who is authorized to collect the same by the same process by which he is empowered to collect the taxes of the city. If such removal be not made within twenty days, as aforesaid, the owner or owners thereof shall pay a fine of five dollars for each and every day that said encroachment is allowed to continue thereafter, which said fine shall be imposed and enforced by the police justice, in the mode prescribed for the collection of other fines.

Oct. 9, 1871.

Ordinances 1869 48. Any person employed in business in the city may put up a sign made of tin, which does not extend over the sidewalk more than three feet from his place of business, and is not less than ten feet above the sidewalk: and may in front of his place of business and next thereto occupy with his goods one-third of the sidewalk. But he shall not suspend his goods or other articles so that they shall extend from the front of his house more than one foot towards the street. And any person putting up a sign or occupying the side-

* The rest of this section was passed as a separate ordinance, October 9, 1871.

walk, or suspending his goods otherwise than is herein authorized, shall pay a fine of not less than one nor more than ten dollars for each offence; and the sign shall be removed by the police. And when a merchant or other person, after doing business on a street or public alley, declines such business and sells by auction his stock of goods; or when the property of a decedent, who at the time of his death was a resident of the city of Richmond or county of Henrico, is sold by his representative; or when property is sold under a deed of trust thereon, made by a person who at the time of executing said deed was such a resident; or when property is levied on in said city or county, and sold therein by an officer under a warrant of distress, execution or other legal process; or when property is sold under the judgment or decree of a court or magistrate, there may, on the day of sale, be occupied with such goods or property half of the sidewalk and a third of the carriage-way next to the house or other place of such sale. And when at the dock or a wharf an auctioneer sells a cargo, half of the sidewalk and a third of the carriage-way next thereto may be occupied with such cargo for three days and no more, unless the sale be necessarily postponed because of the weather; in which case the sale shall be within three days after the cause for such postponement shall cease; and the occupation shall be no longer than half an hour after sunset of the day on which the sale is made. If an auctioneer, or any person in his employment, sell or offer for sale at auction any personal property which shall be in any part (either of the sidewalk or carriage-way) of a street or public alley when he is not authorized by this section, he shall, for every article there offered for sale by him, pay a fine of ten dollars. Ordinances 1869

49. Posts for awnings constructed of either iron or wood may be placed on the curbstone or near the inner edge thereof, so as not to interfere with the free passage of the streets. The diameter of said posts shall not exceed, if of iron, three inches, and if of wood, six inches. The covering shall be of canvas, and shall be so framed and placed as not to reach at its lowest points nearer than within eight feet of the sidewalk. When wood is used the same shall be neatly dressed, and the entire structure in all cases put up and finished in a neat and workmanlike manner. Any person putting up an awning which shall not conform to the provisions

Ordinances 1869 of this section, shall pay a fine of not less than ten nor more than one hundred dollars: and the awning and posts shall be removed by the order of the police justice.

50. There may be erected in front of each tenement one frame with two posts not more than six feet apart, with a cross bar, to which horses may be tied. The said posts may be either of wood or iron, well imbedded in the ground, and shall not be less than four nor more than five feet high above the sidewalk; and if of wood, shall not be less than four inches in diameter at the level of the footway. The said posts shall be placed next to the inner edge of the curbstone, or where the curbstone would be if there be none there, and shall be so arranged with a cross bar or otherwise as not to allow the horse or other animal hitched thereat to go upon or stand on the footway.

51. If any person shall place, or in any manner use, upon the sidewalk of any public street or alley, the carriage-way whereof is paved, any wheelbarrow, hand-carriage, hand-cart, or sled, or shall skate or slide thereon, he shall pay a fine of not less than one nor more than ten dollars. But nothing in this section contained shall prevent any person from passing, with such hand-carriage or cart, across the sidewalk of a street from or to a house or lot, from such street or alley, nor prevent the use on a sidewalk of a hand-carriage to ride or carry infant children.

52. The tenant, occupant, and, in case there shall be no tenant, the owner, or any person having the care of any building or lot of land bordering on any street, lane, court, square or public place within the city, where there is any footway, or sidewalk, shall, after the ceasing to fall of any snow, if in the day time, within two hours, and if in the night time, before nine of the clock in the forenoon succeeding, cause the same to be removed therefrom, and in default thereof, shall forfeit and pay a sum not less than two dollars nor more than ten dollars; and for each and every hour thereafter that the same shall remain on such footway or sidewalk, such tenant, occupant, owner or other person shall forfeit and pay a sum not less than one dollar nor more than ten dollars.

53. Three or more persons shall not stand in a group, or near to each other, on any sidewalk, in such a manner as to obstruct free passage for foot passengers, for a longer time

than twenty minutes, under a penalty of not less than three nor more than fifty dollars; nor more than five minutes after a request to move on, made by the mayor,* or any police officer, under a like penalty. Twenty or more persons, assembled on the streets, alleys or sidewalks, or in or around the market houses, city hall, station houses, or other public buildings or places in this city, shall be deemed to be an unlawful assemblage; and the mayor* may proceed, under the provisions of chapter 191 of the Code of Virginia of 1873, to disperse such unlawful assemblage. Ordinances 1869 May 19, 1870.

54. The owners of lots with houses on them, which according to the plan of the city, adjoin a street in which there is a sewer owned by the city into which it is practicable to enter, or are distant from said street not more than one-half of one side of a square, shall be assessed annually thirty cents for each front foot of such lots respectively, being ten per cent. upon the cost of the sewer estimated at three dollars; the owners of unimproved lots similarly situated with reference to a city sewer, shall be assessed annually fifteen cents for each front foot of the same respectively; and whenever such lots are built upon, the assessment shall be increased to thirty cents per foot, until a connection with the sewer shall have been made. Such owners shall be so assessed notwithstanding there may be on such lots a cellar eight feet below the level of the sidewalk and not capable of drainage into it. The tax so assessed may be commuted at any time by the payment to the treasurer of a sum whereof the assessment is ten per cent. Upon such payment the treasurer shall furnish said owner a receipt stating that the assessment has been commuted, and that the property on which the assessment is thus commuted, shall have a perpetual right of drainage into said sewer without further payment therefor. The engineer of the city shall from time to time return to the commissioner of the revenue a list of the assessments to be made under this ordinance, and the commissioner shall assess said owners respectively with the amounts with which they are reported chargeable, to be collected in the mode prescribed for the collection of city taxes. Said lots shall be assessed for one sewer only, and such as have paid assessments for sewerage, or complied with the requirements under a former ordinance of the city, are exempt under this. But Dec. 11, 1871.

* See note on chapter XX, § 3.

Dec. 11, 1871. when lots assessed under this ordinance shall afterwards be sub-divided as separate lots, and buildings erected thereon with new and additional fronts, such new fronts shall be subject to assessment, and to all the provisions of this ordinance, in like manner as though they had been fronts originally.

July 14, 1873. 55. The said owners of lots, with houses on them, to which the city water is accessible, shall form a connection from their lots respectively with said sewer, or with some other sewer owned by the city, into which shall be carried all waste water, except rain water; and any person failing herein shall be fined not less than five nor more than ten dollars. And whenever any person has made the connection herein required, he shall obtain from the city engineer a certificate thereto, stating that he is thereby entitled to a reduction of the assessment upon said lots to fifteen cents per foot. And the city collector shall receive such certificate as a payment of one-half of any uncollected assessments of thirty cents per front foot of said lot for that fiscal year. The city engineer shall return to the commissioner of the revenue, on the first day of each month, a list of all owners who have made the connection herein required during the preceding month. And the commissioner shall reduce the annual assessment on all such owners from thirty cents to fifteen cents per front foot of the lots from which such connections have been made. The owners of lots not required under this ordinance to form a connection with a city sewer, may form a connection from their lots with any accessible sewer owned by the city, upon permission of the engineer of the city. All owners making such connections shall be assessed fifteen cents per front foot of the lots respectively from which the connection is made, subject to the provisions of the preceding section applicable thereto: provided, however, that in the cases of indigent widows and other persons unable to raise the means necessary to make such connections, and to introduce protecting traps as provided in section sixty, the committee on streets generally may order the work to be done on city account; and the sum of the cost thereof shall be, by the city engineer, charged to the owner, and certified to the auditor, who shall make proper entry thereof on his books, and make out and deliver to the city collector bills for the amount thereof in four equal annual instalments, each to bear interest at the rate of eight per centum per annum till paid, to be by him collected and accounted for as in the collection of city taxes. And the debt thus created shall constitute a lien on the property of the owner from the date of such connection, and so forth, until the whole amount of both principal and interest shall have been paid. July 14, 1873.

56. Whenever the board of health shall deem it important to the health of the neighborhood, or the cleanliness of any lot, or the owner thereof shall desire, that a sewer or drain pipe shall be run from said lot to connect with a public sewer, the president of said board shall report the fact to the city engineer in writing, and the engineer shall give the applicant such information as will enable him to make such connection on the most economical plan, consistent with the requirements of the ordinances of the city, and it shall be the duty of the owner to make the connection as soon as possible after having received written notification from the engineer: provided, the sewer with which the connection is to be made is within half of one side of a square of the property to be drained, and capable of draining the same. Any person failing to make such connection within fifty days after receiving such notice, shall be fined one dollar per day for every day thereafter, until such connection be made. Dec. 11, 1871.

57. Connections may be made directly with a city sewer, or through a private drain or sewer, having a direct connection with a city sewer, upon payment to the owner of said sewer of a ratable proportion of the cost thereof, which is to be ascertained by the city engineer. And all persons making connections either with public or private sewers or drains, shall first obtain permission from the city engineer to enter the street or alley as the case may be, and shall connect at such point and in such manner as he may direct, and shall forthwith cover the sewer or drain with earth, thoroughly consolidating the same as it was before the connection; and in ten days after the connection, shall have such pavement or curbstone as was injured or removed in making said connection so repaired or restored as to be in as good order as it was before; and any one failing to comply herewith shall pay a fine of not less than five nor more than twenty dollars, and every ten days that such failure shall continue shall constitute a distinct offence. And all connections with sewers

Dec. 11, 1871. shall be made in the most substantial manner, and no brick or stone-box drains shall be hereafter constructed, but all private sewers or drains shall be of drain-piping or of brick barrel drains, or such other as shall be approved by the committee on streets, with sufficient stench-traps at their heads; and any person who shall make or cause to be made any defective private sewer or drain, where the same passes under a public highway, shall be fined not less than twenty nor more than fifty dollars upon conviction thereof before the police justice, and the city engineer shall cause said defective sewer to be shut up. If any person shall, either in a street or upon a lot, put any stone, brick or other solid thing into a culvert or sewer, or shall in any way whatever injure, impair or obstruct a culvert or sewer or a fixture thereof, he shall pay a fine of not less than five nor more than twenty dollars. From and after the first of May, eighteen hundred and seventy-two, all connections with public or private sewers or drains shall be protected by traps to be approved by the city engineer. Any person failing to introduce traps at the time specified, shall be fined one dollar per month for the first year, and two dollars per month for each subsequent year, and until the requirements are complied with.

Numbering of houses.

April 10, 1872. 58. All houses within the limits of the city now unnumbered, shall have their proper numbers fixed upon their fronts; and it shall be the duty of the contractor appointed by the committee on streets, to furnish the required numbers, painted upon tin, and secure the same to the unnumbered houses throughout the city; the size and character of numbers, and quality of tin and painting, to be determined by said committee. The contractor shall be paid by the owner or owners of every house so numbered, or their agents, twenty-five cents, and the bill therefor having been presented by the contractor, and such owner or agent refusing to pay the same, the engineer of the city, being satisfied thereof, shall report the fact to the city assessor, whose duty it shall be to add the amount, with twenty-five per centum thereon, to the next tax levy of the property in question, and thereupon the contractor shall be paid said amount of twenty-five cents from the city treasury. And if any occupant, owner or agent, shall remove from any house the number so placed thereon, he shall be subject to a fine of fifty cents for each day, after ten days notice, during which the house shall remain unnumbered. April 10, 1872.

Grade of Broad street.

59. The city engineer, under the direction of the committee on streets, shall, as soon as may be practicable, after the passage of this ordinance, survey, establish and locate the grade of Broad street, from Ninth street, westward, to the corporation limits of the city, and designate the corners, widths and lines of all streets that may cross the same, by locating stones at the proper places, wherever, in his judgment, they may be required. May 13, 1872.

CHAPTER XXXIV.*

CONCERNING STREET RAILWAYS.

Contracts for the privilege of running railway passenger cars on the strbets of the city of Richmond, shall be subject to the following terms, provisions, conditions, restrictions and limitations, viz: Ordinances 1869

1. The contract shall prescribe specifically the streets in which the said railways may be laid down and the passenger cars may run, and the termini, in each street, of said railway, and to which the cars may run; and no part of the said

---

*Chapter XXXV of 1869.

Ordinances 1869 work shall be changed without the consent of the city council. The said contracts shall state what part of the railways mentioned therein shall be with a single and what with a double track, and if with a single track, where the sidings shall be located.

2. If after a single or double track has been prescribed for any part of a railway authorized to be constructed, the company or corporation shall desire to change it, or any part of it, in that respect, they may apply to the city council to be authorized to make the said change. And upon such application the city council shall proceed as is prescribed in the first section; and their act shall, as to the subject to which it refers, have the same binding effect upon the company or corporation, upon their accepting the same, as is prescribed in said section.

3. The said railways and the track thereof shall be constructed on the most approved plan, and the same shall be approved by the engineer of the city before the construction thereof is commenced. And the said railways and tracks shall be constructed under the supervision of the said engineer, who shall see that the same is properly done; and if he shall be of the opinion that the same is not properly done according to the plan approved by him as aforesaid, he shall stop the construction thereof. But the said company or corporation may appeal from the decision of the engineer to the city council, and the parties shall be governed by the decision of the city council upon the question. The said railways and tracks shall be so constructed and laid down as not to impede or obstruct the full flow of water across the streets or down the gutters thereof, and shall conform to the grades of the several streets through which they pass, as the said grades are now or may be hereafter established. And if the company or corporation shall afterwards desire to extend their railway and cars into another street, they shall apply to the city council, stating specially the streets or street into and along which they propose to extend their railway and cars, the points at which they propose to connect with their then existing railway, if the same shall connect therewith, and in any case the points in each street between which they propose to carry their railway and run their cars; and the city council, at any of its regular meetings, or at a meeting adjourned or called for the purpose, and of which purpose

the members shall have notice, may grant the application to extend the railway and run the cars as specified in the application, or may grant the application in part. But no such application shall be acted on without a reference thereof to the committee on streets generally, and until the same is reported upon by them, nor shall their report be finally acted on at the meeting of the city council at which it is made. And the city council may prescribe such additional terms, conditions and restrictions, to the granting of the said application, as they may deem expedient; and the same shall be binding upon the said company or corporation, if they shall accept the privilege of so extending their railways and running their cars. Ordinances 1869.

4. The gauge of the said railway tracks shall be the same as that of ordinary street carriages in use in the city of Richmond, in order to admit of the passage of such carriages upon the tram-plate of said railway. But it shall not be lawful for any person, or owner of any carriage, dray, cart or other vehicle whatever, to obstruct or impede the running of any car on any of said tracks, by occupying or driving on said tracks in front of said car, when by lawful increase of speed or turning out on either side of said tracks, such obstructions or impediments can be avoided, under a penalty of five dollars, recoverable as small debts out of court are recoverable, at the suit of said company or corporation; and all carriages, drays, carts or other vehicles, while running through any of the streets upon which said railway tracks may be laid, shall keep to the right in passing or turning out to permit the cars running on the same to pass, under a penalty of five dollars, recoverable as aforesaid. And it shall not be lawful, without the consent of the company or corporation, to establish any line of carriages, omnibuses or other vehicles of any description whatever (other than the cars of the proprietors of said railways), to be run upon the said railways for the purpose of carrying passengers for pay or hire.

5. The company or corporation, in laying down the said railway tracks, shall restore all pavements and regrade all earth taken up or disturbed in said construction, and shall at all times, under the supervision of the engineer of the city, at their own expense and charge, keep the streets and pavements upon which the tracks of the railways are laid, to the

Ordinances 1869 extent of the portion of said streets covered by said tracks, and for two feet on either side beyond the outside of said tracks, in good and complete repair; and should they refuse to do so for the space of ten days, after having been notified by the engineer of the city, that any portion of their road needs repairing, as herein provided, then the said company or corporation shall be liable to a fine of five dollars for each day they shall fail to repair the same; and the city council may forbid the running of any car or cars upon said road until the same shall be fully complied with; and the city may in all such cases repair such streets when not done by the company or corporation as herein provided, and the expense thereof shall be a debt against the company or corporation, recoverable as debts are now recoverable by the city of Richmond.

6. Should the corporate authorities of the city hereafter determine to pave any street or streets in which such tracks may be laid, and which streets shall not have been paved at the time said tracks were laid, then the proprietors of said railways shall at the same time, at their own cost and expense, pave so much of said streets or street as may be covered by said tracks, and for two feet on either side beyond the outside of said tracks, for the same distance and to the same extent as the remaining portion of the street may be paved by the city.

7. The cars running upon the said railways shall be subject to all the police regulations which are now or may hereafter be contained in the ordinances of the city, in regard to railway cars or other vehicles, so far as they may be applicable thereto. The price of transporting passengers from one part of the city to any other shall not exceed the sum agreed upon in the contract for each passenger; but if the passenger, without leaving the cars, shall return to any point nearer to that from which he started than a point which he has passed, he shall pay a second fare, unless this be occasioned by the line of the route on which he is passing being circuitous. And the said company or corporation shall pay to the proper officer of the city, in consideration of the privilege hereby granted, and in lieu of all charges by the city upon the property and capital stock of said company or corporation for taxes and assessments, ten per centum of the net profits made by them upon the transportation of passengers

within the city limits, payable semi-annually from the time of opening the road to public travel, and the aforesaid sum of ten per cent. of net profits shall be a preferred debt or claim against the road and property of said railway company. They shall also, before placing cars upon their roads, pay into the office of the city treasurer, and annually thereafter, for the use of the city, the sum of five dollars for each and every car intended to run on said railways. Ordinances 1869.

8. The company or corporation shall use cars with suitable brakes thereto, and the cars shall be moved by horses or mules, and there shall not be more than four horses or mules to a car. And if from a want of sufficient number of brakes to any car, or from the carelessness or incompetency of the conductor or driver of such car, the car shall run on said railway track or in the street at a greater speed than is authorized by this or any other ordinance, the said company shall be subject to a fine not exceeding twenty dollars, for the use of the city; and such careless conductor or driver may be subjected to a like fine. The said cars shall not incommode the crossings nor stop at corners of any street or elsewhere to solicit passengers. It shall also be the duty of conductors and drivers of the cars to give ample notice to drivers of vehicles and pedestrians of their approach, and also to afford all reasonable opportunity for them or either of them to avoid collision or accident; and any neglect by them to comply with the provisions of this section shall be punished by a fine of five dollars, to be recovered before the police justice of the city, for the use of the city.

9. It shall be the duty of said company or corporation to employ careful, sober and prudent agents, conductors and drivers, to take charge of their car or cars when upon the road; and for violation of any act of assembly or ordinance of the city on the part of such officer or officers or employees upon said road, the company shall be liable to all fines, forfeitures or damages therefrom: provided, that this shall not be taken as an excuse, or free any such officer or employee from penalties or responsibilities for any such violations or other acts committed.

10. Each car running upon the road shall be numbered, commencing at number one and continuing in regular numerical order; which number shall be painted in some conspicuous place upon both sides of the car. For any neglect

Ordinances 1869 to comply with this provision, the proprietors shall be punishable by a fine of ten dollars, to be recovered on complaint before the police justice of the city, and for the use of the city.

11. After a company or corporation shall have been authorized to construct a railway and run their cars in any street of the city, said company or corporation shall not cease to run their cars therein as agreed on, without the consent of the city council, applied for and obtained in the manner prescribed in section three. And upon the failure of said company or corporation for six months to run their cars in any street as said company or corporation has been authorized to run its cars, said company shall forfeit so much of its railway on said streets as they have failed to run their cars upon, and the right of said company or corporation to run their cars in that part of the street shall cease; and the city council may grant the privilege to another company or corporation to run their cars therein or in any part thereof; or may have the railway taken up and the material thereof sold, and after paying all expenses arising therefrom, pay the balance, if any, to said company or corporation.

12. The privilege granted to any company or corporation to construct railways and run cars in the streets, shall continue for such term of years, from the date of the grant, as shall be fixed by the city council, unless the same shall be forfeited under the preceding section. At the expiration of that period, the city council may extend the said privilege to said company or corporation for another period, to be fixed by the city council, upon such terms, conditions, restrictions and limitations, as may be agreed upon by the council and said company or corporation; and if the city council shall fail for one year to give notice to said company or corporation of its purpose to insist upon a new contract, the assent of the city council to the continuation of the privilege of said company or corporation for a period of fifteen years, upon the terms, conditions, restrictions and limitations, on which they held said privileges at the expiration of the first period fixed, shall be presumed. But if the city council shall refuse to continue to said company or corporation the privileges held by them during the period fixed, upon the terms on which they were held during that period; or if the city council and said company or corporation cannot agree upon the

terms upon which the said company or corporation may continue to run their cars in the streets of the city, the city council shall have the right to take, and shall take, the railways and fixtures thereto lying within the city, and the lots and buildings thereon and appurtenances owned by said company or corporation, and used and held as a part of its capital, and the cars of said company or corporation used upon its railways in the city; and the price to be paid therefor shall be fixed by arbitrators, one of whom shall be appointed by the city council, and the other shall be appointed by the said company or corporation; and if they shall fail to agree, by an umpire mutually agreed upon by them. And in fixing the price of said property the same shall be valued as property, to be used for the purpose for which it was provided, and in its then place and condition; but the value of the privilege of running passenger cars in the streets of the city shall not be estimated as a part of the value of said property. Ordinances 1869

13. If the said company or corporation does not within two years from the date of the contract, construct the railways provided for in it, as agreed upon therein, the said contract shall be void and of no effect; and the city council may grant the privilege of laying down railways and running cars thereon in said streets to another company.

14. A grant to one company of the privilege of laying down railways and running cars thereon in one or more streets of the city, shall not prevent the city council from granting the like privilege to another company or companies in other streets. But the privilege shall not be given to two or more companies to run their cars in the same street, except at the crossing of streets, and only for the purpose of crossing a street. And when one company is authorized to lay their railway along a street, so that said railway will cross the railway of another company which has been first authorized to lay down its railway, the company crossing such railway shall, at its own expense and under the direction of the engineer of the city, make the necessary alterations in the railway which is to be crossed.

CHAPTER XXXV.*

CONCERNING WAGONS, DRAYS, CARTS AND HACKS.

Ordinances 1869 1. No wagon, dray, cart, hack or other wheel-carriage shall be kept or employed in the city for hire, directly or indirectly, unless the owner or keeper thereof obtain a license therefor, as hereinafter mentioned. The time for which the license is issued shall be until the first day of February next following the date thereof. Before such license is issued, the applicant shall give bond in the sum of three hundred dollars, payable to the city of Richmond, with surety approved by the auditor, conditioned that all articles entrusted to the owner, keeper or driver of any such vehicle, and all persons taken in or upon the same, shall be faithfully transported and delivered. On every such bond suits may be brought, from time to time, in the name of the city, for the benefit of any person injured by any breach of the condition, as often as any such breach may be alleged, until damages shall be recovered for such breaches equal to the penalty of the bond. And a like license shall be taken out by the owner of any wagon, dray or cart which is employed on any streets of this city in the business, or for the private use or benefit of such owner, unless the same be exclusively employed in transporting fuel, provisions, manure or other things to be used only at the owner's farm or dwelling.

Jan. 26, 1874. 2. Before issuing such license, there shall be paid to the treasurer the tax required by the twentieth section of the

* Chapter XXXVI of 1869.

thirteenth chapter.* The auditor may issue such licenses for the unexpired portion of the year, at a ratable proportion of the tax: provided that the same shall not be less than for a license for three months. But no such license shall be issued for a cart or wagon employed in transporting wood, coal or coke, unless the applicant shall produce a certificate from the inspector of carts and wagons, as provided in the seventh section of this ordinance, and the license tax shall be in lieu of general property tax on all vehicles so licensed. Jan. 26, 1874.

3. The auditor shall furnish to the owner or keeper of every licensed vehicle a painted sign, showing the number of the vehicle, and the year for which the license is issued. The same shall be permanently placed by the owner or keeper, if the vehicle be a dray, on each shaft; and if a wagon or cart, on each side, unless the sides be movable, in which case they shall be placed on the frame on each side; and if a hack or other licensed vehicle for the transportation of passengers, in some conspicuous place on each side of said vehicle. Ordinances 1869

4. Any person who shall keep or employ in this city a wagon, cart, dray, hack or other wheeled-carriage, without a license therefor, when a license is required to be taken out for it, or who shall fail to have the painted sign thereon, as required by this ordinance, shall pay for every such offence a fine of not less than ten nor more than twenty dollars; and each day that the same shall be so kept or employed shall be a distinct and separate offence.

5. The unexpired term of any license granted under this chapter, may be transferred, by assignment on the back thereof, by the person to whom it was issued, provided that the assignee of such license shall execute the like bond as was required of the assignor; and then a new license shall be issued to the assignee for the unexpired term of such license, who shall cause a painted sign to be placed thereon, in the same manner and under the same penalty for failing so to do, as if the original license had been granted to him.

6. Whether a vehicle be licensed or not, neither coal nor dirt shall be transported therein, unless it be so tight and have such a tailboard thereon, as will prevent the waste of

* The taxes fixed in this ordinance are the same as those prescribed in the thirteenth chapter, and it is deemed unnecessary to repeat them here.

Ordinances 1869 the coal or dirt. For every violation of this section there shall be a fine of ten dollars.

7. The city council shall appoint* an inspector of carts and wagons employed in transporting wood, coal or coke, who, when applied to, shall examine such cart or wagon, and on examination, if he find himself justified in so doing, shall give a certificate that the vehicle is tight and in proper order to prevent the waste of coal or coke; and if it be a cart, that it contains twenty-five bushels when not loaded above, but leveled to the mark of full measure or loading. The said inspector shall be paid fifty cents for each certificate.

8. The inspector may at any time examine any cart or wagon, and if he shall find that its dimensions are not such as to contain the proper quantity when leveled to the mark of full measure or loading, he shall report the fact to the police justice and the auditor; and thenceforth the license for such cart or wagon shall be forfeited, and the owner or keeper thereof shall pay a fine of not less than ten nor more than twenty dollars. And if coal or coke be wasted on a street or public alley from a cart, wagon or other vehicle, whether the same be transported for consumption or not, the owner or keeper of such wagon, cart or other vehicle shall pay a fine of ten dollars.

9. The person for whom a load is carried shall be charged therefor no higher rates than are allowed by this chapter, and shall pay these rates, or sign a ticket expressing the place from which and to which the load is to be carried. Any person refusing to pay such rates or sign such ticket, and the owner or keeper of a vehicle who, or whose driver, charges a higher rate, shall for every such offence pay a fine of five dollars. A like fine shall be paid for refusing to carry a load or part of a load, when not engaged; and the burden of proof of such engagement shall be upon the owner of the vehicle; but in such case the proper charge for carrying shall be paid, if demanded, before taking on the load.

10. The charge for a load on a wagon, dray or cart shall be as follows: for carrying it five squares or less, twenty-five cents; and for each square over five, two cents additional.

11. The charge for the use of a hack or other wheeled-carriage kept for hire, shall be as follows: For carrying a person therein not more than ten squares, fifty cents; and

---

*See note on chapter IV, § 2.

for each additional square, five cents: provided, that the whole charge for carrying one person to any part of the city shall not exceed one dollar. The charge for carrying not more than four persons shall not for the whole exceed one dollar and fifty cents, unless more than one hour be employed, and shall then only be one dollar and fifty cents for the first hour, and fifty cents for each succeeding hour. The charge for a hack to attend a funeral procession shall not exceed three dollars and fifty cents; and no charge shall be made for children under three years of age. For carrying persons between ten o'clock at night and daybreak, an additional charge of one-half the above rates may be made, and no more. For baggage, the charge shall be twenty-five cents for each trunk carried outside, and nothing shall be charged for any article carried inside or for any carpetbag or basket. Ordinances 1869

12. The load for single carts shall not exceed one thousand five hundred pounds, and their width of tires shall not be less than two inches. The load for single drays or trucks shall not exceed two thousand and five hundred pounds, and their width of tires shall not be less than two inches. The load for double carts, drays or trucks shall not exceed three thousand pounds, and their width of tires shall not be less than two inches. Three or four horse wagons or trucks shall carry a load not exceeding five thousand pounds, and their width of tires shall not be less than two and a half inches. Wagons and trucks, carrying a load exceeding five thousand pounds and not exceeding six thousand pounds, shall have tires not less than two and a half inches wide. Railroad cars, unless moved upon permanent or shifting tracks, shall pass over the streets upon eight wheels with flat tires not less than six inches wide, or upon four wheels with tires not less than ten inches wide. Portable engines, exceeding ten thousand pounds, shall be moved on four wheels with tires not less than six inches wide. Locomotive and stationary engines and heavy ordnance, exceeding five tons, shall be moved on four wheels having tires not less than six inches wide. Any piece of machinery or other indivisible article shall be transported upon wheels having tires corresponding in breadth to the weight of the piece of machinery or article in the ratio specified for cars, engines or ordnance. The owner of any cart, dray, truck or wagon, Jan. 8, 1872.

Jan. 8, 1872. and the manufacturer or transporter of any cars, engines, machinery or other article, who shall fail to comply with the restrictions imposed by this chapter, shall, for every such offence, be fined not less than ten nor more than twenty dollars. Nothing in this section shall apply to vehicles used by farmers or others living in the country, coming into the city with produce or fuel.*

Ordinances 1869 13. A copy of the rates for hacks and other wheeled-carriages shall be kept by the driver of every such hack or carriage, and he shall exhibit the same whenever called for by any person employing or using said hack or carriage. And if he shall fail to exhibit the same when so required, or if for carrying a person or baggage there be charged more than is allowed by this chapter, the owner or keeper of the vehicle, for every day of such failure, or for every time of such charge, shall be fined not less than five nor more than twenty dollars.

14. If any person desiring the use of a hack or any public vehicle kept for the purpose of taking persons, for hire or compensation, from one place to another within this city, shall tender to the owner, keeper or driver of such hack or vehicle the proper charge, according to the rates established by this chapter, for the use and service thereof as required, and the owner, keeper or driver shall fail or refuse to render the service so required, he shall be fined not less than ten nor more than twenty dollars, unless the keeper, owner or driver of such hack or vehicle shall, upon summons or warrant, appear and by proof show good cause to the contrary; and no prior engagement of the use or service of such hack or other public vehicle shall be taken as good cause for such failure or refusal, unless upon the trial of the offender he shall make it manifestly appear with whom the prior engagement was made, and the place to which the said hack or such other vehicle was engaged to go, and that there was not, by the use of ordinary diligence, time to render both services: provided, however, that between the hours of ten o'clock P. M. and daylight, when his horses are put up in his stable, he shall not be compelled to bring them out; but if he does consent to carry the person or persons calling upon him, he

*Parts of this section allowing the Tredegar company to carry cars built by them through certain of the public streets during a limited time, and requiring changes as to tires of wheels to be made before 1872, are omitted as now out of date.

shall do so at the rates fixed in this chapter, under the penalty aforesaid. Ordinances 1869

15. The mayor* shall, from time to time, designate such place or places as he shall deem proper, at which hacks or other carriages may stand waiting for employment. The owner or driver of any hack or other carriage which shall stand waiting for employment at any other time or place than shall have been designated by the mayor, shall be fined not less than five nor more than twenty dollars for each offence. June 15, 1870.

16. The mayor is hereby authorized to make regulations and give directions respecting the places or positions to be occupied by hacks or carriages at the public stands, or at any railroad depot, steamboat landing, canal packet landing, theatre or other place of public entertainment, when they may be attending for passengers, and the route they shall go when going to or leaving any such place; and if any owner, driver or other person having the care of any such carriage, shall refuse to obey such regulations or directions, he shall be liable to a fine of not less than five nor more than twenty dollars for each offence.

CHAPTER XXXVI.†

CONCERNING ANTHRACITE COAL.

Sec.
1. To be sold by weight; two thousand pounds to be a ton; penalty for violation.

1. Anthracite coal shall be sold by weight of two thousand pounds to a ton. Any violation of this ordinance shall be punished by a forfeiture of the coal to the city, and by a fine of not less than ten dollars and not exceeding twenty-five dollars. All ordinances and parts of ordinances conflicting with the foregoing are hereby repealed. Ordinances 1869

---

* See note on chapter XX, § 3.

† Chapter XXXVIII of 1869. The thirty-seventh chapter of that revisal, "Concerning the measuring of lumber," was repealed May 6, 1870.

CHAPTER XXXVII.*

CONCERNING THE MEASURING OF GRAIN.

Ordinances 1869 1. There shall be appointed by the city council a measurer of grain, who shall hold his office for the term of. two years, and until his successor is qualified, unless sooner removed.† Before entering on the duties required of him, he shall take the following oath, to wit: "I do solemnly swear that I will, to the best of my skill and judgment, render equal justice to all who may be interested in the discharge of the duties of my office;" and shall also give bond in the penalty of one thousand dollars, with security approved by the council.

2. Every person who shall bring to this city, for sale or barter, grain of any kind, potatoes, or any other article hereinafter mentioned, to be sold by solid measure (if over ten bushels), may apply to the measurer of grain to weigh the same.

3. When any article is provided for in this chapter to be sold by solid measure (except Irish potatoes when sold by the barrel), if either the buyer, seller, or party transporting to or from the city, require the article to be weighed by said measurer, and the other contracting party refuse to have the same so weighed, the party refusing shall pay a fine of twenty dollars.

4. The measurer shall weigh and ascertain the number of bushels of any article mentioned in this chapter, according to the standard herein named; and his certificate shall be binding on both parties as to the number of bushels, to wit: wheat, sixty pounds; corn, shelled, fifty-six pounds; corn, on the cob, seventy pounds; oats, thirty-two pounds; rye, fifty-six pounds; barley, forty-eight pounds; corn meal, fifty pounds; peas, sixty pounds; beans, sixty pounds: buckwheat, forty-eight pounds; clover seed, sixty-four pounds; timothy seed, forty-five pounds; flax seed, fifty-six pounds; hemp

* Chapter XXXIX of 1869.

† See note on chapter IV, § 2.

seed, forty-four pounds; Irish potatoes, sixty pounds; sweet potatoes, fifty-six pounds; onions, fifty-six pounds; bituminous coal, seventy pounds. If either seller or buyer of any such article refuse to be governed by this ordinance, he shall pay a fine of twenty dollars. It shall be the duty of said measurer to test the scales used by him at least once a week, and oftener if required. Ordinances 1869

5. The said measurer may appoint one or more deputies, who (when approved by the city council) may, after taking an oath faithfully to discharge the duties of his office, discharge any duties of his principal, but the principal shall be liable therefor; and any such deputy may at any time be removed from office by the principal or by the city council.

6. The said measurer shall receive for his services one-half cent per bushel; and the buyer and seller shall each pay one-half of the said fee, except in those cases where one of the parties does not reside in this city and the party transporting the grain requires the same to be weighed, when the seller or shipper shall pay the whole fee aforesaid.

7. The said measurer shall quarterly, to wit, on the first day of January, first day of April, first day of July, and first day of October in each year, return to the auditor an account of the number of bushels of each article weighed, and the amount received by him, verified by oath. He shall also cause to be published, at his cost (in a newspaper of this city), a statement of the number of bushels of each article mentioned in said report. If he fail for ten days to return such account, and make such publication, he shall pay a fine of ten dollars; and each subsequent day shall be a distinct offence.

CHAPTER XXXVIII.*

CONCERNING THE WEIGHING OF LONG FORAGE AND OTHER ARTICLES.

Ordinances 1869 1. There shall be appointed by the city council a weigh-master for each of the first and second markets, who, before acting in his office, shall give bond in the penalty of one thousand dollars, with surety approved by the city council.†

2. The weigh-master for each market shall have the care of the city scales and balances at or near the market for which he is appointed; and he shall keep the same for public use. In person, or by a deputy approved by the city council, he shall from sunrise to sunset of every day (except Sunday) attend the place at which the scales and balances under his care are kept, and weigh such articles as may be brought to the said place to be weighed.

3. The toll-gatherer of the James River and Kanawha company may, with the assent of that company, act as weigh-master near the basin of the James river canal, provided he shall, before acting as such, give bond in the penalty of one thousand dollars, payable to the city of Richmond, with surety approved by the city council, and with condition faithfully to account for and pay to the city such part of the fees received by him under this ordinance, and at such time and in such manner as is hereby required. If, before said bond is given and approved, the said toll-gatherer, or any person in the employment or under color of the authority of said company, shall weigh an article in any case in which the said company is not allowed by its charter to have such weighing done, such toll-gatherer or other person shall pay a fine of not less than two nor more than twenty dollars. After said bond is given and approved, there shall, for weigh-

* Chapter XL of 1869.

† See note on chapter IV, § 2.

ing done by said weigh-master, be paid him fees in every case in which the said company is not allowed by its charter to have such weighing done. Ordinances 1869

4. Forage in bales and bundles, brought by water, may be weighed at a place other than is before mentioned, provided proper balances for the purpose and the necessary labor be furnished by the owner at such place. If such place be at the dock or in James river, the weigh-master for either the first or second market may act; and the profits arising therefrom shall be equally divided between the said weigh-masters.

5. When hay, fodder, oats, shucks or other long forage is brought to the city, the same shall be examined, weighed and certified by a weigh-master, according to the provisions of this chapter. And if such hay be in bales, the weigh-master, after a satisfactory inspection thereof, shall mark each bale with the quality of the hay contained therein, either as "number one," "number two," or "refused," and shall moreover mark it with the weight of the hay, exclusive of the wood or other wrapping around or about it. If the person offering such hay for inspection shall request it, the weighmaster shall unpack it, and weigh the hay and the wood or other wrapping separately, and then repack the same, such person furnishing as many hands, at his own charge, to assist the weighmaster as may be necessary; otherwise the weighmaster shall make such deduction from the gross weight for the wood or other wrapping as he may deem reasonable. The weighmaster's certificate in such case shall be special, stating the weight and quality of the hay. Moreover he shall carefully remove from the bale any marks of its weight or quality other than his own.

6. Any person who shall sell or store for sale such hay, fodder, oats; shucks or other long forage, before it is weighed and certified by a weighmaster, and in case such hay be in bales before it is inspected and marked as aforesaid, or shall when it is brought in a vessel remove it any greater distance than is necessary to have it weighed, shall pay a fine of not less than two nor more than twenty dollars per bale, unless it be a case in which the owner of the land upon which the article was grown has brought it to this city for his sole and exclusive use, or be such a case of hay sent to this city in bales by a farmer of the state as is contemplated by the act

Ordinances 1869 of assembly passed the twenty-second of March, eighteen hundred and forty-seven, and mentioned in section nineteen, article twelve of the charter of the city.

7. Upon receiving the fee hereinafter mentioned, the weighmaster shall grant a certificate of the article weighed, specifying the owner's name, at whose instance it is weighed, and its true weight, exclusive, when forage is weighed, of the wagon or other article containing it and of any wood around or about such forage. And he shall date and sign said certificate, and in a book kept for the purpose make an entry of the article, placing each species of long forage in separate columns, which entry shall correspond with the certificate. He shall also, when a bundle of hay is weighed by him, mark its weight upon the binding of such bundle. If any person alter said certificate or mark he shall pay a fine of twenty dollars.

8. When the weighmaster, on examining an article, deems it not merchantable, he shall so mark it, and his certificate shall be special, stating the quality and condition of the article, or what deduction will render the residue merchantable.

9. The fees to be paid the weighmaster shall be for hay, whether loose or in bales, fodder, oats, shucks or other long forage, two and a half cents per hundred pounds; and for any other article, a cent and a half per hundred pounds.

10. Every weighmaster shall, quarterly, on the first day of every January, April, July and October, return to the auditor an account, verified on oath, of his receipts for fees within the preceding three months, and after deducting three-fourths thereof, as a compensation for his services, shall pay the residue to the treasurer. If a weighmaster fail for five days to render such account or to make such payment, the auditor shall report such default to the city council at its first meeting thereafter.

CHAPTER XXXIX.*

CONCERNING THE GAUGING OF LIQUORS.

1. There shall be appointed by the city council a competent person, who shall be called inspector and gauger of liquors.† Feb. 20, 1871.

2. It shall be the duty of the inspector and gauger so appointed, to provide himself with the most approved instruments for ascertaining the capacity of a barrel, hogshead, cask or other vessel, and the quality or proof of spirituous liquors, and when called upon for that purpose shall attend with the same in any part of the city, and there gauge and ascertain the contents of any barrel, hogshead, cask or vessel, and examine the quality and proof thereof, and mark on such barrel, hogshead, cask or other vessel near the bung, the capacity in gallons and fractions of gallons, and on the head, with chalk, the capacity and ullage.

3. If any person shall alter, deface or change any of the marks or characters made by the inspector aforesaid, or shall on any cask which has not been gauged and inspected, put a mark similar to, or in imitation of the gauger's mark, thereby to deceive and defraud the purchaser of distilled spirits, wines or other liquid merchandise so gauged and inspected, he shall, for each offence, pay a fine of not less than twenty dollars, together with cost of prosecution.

4. Any person may sell, export or otherwise dispose of any foreign or domestic liquors, in casks—rum, wine, molasses or other liquid merchandise, in said city, without having the same gauged or inspected; but in cases of difference between buyer and seller, as to the quantity and quality, either party may call in the inspector and gauger, and his judgment shall bind the parties; the party in error paying the gauger's fees.

* Chapter XLI of 1869.

† See note on chapter IV, § 2.

Feb. 20, 1871. 5. The said gauger and inspector shall, for his services, be entitled to demand and receive from the person or persons employing him as aforesaid, compensation as follows: For gauging and inspecting every barrel, hogshead, cask or other vessel, the sum of fifteen cents.

6. No person engaged in vending or trading in, or manufacturing casks or liquors, individually, or as agent, clerk or employee of a trader, vender or manufacturer of said articles, or either of them, shall be entitled to a license to act as gauger.

7. The inspector and gauger may appoint one or more deputies, who, after being approved by the city council, and taking an oath faithfully to discharge the duties of the office, may perform any of the duties of his principal; but the principal shall be accountable for the official conduct of such deputies.

8. The person so appointed inspector and gauger of liquors shall, before entering upon the duties of his office, take and subscribe an oath or affirmation faithfully and impartially to execute the duties of his office.

9. The city council shall have power, at any time hereafter, to appoint one other inspector of liquors, if it shall by said council be deemed necessary, who shall be subject in all respects to the provisions of this chapter: provided, inspection or gauging under this chapter shall in no case be compulsory upon the buyers or sellers of any liquors herein mentioned, unless the same has been agreed to by mutual consent of the parties.*

*It is difficult to say exactly what this proviso means. The probable meaning seems to be, that it is to be entirely optional with the parties whether there shall be any inspection or gauging of liquors. But if the persons proposing to buy and sell agree to have such inspection or gauging, and call in the inspector and gauger, then, and only then, they must be bound by his judgment. If this is the meaning, however, it takes away the power given by section four to either party, in cases of difference, to call in the inspector and gauger and have his decision made binding upon both. Whatever may have been the intention of the proviso, it certainly needs clearer expression, and some change to reconcile the two sections.

CHAPTER XL.*

CONCERNING POWDER, DANGEROUS LIQUIDS, NITRO-GLYCERINE, &C.

Powder.

1. Not more than fifty pounds of powder shall be transported in the city at one time, except by a military company, or in a vehicle constructed as the engineer of the city shall prescribe. Ordinances 1869.

2. The master of a vessel or steamer arriving in the port of Richmond with more than fifty pounds of powder on board, shall forthwith report the fact to the harbor-master, and take such berth as he shall assign.

3. The head man of a boat arriving in the city by the canal or river with more than fifty pounds of powder on board, shall forthwith report the fact to a police officer, and take such berth in the basin or canal as he shall direct. No fire shall be used on board of a boat having such quantity of powder on board.

4. When any person delivers more than fifty pounds of powder to a vessel, steamer or canal boat, he shall notify forthwith the harbor-master of such delivery to a vessel or steamer, and a police officer of such delivery to a canal boat, and the harbor-master shall assign a proper berth to the vessel or steamer, and the police officer shall do the same to the canal boat.

5. No person shall keep in the city longer than twenty-four hours more than two pounds of powder, except in tin canisters, or more than twenty-five pounds elsewhere than in a magazine, which shall be approved by the city council.

---

* Chapter XLII of 1869.

Ordinances 1869 6. Violations of sections one, two, three, four and five, by any person mentioned therein, shall be punished by a fine of not less than five nor more than fifty dollars.

7. The committee on public grounds and buildings shall have supervision of the powder kept in or near the city, and may prescribe such regulations for the reception, storage, delivery and transportation of powder, as the public safety requires. The engineer of the city shall inspect annually the vehicles used for the transportation of powder, and report their condition to the said committee, who may require such changes and repairs to be made in the same as they deem necessary.

Dangerous Liquids.

Oct. 14, 1872. 8. It shall be unlawful for any person, persons or corporation, to store or keep for sale, within the corporate limits of the city of Richmond, any gasoline, naptha, benzine, camphene, spirit gas, burning fluid or spirits of turpentine, exceeding a quantity of five barrels, of fifty gallons each; and it shall be unlawful to keep for sale, or on storage, any refined carbon oil, kerosene, or other products, for illuminating purposes, excepting such articles as will stand a fire test of one hundred and ten degrees of Fahrenheit, according to the method and directions of John Tagliabue, as explained in his work on the same, and it shall not be lawful to keep any of said articles, exceeding one barrel of fifty gallons, in any part of a building except a cellar, the floor of which shall be five feet below the grade of the adjacent streets; and no gasoline, naptha, benzine, carbon oil, camphene, spirit gas, burning fluid, or spirits of turpentine, shall be kept or stored in front of any building, or on any street, alley, wharf, lot or sidewalk, for a longer time than is sufficient to receive in store or in delivering the same, provided such time shall not exceed six hours.

April 21, 1871. 9. The inspector and gauger shall, at his own expense, provide himself with the necessary instruments and apparatus for testing the quality of said articles named in the preceding section; and it shall be his duty to examine and test the quality of all said oils and products, and if upon such testing and examination, the oils so tested and examined shall meet the requirements of this chapter, he shall brand the same with the date of examination, his name and this device, "Approved;" but if the oil so tested shall not meet the requirements of this chapter, he shall brand the same "Condemned;" and it shall be unlawful for the owner thereof to offer the same for sale within the limits of the city, for illuminating purposes. April 21, 1871.

10. The inspector and gauger may collect from the party so employing him, for inspecting and gauging each package, cask or barrel, the sum of twenty-five cents.

11. Any person, persons or corporation, who shall violate either of the provisions of sections eight and nine of this chapter, shall be subject to a fine of not less than one hundred dollars, nor more than five hundred, one-half of which shall go to the informer, and the penalties for such violation may be recovered in any court of competent jurisdiction.

Nitro-glycerine and other Explosives.

12. Nitro-glycerine shall not, nor shall any explosive compound of which it is a component part, be brought into the city, or manufactured or kept within the same. Any person offending against this section shall be fined not less than five hundred dollars for every offence. July 14, 1873.

13. No person or persons shall bring into the city, keep for sale, offer for sale or barter, torpedoes or fire crackers of an extra size under any name whatsoever, nor any fire-works in which nitro-glycerine forms a constituent part, under a penalty of not less than twenty nor more than one hundred dollars. The chief of police shall have power to determine what size of torpedoes or fire crackers may be offered for sale under this ordinance. Dec. 13, 1869.

CHAPTER XLI.*

CONCERNING PORT WARDENS, AND THE SPEED OF STEAMBOATS.

Ordinances 1869 August 1, 1874.

1. There shall be appointed by the city council for the port of this city four port wardens, each of whom, before acting in his office, shall give bond in the penalty of five hundred dollars, with surety approved by the council.† On any of said bonds suit may be prosecuted from time to time, in the name of the city, for the benefit of any person injured by any breach of the condition, as often as any such breach may be alleged, until there shall be recovered for the breaches damages equal to the penalty of the bond. The said port wardens shall continue in office until their successors are appointed.

Ordinances 1869

2. Two of the port wardens, when called on by the owner or master of or any person interested in a vessel, which, or its sails or rigging, arrives in the port in a damaged state, shall inspect such vessel, sails and rigging, and assess the damage, and upon receiving for their services a fee of six dollars, grant a certificate of said damage.

3. If a captain or master of a vessel arriving in the port shall enter his protest before the hatches of his vessel shall have been removed, or if he shall, within twenty-four hours after his vessel shall have been moored to a wharf, give notice to two of the port wardens that he has entered his protest before removing the hatches, the two port wardens called on by said captain or master shall inspect the condition and storage of the cargo, and on receiving for their services a fee of three dollars, grant a certificate stating whether, in their opinion, said cargo has been properly stowed, and whether damaged or not.

4. When a captain or master of a vessel shall have removed the hatches of his vessel to land a cargo at Norfolk,

*Chapter XLIII of 1869.

†See note on chapter IV, § 2.

or any port on James river, and shall produce to two port wardens satisfactory evidence of his having at the time called for an inspection in regular manner, he shall be entitled to a further inspection; and the two port wardens shall proceed therewith. Ordinances 1869.

5. When the two port wardens, on inspecting the cargo, find the same or any part thereof damaged, they shall immediately give notice to the consignee or the owner thereof, or person interested therein, and if requested by him, shall assess the damages to the cargo or such part of it as is damaged, and on receiving three dollars from the consignee, if there be but one, and one dollar from each consignee, if there be more than one, shall grant a certificate of their assessment to the consignee or owner of each separate shipment, or the person interested therein.

6. When two port wardens disagree, a third shall be called on, and of the two, that opinion to which the third approximates the nearest shall be taken as the judgment. The fees of port wardens shall be equally divided among those rendering the services.

7. When a cargo, or any part thereof, is abandoned to the underwriters, the port wardens shall take charge of the same, and after giving, in one or more of the newspapers of the city, such notice of the time and place of sale, as in reference to the nature and condition of the damaged articles they may deem advisable, shall sell what is so abandoned, at public auction, and after deducting the cost of advertising, necessary expenses for labor and for their services a commission of one and a quarter per centum, shall faithfully account for and pay the residue to the parties entitled.

8. The port wardens shall keep a record of their proceedings, and annually, at the first meeting of the city council in July, return an account, on oath, of their receipts within the preceding year by virtue of their offices. If they fail to make such return, neither of them shall be capable of being re-elected, unless he satisfies the council of his inability to make it.*

9. The captain or commander of every steamboat coming into or departing from the port of this city, shall, on its ar-

* The return required by this section of the old ordinance was, in part, a preliminary to the annual election of port wardens. Now, it can only have that use every second year; but in order to that, the return must be made to the *first* meeting in July.

Ordinances 1869 riving within half a mile of the port, or while it is not more than half a mile from the port, retard its speed to one-half its usual rate, or fourteen revolutions of its wheels per minute. If he fail so to do, he shall pay a fine of ten dollars.

CHAPTER XLII.*

CONCERNING THE EMPLOYMENT OF PRISONERS IN THE CITY JAIL.

July 18, 1870. 1. The police justice may, by his warrant directed to the keeper of the jail of the city, order such persons as he may designate, and as are liable to be employed under the act of the general assembly, passed February twenty-sixth, eighteen hundred and fifty-six, and entitled "An act for establishing a workhouse in the city of Richmond," to be employed on the public works of the city.† In said warrant shall be specified the names of such persons, the number of days and the hours of the day during which such persons shall be so employed; and for sufficient cause to him appearing, the police justice may supersede his said warrant, when the said employment of such persons shall cease. Such persons shall be employed on the same works, and in like manner, with the city hands, but shall be furnished while so employed by the keeper of the city jail with proper food, clothing and lodging, in like manner with the other prisoners committed to the jail.

2. The board of police commissioners may appoint one or more persons, not to exceed four, to attend the prisoners whilst at work, and passing and re-passing from the jail to the place of employment. It shall be the duty of such persons so appointed, to enforce orderly behavior and obedience

---

* Chapter XLIV of 1869.

† The words "under the management of the overseer of the public hands" closed this sentence in the ordinance of July 18, 1870. There being no such office, the sections creating it (Ordinances of 1869, chapter XXXIV, § 10, 11) having been repealed, the words quoted are omitted. See notes on chapter XXXIII, § 8, and § 2 of this chapter, relative to this repeal.

of the prisoners* when out of the custody of the jailor; and for this purpose they may command any person or persons to aid and assist in apprehending and securing such prisoners. Should any person, when required to aid and assist in apprehending and securing a prisoner as aforesaid, neglect or refuse so to aid and assist, such person shall pay a fine not exceeding ten dollars for every such offence. July 18, 1870.

3. For the more perfect security of the prisoners, the engineer of the city shall have provided a chain and ball for each prisoner that may be worked on the streets, to be affixed to his leg before leaving the jail, and not to be taken off until returned to jail.

4. Any person charged with and duly performing the police duty provided for in the second section of this ordinance, shall, on the certificate of the board of police commissioners that he is justly entitled thereto, be paid the same compensation as a permanent policeman.

---

*After the words "obedience of the prisoners," there followed in this ordinance the words "to the overseer." There being no such officer, the last three words are omitted. The persons to be appointed under this section seem to be the only persons now authorized to take any control of the prisoners while at work out of jail, and as there is now no officer to whose orders they are to enforce the obedience required, the ordinance seems essentially defective.

Title 7.

NUISANCES.

CHAPTER XLIII.*

CONCERNING ANIMALS GOING AT LARGE.

August 1, 1870. 1. No hog or pig shall be kept on any lot or allowed to go at large within the limits of the city: provided, that in the wards Marshall, Jefferson, Monroe and Clay, upon special application, the city council shall be at liberty to grant special permission to the owners to keep such animals, upon such terms as the city council may by resolution prescribe. Any person violating the provisions of this section shall pay a fine of not less than two nor more than twenty dollars; and such hog or pig kept or going at large without such permission shall be forfeited.

Ordinances 1869 2. No dog or bitch shall be permitted to go at large in any street, lane or alley in the city, until the owner or keeper thereof shall have paid the tax and obtained the license required by the twentieth section of the thirteenth chapter. And the owner or keeper thereof shall be required to muzzle every such dog or bitch during the months of May, June, July, August and September of each year. And for any failure to comply with the provisions of this section, the owner of such dog or bitch shall pay a fine of not less than ten nor more than twenty dollars.

---

*Chapter XLV of 1869.

3. The license to be granted by the auditor under the preceding section and the chapter therein referred to, shall expire on the first day of February next after the same is given. The auditor shall keep a record of all such licenses, and furnish each person taking such license with a medal, with the number of such license stamped thereon (the shape of the medal to be changed each year), which shall be kept about the neck of the dog attached to a collar, with the owner's name engraved or written thereon. If any person shall attach such medal to the collar of any dog without having obtained such license according to this ordinance, he shall pay a fine of not less than five nor more than twenty dollars, and said dog shall be killed. Ordinances 1869

4. Every unlicensed dog found going at large off the lot or premises of the owner or keeper of such dog, shall be taken and killed as directed by this ordinance: provided, that any unlicensed dog may be redeemed by his owner, or any other person for him, paying the police officer having the custody of such dog five dollars, for the use of the city, at any time before sunset of the day on which said dog is taken. The owner or keeper of every unlicensed dog or bitch shall be liable to a fine not exceeding five dollars. The occupant of any lot or premises on which an unlicensed dog or bitch shall be harbored for a period of ten days, shall be deemed the owner or keeper of such animal. One-half of the fine collected for any violation of this ordinance shall be paid to the informer. Nov. 25, 1872.

5. If any person shall permit any dangerous or vicious animal, owned or kept by him or her, to go at large with or without a license, he shall be fined not less than one nor more than twenty dollars; and such animal may be killed by order of the police justice if, after twenty-four hours' notice, such animal is not removed beyond the limits of the corporation by the owner thereof. No butcher's dog shall appear or be brought into the markets on any account; and any such dog being found at or in any market-house in this city shall be taken and considered within the meaning of this ordinance as a vicious animal going at large. Ordinances 1869

6. If any person shall unlawfully and without necessity kill a licensed dog, not vicious or dangerous, without authority from the owner of such dog, or shall steal or take away such dog, with intent fraudulently to deprive the owner or

Ordinances 1869 keeper of the use of such dog, he shall be fined twenty dollars.

7. If any person shall suffer his cow or calf to be in any street or public alley of this city in the night time, he may be fined not less than one nor more than five dollars.

Nov. 25, 1872. 8. If any owner or other person having the custody of any horse, mule, swine or goat, shall turn loose or permit the same to go at large in any public street or alley, he shall be fined not less than one nor more than five dollars, and every such hog or goat shall be taken and sold for the use of the city. But nothing in this chapter shall be so construed as to subject any visitor or resident in the city to any fine or forfeiture for ten days after the arrival of his or her dog therein; nor to prevent the owner or keeper of any animal (not vicious or dangerous) from driving it through the streets or alleys in coming into, going from or passing through the city. Nor shall this section apply to any goat, for which the owner thereof has obtained a license from the auditor for keeping the same, for the time allowed by said license. But the said license shall only be obtained upon the certificate of the family physician, declaring that goat's milk is absolutely essential to the health of a member of said family, and fixing a period during which he conceives it will be so essential. A fee of one dollar shall be paid for every such license.

Ordinances 1869 9. If any person shall cruelly beat or torture any horse, mule, dog or other animal, whether his own or that of another, he shall be fined not less than five nor more than twenty dollars.

10. The officers of police shall take up and secure hogs, dogs and goats going at large in violation of this ordinance. The mayor* may, as often as he sees occasion therefor, require to be sent through the city as many of the city hands, carts and horses as he may deem necessary, furnished with the fixtures and apparatus provided therefor, and put therein all hogs, dogs and goats so found at large. Such of the police officers as the mayor may direct shall accompany said

*See note on chapter XX, § 3. Probably this special matter of police was not designed to be left as here; but there is nothing about it in later ordinances, and the compiler was uncertain to what officer it should be assigned, whether to the police justice or the chief of police. If to the latter, a change of the ordinance it not essentially necessary, as that officer is already subject to the mayor's orders as to all police matters not regulated by the police board.

carts; and any person who shall prevent a hog, dog or goat from being taken under this ordinance by said officer, shall pay a fine of not less than one nor more than twenty dollars. Every hog, dog or goat taken up under this ordinance shall be removed to a place of deposit to be provided by the mayor, and any such dog shall be kept until sunset of the day on which he was taken up, unless sooner redeemed. The owner of such dog so taken up, or, on his failure until sunset, any other person may redeem such dog by paying to the police officer having such dog in charge, five dollars; but every dog not redeemed shall, under the direction of the mayor, be conveyed beyond the corporate limits at least five hundred yards, and there put to death and buried; and every hog or goat taken up shall be sold at public auction by a police officer, for the use of the city, at such time and place as the mayor may direct. Ordinances 1869.

11. Every police officer receiving money for dogs redeemed, or for hogs or goats sold under this ordinance, shall account for the same in the mode prescribed by the twenty-second section of the ordinance concerning the police.

CHAPTER XLIV.*

CONCERNING VARIOUS NUISANCES.

Ordinances 1869

1. If any person shall put or cause to be put into the canal, locks or dock, or any basin of the James river and Kanawha company, or upon the margin of James river, within the corporate limits of this city, or the pond of the water works, the carcass of any animal, filth or nuisance of any kind, he shall be fined not less than five nor more than fifty dollars. And the like fine shall be imposed on the said company, if it shall suffer or permit any boat with offensive stagnant water or other nuisance therein to remain more than twenty-four hours in said canal, locks, dock or basin; and the captain or owner of such boat may also be fined not less than five nor more than twenty dollars. Every such nuisance when suffered to remain as aforesaid by the said company, shall be removed at the expense of the said company, by an officer of the police, or at the expense of the person so putting or causing it to be put, if he be known, otherwise at the expense of the city.

2. If any person shall put or cause to be put into any cellar or house, or upon any other private property not owned

* Chapter XLVI of 1869.

or occupied by him, any filth or nuisance of any kind, he shall be fined not less than one nor more than twenty dollars. Ordinances 1869

3. If any person shall employ any person other than those appointed by the city council to remove from any house or lot, or any other place, any filth or other nuisance, and such person shall waste the same in the street or alley, or shall put or cause the same to be put into or upon any land or place mentioned in either of the preceding sections, the person so employing such person and the said person shall each be fined not less than two nor more than twenty dollars.

4. If any person shall have or suffer any noxious, unwholesome or offensive matter, stagnant water or nuisance of any kind, in any house or cellar, or upon any other private property owned or occupied by him, he shall be fined not less than one nor more than twenty dollars: provided, however, that if any such nuisance be caused or arise from the want of proper and sufficient draining, the occupier of any lot or tenement, if he be not the owner thereof, shall not be fined for such nuisance, if immediately after the existence of the same he give notice thereof to the owner; and unless, after such notice, the owner abate or remove such nuisance by proper and sufficient draining or otherwise, within such time as the police justice may prescribe, he shall be fined not less than ten nor more than fifty dollars.

5. Upon the complaint of any citizen or information given by any police officer to the police justice, that a privy is so placed as to be offensive, he may, upon summons returned executed against the owner, order such privy to be removed.

6. If any person shall erect, have or keep any slaughter-house or distillery in this city, he shall on proof thereof be held guilty of a nuisance, and be fined not less than twenty nor more than fifty dollars for each day the said nuisance shall continue.

7. If a person shall, within two hundred feet of a dwelling house, without permission of the owner or occupier thereof, burn any lime-kiln or brick-kiln, he shall pay a fine of not less than one nor more than five dollars for every hour the same may be burning.

8. On complaint to the police justice that unslacked lime has been stored on premises within fifty feet of any house in this city, he shall issue a warrant, directed to three free-holders, to examine the said premises. If they deem it dan-

Ordinances 1869 gerous that the lime should be stored on said premises, the owner or occupier shall remove the same within twelve hours after being notified thereof. If he shall fail so to do he shall pay a fine not exceeding ten dollars; and for each hour thereafter that the same continues to be stored, he shall pay a fine of not less than two nor more than twenty dollars.

9. A stove pipe passing in or through a floor, partition, roof or side of a house, shall be enclosed the whole of such passage in earthenware or mortar or tin casing filled with sand, and if passing through a window, shall be enclosed with tin or sheet-iron; it shall extend two feet beyond the roof or side of the house, and if through the side of the house, it shall be capped with a cross pipe at least eighteen inches long: and no stove pipe shall project into a street. If any person put up, construct or use in any building in this city, any stove pipe otherwise than according to and in conformity with the foregoing directions and regulations, he shall be fined not less than five nor more than twenty dollars; and each day that the same shall continue shall be a distinct offence, and punishable as such by a fine of twenty dollars.

10. If any person shall put fire to a chimney to clean it, except in the day time, and whilst the roof of the house to which it is attached is well covered with snow, or whilst it is raining, and the roof thoroughly wet thereby; or if the chimney of any house shall take fire from not having been properly cleaned, the occupier of any such house shall be fined not less than two nor more than five dollars.

11. If any person shall sell, or expose for sale, in this city, any torpedoes, popcrackers, squibs or other fireworks of any kind whatever, except in packages containing each at least one hundred, or shall, without permission in writing from the mayor, discharge or set off, in any street or alley of the city, any balloon, rocket, torpedo, popcracker, fireworks, or any combination of gunpowder, or any other combustible or dangerous material; or if any person shall, except under the thirty-ninth section of the chapter concerning streets, without necessity, fire or discharge in this city any cannon, gun, pistol or other fire-arms of any kind, shall make therein any unusual noise, whereby the inhabitants thereof may be alarmed, or raise or fly a kite in this city; or if any auctioneer shall use any bell or herald to notify the public of any

sale, except of real property, every such person herein offending shall pay a fine of not less than one nor more than twenty dollars. Ordinances 1869

12. No person, firm or incorporated company shall keep in any house in the city any loaded shell or shot, or any explosive material of any sort not authorized by ordinance. And any person, firm or incorporated company violating the provisions of this section, shall be fined not less than twenty nor more than one hundred dollars; and each day on which the same is so kept in the city shall be a distinct offence, and punishable as such.

13. Every hotel keeper and keeper of a restaurant, lager beer saloon, or other place where ardent spirits, beer, cider or other drinks are sold or given away, shall close the bar where such drinks are sold or given away, every Sunday during the whole day. At all times when such bar shall be open, the license under which the business is conducted shall remain posted in some conspicuous place in the bar-room. And any person violating any provision of this section shall be fined not less than ten nor more than five hundred dollars. March 23, 1874.

14. If any person shall, by swimming, bathing, or in any other way, indecently expose his person, or any part thereof, to the public view, or cause any person so to do within this city, or the river adjacent thereto, he shall be fined not less than one nor more than twenty dollars. Ordinances 1869

15. If after the city council, on the petition of the owners of not less than one-fourth of the ground included in any square in the city, shall have prohibited the erection in such square of any building, or of any addition to any building, more than ten feet high (unless the outer walls thereof be made of brick and mortar or stone and mortar), it be alleged by an officer of police or any citizen, to the police justice, that any person has erected any building or addition contrary to such prohibition, the said police justice shall have the said person summoned before him; and upon proof that a building or addition has been erected contrary to such prohibition, shall order him to remove the same. And if it be alleged in like manner to the police justice that any building or wall of any kind hath become dangerous to citizens or to adjoining property, by dilapidation or otherwise, he shall in like manner have the owner thereof, or his agent, summoned

Ordinances 1869 before him; and upon proof that the said building or wall, or any part thereof, is dangerous as aforesaid, shall order the said owner or agent to remove or repair the same, or so much thereof as is dangerous as aforesaid.

16. Hereafter no wooden building shall be erected in the city, nor shall any wooden addition be made to any building already erected, without permission first had and obtained from the council. Any person violating this section shall be fined not less than twenty nor more than fifty dollars; and for every day it shall remain after the first fine is imposed, it shall be a distinct offence and punishable as such.

17. Upon its being alleged by a citizen or any officer of police, to the police justice, that ground in the city owned by a non-resident thereof, and not occupied by any person residing thereon, is subject to be covered by stagnant water, or that such owner permits or suffers any offensive or unwholesome substance to accumulate or remain thereon, reasonable notice of such allegation shall be given by the said police justice to the said owner or his agent, if any he has: and in case he has no such agent, by publication for not less than four weeks in a newspaper printed in said city. The said police justice shall communicate to the city council the fact of such allegation and notice, that they may cause such ground to be filled up, raised or drained, or to cause such substances to be covered or removed therefrom, and to collect the expense of so doing from the owner or owners, occupier or occupiers, or any of them, by distress and sale, in the same manner in which taxes levied upon real estate for the benefit of said city are authorized to be collected.

18. In every case arising under the preceding sections of this ordinance, except under the seventeenth section, the police justice, in addition to any fine he may impose, may, in his discretion, order the nuisance complained of to be abated or removed, whether specially so directed or not, and shall prescribe the time within which such order shall be executed; and if any person shall, after notice of such order, fail or refuse to obey the same within the time prescribed (not in any case to exceed ten days), he shall be fined not less than ten nor more than twenty dollars for each day that such nuisance shall thereafter exist or remain; and he may moreover cause such nuisance to be abated at the cost of the person offending. If such cost shall not exceed one hundred

dollars, he may issue execution therefor against the goods and chattels of the offender, for the use of the city; and when such expense shall exceed one hundred dollars, an account thereof shall be filed by the police justice with the auditor, who shall proceed forthwith to collect the same by suit for the like use. Ordinances 1869

19. Any person driving over the free bridge between Richmond and Manchester at a speed faster than four miles per hour, shall pay a fine of ten dollars for each offence, upon conviction before the police justice, one-half to go to the informer, and every violation shall constitute a distinct offence. July 14, 1873.

20. It shall not be lawful for bands of musicians to parade the streets performing on musical instruments, between the hours of eleven o'clock in the forenoon and two o'clock in the afternoon of Sunday. Every person violating this section shall be guilty of a misdemeanor, and upon conviction thereof before the police justice, be fined not more than twenty nor less than five dollars.

21. No furnace for melting iron or other metals, or making glass, and no stationary steam engine, designed for use in any mill for planing, or sawing boards, or turning wood, or for any other purpose; or in which any other fuel than anthracite coal is used to create steam, shall be erected, or put up to be used in this city, unless a permit therefor shall have been first granted by the city council, prescribing the place where the building in which such steam engine or furnace is to be used, is located, or where the same shall be erected; the materials and construction thereof, with such regulations as to height of stacks or chimneys, as to prevent the use of the same from being offensive to the occupants of adjacent property; and such protection against fire as they may deem necessary for the safety of the neighborhood. May 15, 1871.

22. The committee on the fire department, (or such officers or committee as the city council shall otherwise designate), may, after notice to the parties interested, examine any furnace, steam engine, or steam boiler in use in this city, and for that purpose may enter any house, shop or building, and if upon such examination it appears probable that the use of such engine or boiler is unsafe, or that the furnaces, stacks or chimneys thereof, are liable to set fire to adjacent property, or to create a nuisance to those residing in the vicinity, they may issue a temporary order to suspend such

May 15, 1871. use, and shall make a report of their action, with a statement of the reasons therefor, to the next meeting of the city council thereafter.

23. If after giving the parties interested, so far as known, an opportunity to be heard, the council shall adjudge such engine, boiler or flues, to be unsafe or defective, or unfit to be used, they shall prohibit the use thereof, until the same be rendered free from the objections cited in the twenty-second section.

24. If after notice to the owner, or person having charge thereof, such engine or boiler is used contrary to either of such orders, it shall be deemed a common nuisance, without other proof thereof than its use, and he or they shall be fined not less than ten nor more than fifty dollars for each day the said furnace, engine or boiler is so used.

Title 8.

THE POOR.

CHAPTER XLV.*

CONCERNING THE POOR OF THE CITY.

1. The committee for the relief the poor shall have the government, control and direction of the almshouse and grounds, and of any other buildings and grounds which may be acquired or used for the benefit of the poor of the city. It shall likewise have the government, control and direction of all the officers, agents, nurses and other employees connected with the institution, and of the poor receiving aid or relief from the city; and except the superintendent of the almshouse, it shall appoint all such officers, agents and employees, prescribe their duties and fix their compensation. And it may prescribe the duties of the superintendent. Ordinances 1869

2. To carry out the foregoing powers and duties, the committee shall prepare rules and regulations for the government, direction and control of the institution and of the offi-

* Chapter XLVII of 1869.

Ordinances 1869 cers, agents, employees and inmates connected with it, which shall be submitted to the city council; and when or so far as they may be approved by the council, they shall have full force and effect as if embraced in this ordinance. And if at any time the committee shall be of opinion that other rules and regulations should be made, or those in force should be changed, such additions and changes shall be prepared and submitted to the council; and when approved, shall have the same force and effect as if they had been originally adopted.

3. The officers of the institution shall be a superintendent of the almshouse, who shall be elected by the city council,* a physician, a matron of the almshouse, and a matron of the hospital. The superintendent of the almshouse shall also be superintendent of the city hospital and keeper of the Shockoe Hill cemetery. The salary of the superintendent shall be fixed by the city council. The physician of the almshouse shall also be the physician to the city hospital, and shall have all the powers and perform all the duties devolved upon the physician of the hospital by chapter twenty-six of the city ordinances. Before the superintendent shall have authority to act as such, he shall enter into bond with security to be approved by the city council, in the penalty of five thousand dollars.

4. The committee may remove any officer, agent or employee engaged in the institution except the superintendent, and they may, for any misconduct or neglect of duty, suspend him from the performance of his duties, and report the fact to the city council; and for this purpose shall call a meeting of the city council within three days.† And the city council shall either restore him or dismiss him from his office, as his conduct shall merit.

5. Any person who has lived in the city for one year at the time, may by himself or herself, or another person, apply to one of the committee of the ward in which such applicant lives, for relief either for such applicant or his or her family; and if the said member of the committee shall be satisfied that the applicant or the family are proper subjects for the almshouse, he shall give to such applicant an order to the superintendent, directing him to receive the applicant, or the family,

* See note on chapter IV, § 2.

† This call of the committee would seem to require a joint meeting of the two branches of the council.

as the case may be, into the almshouse; and upon presentation of such order to the superintendent, he shall receive the person or persons who are embraced in it, and provide for them until the physician of the almshouse shall make his next visit. He shall then report the case to the physician, who shall examine the parties; and if he shall be of opinion that he or they are proper subjects for the almshouse, he shall endorse the order to that effect, and the party or parties shall be permitted to remain. But if the physician shall be of opinion that the party or parties are not proper subjects for the almshouse, he shall endorse the same on said order; and the superintendent shall thereupon dismiss them; and said party or parties shall not be again admitted to the almshouse for the same cause, except by the order of the committee. Ordinances 1869.

6. No out-door relief shall be given except in the most urgent cases, in which a physician attending on the person for whom application for relief is made, shall state in writing, or a member of the committee for the ward, upon his own view, shall be of opinion, that the person cannot be removed to the almshouse without endangering his life. In such case and upon such statement the members of the committee in that ward, acting together, may order such relief as they shall deem necessary; and shall report the case to the committee at its next meeting. And if in such case it is necessary to expend money immediately, they may give an order on the auditor for the amount.

7. In cases in which a person who has not lived in the city for a year, is in the city sick and destitute, or not in a condition to provide for him or herself, or his or her children, he, she or they may be sent to and received and examined and treated at the almshouse in the mode prescribed in the fifth section of this chapter, but shall only remain there until he or she has recovered from his or her sickness, or is in a condition to provide for him or herself, or the children. But the superintendent may, with the concurrence of the physician and the committee, discharge them at any time. And if any person is in the city sick and destitute, or if any destitute female and children, unable to provide for themselves, are in the city, and are likely to become chargeable to the city, the committee may send such persons to their homes; and the expense of so doing shall be paid by the auditor, upon the order of the chairman.

Ordinances 1869 8. The committee shall hold monthly meetings at the almshouse, on such day as may be fixed by them. At these meetings the superintendent and physician shall lay before the committee a statement of the supplies and an estimate of their cost, which will be needed in their departments respectively, up to the end of the second succeeding month; and the committee shall determine which and how much of said supplies shall be purchased, and may fix a price therefor, which shall not be exceeded; and the committee may authorize the purchase of supplies for a longer period than one month, if they deem it expedient. When the committee have ascertained and entered on their journal the amount which will be necessary to be expended for the expenses of the institution during the next month, they may, if they shall deem it expedient, authorize the chairman to draw upon the auditor, on a copy of the resolution, in favor of the superintendent and physician respectively, for the amount which the committee has fixed for expenses in their respective departments during the next month; and the clerk of the committee shall, immediately after the meeting, report to the auditor the amount fixed upon for said expenses, and the resolution authorizing the chairman to draw upon him in favor of the superintendent and physician.

9. At each monthly meeting of the committee, the superintendent and any other officer or agent empowered by the committee to make any contract which involves the expenditure of money, shall present his accounts for the transactions of the previous month, with his vouchers; and after the same has been examined by the committee, and the committee is satisfied of its correctness, or so far as the same is ascertained to be correct, it shall be approved; and if any money is due thereon from the city it shall be paid by a draft of the chairman upon the auditor; and in every case a copy of said account shall be returned to the auditor: provided, that the expenses of the institution for the said previous month do not exceed the amount to which the city council may have restricted the expenditure, or which they may have appropriated for the relief of the poor, if a specific appropriation has been made for that purpose.

10. The committee shall keep a record of its proceedings, and for this purpose may employ a clerk, and make him a per diem allowance for his services. The clerk shall certify

to the auditor of the city the names of the several officers appointed by the committee under the first section, and the amount of compensation allowed to each. And the said officers may draw the same in monthly instalments, upon application to the auditor. Ordinances 1869

11. The committee shall report annually to the city council, at its first meeting in March; in which report they shall state the number of persons provided for in the year, showing how many were white and how many colored, for what length of time and where each was provided for or assisted, the name of each, and the amount expended by the committee for the year for the support of the poor, distinguishing the amount expended for those at the almshouse or other building used for their lodging, from the amount expended for outdoor relief; and whether any, and if any, how many, and which were kept at work, and for what length of time. They shall also state the amount expended in repairs of buildings or otherwise, not embraced in the amount expended for the support of the poor proper. They shall also make such recommendations, upon any or all of the objects included within the sphere of their powers and duties, as they shall be of opinion should be acted on by the council.

12. In respect to all matters not provided for in this chapter, the committee shall have the power and perform the duties vested in and required of overseers of the poor by the fifty-first and one hundred and twenty-second chapters of the Code of eighteen hundred and seventy-three, so far as the same are not inconsistent with this ordinance. And if, in executing any power or duty under the said chapters of the Code of eighteen hundred and seventy-three, it shall be necessary to act as overseers of the poor, they shall be such for that purpose, and they shall act with the organization they have as a committee, the chairman acting as the president of the board.

CHAPTER XLVI.*

CONCERNING BEGGARS.

Police officers to inform committee for relief of the poor of persons begging.

Ordinances 1869 It shall be one of the duties of the police officers of the city to give to some member of the committee for the relief of the poor such information in relation to every person going about begging, or staying in any street or other place to beg, as will enable such committeeman to proceed in the case, according to chapters fifty-one and one hundred and twenty-two of the Code of Virginia.

CHAPTER XLVII.†

CONCERNING VAGRANTS.

Ordinances 1869 1. Every railroad company, and every captain or master of a steamboat or vessel, which or who shall bring to the city of Richmond or to the port thereof from another state or country any person not having ostensible means for his or her support, shall, before such person shall be permitted to leave the cars or the vessel, enter into bond to the city in the penalty of five hundred dollars, with condition to pay to the city any sum or sums of money which the city may expend during the next twelve months from the date of such bond for the support or care of such person. And if such railroad company, captain or master of a steamboat or vessel, shall fail or refuse to give such bond, such company, captain or master shall be required to keep such person in the depot of such company, or on board of his vessel, until such person

* Chapter XLVIII of 1869.

† Chapter XLIX of 1869.

shall be taken back beyond the limits of the state by the company, captain or master who shall have brought him to the city. Ordinances 1869

2. If any railroad company, captain or master of a steamboat or vessel, shall fail to comply with the preceding section, or shall bring any such person as is therein mentioned near to the city, and permit him to leave the cars, or his steamboat or vessel, and such person shall come into the city, such railroad company, captain or master shall be fined twenty dollars for each person; and every day that such person shall remain in the city shall be a separate offence.

3. It shall be the duty of the police of the city to arrest all persons having no ostensible means of support, who shall have come to the city within the preceding six months, and all persons known as robbers and pickpockets, who have come from other states within the same period, and to take them before the police justice; and if the police justice shall be satisfied that they are such persons as herein described, he shall, in the case of persons other than robbers, pickpockets or professional thieves, commit them to jail until they can be sent back to the place from whence they came, if their former residence be ascertained, and if not, then to some place out of the state; and in the case of robbers, pickpockets, or persons known as professional thieves, the police justice shall, if he he satisfied that they are such, and have been in the city more than six months, commit them to jail in default of security for good behavior for a term not exceeding twelve months, or send them back to the place from whence they came, if it can be ascertained, and, if not, then to some place out of the state. August 8, 1870.

4. If the police justice can ascertain by whose steamboat or vessel, or by what railroad, such persons were brought to the city or near it, he shall have them put on the cars of such railroad or on such steamboat or vessel; and it shall be the duty of such railroad company, or the captain or master of such steamboat or vessel, to take back such persons at their own expense or the expense of the persons themselves; and if such persons cannot be put on such cars or vessels, they shall be sent out of the state at the expense of the city.

5. Any railroad company or captain or master of a steamboat or vessel, which or who shall refuse to receive such per- Ordinances 1869

Ordinances 1869 sons brought to the city or near thereto upon their cars, steamboat or vessel, and to take them back, shall be fined twenty dollars for each person.

6. If any person described in the first or third sections of this chapter shall return to the city after having been sent away, he shall be placed in the chain-gang of the city and compelled to work upon the streets.

Title 9.

EDUCATION.

CHAPTER XLVIII.*

CONCERNING THE PUBLIC FREE SCHOOLS.

School districts.

1. The city of Richmond shall be divided into three school districts: the first embracing all the corporate limits east of the line of the centre of Seventeenth street; the second all between the centre lines of Seventeenth and Fourth streets; the third all west of the centre line of Fourth street. May 15, 1871.

Trustees.

2. There shall be chosen by the council, as soon as convenient after the passage of this ordinance, three trustees for each of said school districts, the first to continue in office three years, the second two, and the third one year, and until their successors shall have been chosen and accepted their

*Substituting chapter L, of 1869, concerning public schools. Chapter XLVIII, of 1869, concerning beggars, is XLVI of this collection.

May 15, 1871. offices. The said trustees shall constitute and be called the school board of the city of Richmond, and shall have all the powers conferred on such board by law.

3. Vacancies arising in said board, by expiration of the term of office, or by failure to accept office, shall be filled by the city council. Vacancies arising from any other cause shall be filled by the board itself. The failure of a trustee to attend three consecutive meetings of the board next after his appointment shall be regarded a refusal to accept said appointment, and the fact shall be certified to the city council by the city superintendent, when the council shall fill the unexpired term.

4. The mayor shall be ex-officio president of the board, but shall have no vote except in case of a tie.

5. The school board may appoint a secretary, who may be a member of the board, and prescribe his salary, subject to the approval of the city council. He shall continue in office one year, and until his successor is elected and qualifies; and shall perform such duties as the board may, by resolution, prescribe.

6. The school board shall appoint and remove teachers of the public schools, fix their salaries, and prescribe their duties. It shall have charge of, and keep in repair all buildings necessary for public education; shall provide books, furniture and apparatus, and whatever else may be necessary for public instruction; but no member of the board shall be concerned, directly or indirectly, in constructing, repairing or furnishing the said buildings, or any of them; or in the profits of any contract whatever connected with public education in the city of Richmond. The board shall have power to make such rules for its government, not inconsistent with law, as it may deem proper.

7. The school board shall hold regular meetings at least once a month, at such times and places as it may prescribe. It may change such times and places at its pleasure, and may provide for the call of special meetings, as it may deem proper.

8. The school board shall keep a journal of its proceedings, which shall always be open to the inspection of the president of either branch of the city council, or any committee thereof charged with that duty.

9. The school board shall, on or before the first Monday in February of each year, report to the city council, an estimate in convenient detail, of the amount of money needed for the conduct of the public schools, during the year following that for which appropriations will have already been made; and shall as soon after the close of each scholastic year as practicable, make report to the city council of the condition of public education in the city, with such recommendations regarding the same as to it may seem proper. May 15, 1871.

10. The school board shall, as soon as practicable, provide for the establishment of a higher grade of schools, and for a high and normal school, and shall have power, and it shall be its duty, to provide for as thorough a system of public education as the means provided for that purpose will admit.

The City Superintendent.

11. The city superintendent appointed by the state board of education shall be superintendent of the public free schools of Richmond, and shall, in addition to the duties required of him by general law, perform such other duties as may be imposed on him by the school board. He may be present at the sessions of the board, and may participate in its discussions, but shall not be allowed to vote.

12. He shall receive for his services, out of the city treasury, the sum of sixteen hundred and fifty dollars per annum, payable as other salaries are provided to be paid by law.

13. The city superintendent shall, as soon after the expiration of each scholastic year as possible, report to the board the condition of the public schools.

The Lancasterian School.

14. The school board shall be the trustees of the Lancasterian school, and shall take steps to incorporate said institution, in such manner and on such conditions as the board shall deem advisable, into the public free school system of the city, subject to all laws and ordinances governing the same: providing, however, that during the session at present in progress, no change shall be made in conducting the said school.

May 15, 1871. 15. The school board shall have all the powers and perform all the duties heretofore conferred by act of assembly or by ordinance upon the trustees of the Lancasterian school, from and after the first day of July, eighteen hundred and seventy-one.

The First Normal School.

16. The school board shall have power, in their discretion, and on such terms as may be agreed on between them and the trustees of the first normal school, to take charge of said school, and incorporate it into the public free school system of the city, subject to all laws, ordinances and regulations governing the same.

School Property.

17. All buildings, grounds and property, of every description, used for the purposes of public education, and purchased with money appropriated by the city council, or received from any other source, unless on different conditions, shall be the property of the city of Richmond.

The School Fund.

18. All funds received, from whatever source, or appropriated by the city council for the purposes of public education, shall be deposited with the city treasurer, who shall keep a separate account of the same. Such funds shall be paid out on the warrant of the auditor, which shall be issued only on drafts signed by the mayor, and countersigned by the secretary of the board, which drafts shall on their face show the person for whom or on what account they are drawn.

19. The city treasurer shall furnish the school board once a month with a statement of the account of the school fund.

Title 10.

HUSTINGS COURT, CITY ATTORNEY, AND JUSTICES OF THE PEACE.

CHAPTER XLIX.

OF THE HUSTINGS COURT.*

1. In addition to the powers and authority vested in the hustings court for the city of Richmond by the laws of the state, the said court shall have appellate jurisdiction, to hear and determine appeals from the police justice, in all cases in which the constitutionality or validity of any ordinance of the city shall be drawn in question, or where a fine shall be imposed, or the application for a fine shall be refused for a nuisance, or an order made or refused for abating it, if the alleged nuisance is caused by the pursuit of any trade or manufacture, or by the occupation of the streets and alleys of the city under a colorable and bona fide claim of title; and such appeal shall be as well for the city as for individuals or corporations, and shall be allowed in the same mode and upon the same terms as other appeals from the judgment of the police justice are allowed. Ordinances 1869 ch. 3, §§ 8, 9, 10.

---

* This was chapter III in the Ordinances of 1869, "Of the Election of Judge of the Court of Hustings." The first seven sections, relating chiefly to the election, have been superseded by the state law, (Code of 1873, ch. 49, § 22,) and only the remaining sections are given, the last two, as modified by the state law. Of the omitted setions, the seventh and last formerly fixed the judge's salary, which is now provided for by the Code of 1873, ch. 49, § 41. Chapter III of this collection contains the Ordinance concerning the Mayor. Chapter XLVII, concerning Vagrants, corresponds with chapter XLIX of 1869.

Code of 1873, ch. 154, § 27.

2. During the absence of the judge, or his inability from any cause to hold a term of his court, or to sit in any particular case, or to discharge any duty required by law, the said term may be held, or said cause tried, or said duty performed, by any circuit judge, or by the judge of the chancery court of the city of Richmond: provided, however, that no extra compensation shall be allowed therefor.*

Code of 1873, ch. 154, § 26.

3. The said hustings court shall be held by the judge in the city hall of the city of Richmond, unless otherwise ordered by resolution of the city council; and there shall be a term of said court for each month in the year, except the month of August, commencing on the first Monday in the month, and continuing so long as the business before the court may require.

CHAPTER L.†

OF THE CITY ATTORNEY.

1. There shall be elected by the city council an attorney for the city, who shall be a resident citizen thereof, and who shall have been admitted to practice in the courts of the commonwealth. He shall hold his office for the term of two years, unless sooner removed, and until his successor shall be appointed and qualify.

June 15, 1870.

2. The said city attorney shall have the management, charge and control of all the law business of the city, and be the legal adviser of the mayor, city council, or any committee thereof, and of the several departments of the city government, and when required, shall furnish written or verbal

---

* The provisions of this and the next section are changed to conform to the sections of the Code noted in the margin. By the 15th section of the same chapter of the Code, another method of supplying the judge's place, in certain of the cases referred to, is authorized; making it proper that the permissive form used above, in the second section, should be retained.

† Amending and reordaining chapter LIV of the city ordinances [of eighteen hundred and sixty-nine], concerning the city attorney. The chapter thus reordained was entitled "concerning the attorney, clerk and sergeant." Its provisions relating to the clerk and sergeant are therefore repealed by their omission, and the re-enactment of what relates to the attorney as the whole chapter.

opinions upon any subjects involving questions of law submitted to him by them. June 15, 1870.

3. It shall be the duty of said city attorney to draft all bonds, deeds, obligations, contracts, leases, conveyances, agreements, and other legal instruments, of whatever nature, which may be required of him by any ordinance or order of the city council, or which by any ordinance or order heretofore passed, may be requisite to be done and made by the city, or which may be required by any person or persons contracting with the city in its corporate capacity, and which, by law, usage or agreement, the city is to be at the expense of drawing. It shall also be his duty to commence and prosecute all actions and suits to be commenced by the city before any tribunal in this commonwealth, whether in law or equity; and also to appear in, defend and advocate the rights and interests of the city, or any of the officers of the city, in any suit or prosecution for any act, in the discharge of their official duties, wherein any estate, right, privilege, ordinances or acts of the city government may be brought in question. When the mayor shall direct a prosecution for a nuisance, he shall appear for the prosecution when the case shall come into court; and if the police justice shall require it, he shall appear in such cases before him for the prosecution; and he shall perform such other duties as are or may be required of him for the city by any ordinance or resolution of the city council.

4. In full compensation for his services, the city attorney shall receive a fixed salary of two thousand dollars per annum, payable monthly. In all cases, however, when his attendance may be required out of the city, his reasonable traveling expenses shall be allowed him.

CHAPTER LI.*

CONCERNING JUSTICES OF THE PEACE.

Their fees and compensation.

The justices of the peace of this city shall be entitled to receive the same fees and compensation for their services as July 11, 1870.

---

*New chapter. Chapter LI of 1869 related to the Lancasterian school, now incorporated with the public free schools under chapter XLVIII.

July 11, 1870. are now allowed by law to the justices of the peace of the several townships of the state, and shall also be allowed a fee of fifty cents against the complainant for issuing every warrant of arrest or other process for the commencement of proceedings for a violation of city ordinances or any other criminal prosecution; which fees the said justices shall be entitled to demand before issuing any such warrant or process.*

---

* This ordinance was adopted on the day of the passage of sections 106 and 107 of the charter, and probably without reference to them. It seems doubtful whether the issuing of process by a justice of the peace for proceedings for a violation of city ordinances is consistent with those sections.

Title 11.

CORONER AND SURVEYOR, AND ALLOWANCES TO JURORS.

CHAPTER LII.

CONCERNING THE CORONER OF THE CITY.

1. A room with the necessary furniture and fixtures shall be provided under the direction of the committee on police, to be under the control and management of the coroner of the city, for the use of the said coroner in taking inquests, and in the making of post-mortem examinations, and discharging any other duties of his office. **Ordinances 1869**

2. The coroner shall report semi-annually to the city council all cases in which he shall be called upon to examine a dead body, and shall examine the same, stating the nature of the case and the apparent cause of the death.

3. For all cases in which the coroner shall be called upon to examine a dead body, and shall examine the same, but shall not consider it a proper subject for an inquest, he shall be entitled to a fee of five dollars for each case.

4. When an inquest is held over a dead body, in addition to the fee allowed by law, when the inquest is prolonged in consequence of the want of or search for witnesses, and so forth, he shall be allowed a per diem of five dollars while actually engaged in such inquest. And whenever the coroner shall deem a post-mortem examination necessary, and the same is made, he shall be allowed the sum of twenty-five dol-

Ordinances 1869 lars for such post-mortem examination, whether made by himself, if he is a physician, or some other physician; and this allowance shall be in full of any allowance by the hustings court of the city for this object; and any such allowance shall be paid by himself.

5. Where the coroner is called to see a dead body, and there are no friends of the deceased who will bury the same, he shall have the body decently buried, and shall be allowed the reasonable expenses attending said burial. But this section shall not apply to cases provided for by the ninth section of chapter one hundred and ninety-seven of the Code, edition of eighteen hundred and seventy-three.

CHAPTER LIII.

CONCERNING THE SURVEYOR OF THE CITY.

1. The duties of the city surveyor shall be the same within the city as those of a county surveyor in a county, as prescribed by the laws of the state. For any service performed by him in the city, by virtue of his office, he may charge the party at whose instance such service is performed, at the rate, for each hour necessarily taken by him, of one dollar and fifty cents for the first hour, and of one dollar for each succeeding hour so taken; and when he performs a service, the whole fee for which, at this rate, would be less than one dollar, he may charge therefoı one dollar, instead of at the rate aforesaid. What is allowed in this section to the surveyor shall be deemed full compensation, not only for his own services, but also for the services of any chain carrier or assistants that he may employ.

2. The city surveyor shall keep his office in such place in the city as the council may designate. His books of record and other official papers shall be kept in his said office. He shall reside in the city and be in his office at least one hour each day, Sundays, Christmas day, the first day of January, the fourth of July and twenty-second of February excepted.

3. The cost of any books procured by the surveyor of the city, shall be paid by the auditor when directed by the city council. Ordinances 1869.

CHAPTER LIV.*

CONCERNING ALLOWANCES TO JURORS.

1. Hereafter the auditor of the city shall be authorized to pay to the sheriff of this city the amounts due to jurors for services rendered in the circuit and chancery courts, and to the sergeant of this city the amounts due to jurors for services rendered in the hustings court, upon orders of said courts, certified by their respective clerks. Oct. 14, 1874.

2. The said auditor shall not pay any amount for jury service, in any of the afore-named courts, to any person other than the officers named in the foregoing section, or their legally qualified deputies, and then only upon such orders as are mentioned in said section.

---

*New chapter. Chapter LIV of 1869 was concerning the Attorney, &c. Chapter L of this collection, concerning the City Attorney, is the substitute for that chapter.

Title 12.

OFFENCES.

CHAPTER LV.

CONCERNING INJURIES TO REAL PROPERTY.

June 15, 1870. 1. If any person shall willfully destroy, injure, or in any manner deface any church or other house of public worship, or other public building in this city, belonging to this city or state, the county of Henrico or the United States, or any enclosure thereof, or any tree or plant set on the outside of any such enclosure appurtenant thereto, or shall willfully destroy, injure or deface any tree, shrub or other thing within any such enclosure, he shall be fined not less than one hundred nor more than two hundred dollars. And if any person, other than the owner, shall willfully destroy, injure or deface any other house or building not his own, or the enclosure around any other lot not his own, or any tree, shrub or flower within the same, he shall be punished by like fine; and this section, with the assent of the governor, shall apply not only to the capitol square and the government house, but to all other enclosed grounds and buildings in this city belonging to the commonwealth, and to the enclosures thereof, and the trees, shrubbery and other things therein.* June 15, 1870.

2. If any person shall wilfully destroy, injure or in any manner deface any grave, tombstone or monument in any public or private cemetery in this city, or if any person, other than the owner, shall wilfully destroy, injure or deface any fence or enclosure thereof, or any tree, shrub, flower or other thing within such cemetery, he shall be fined not less than two hundred nor more than five hundred dollars; or, if the fine be not paid, imprisoned for not less than thirty nor more than ninety days. And if any person, other than the owner, shall pluck, take or remove from such cemetery any flower, wreath, vine, plant or other ornament, he shall be fined not less than five dollars nor more than one hundred dollars; or, if the fine be not paid, imprisoned for not less than thirty nor more than ninety days.

3. The superintendent, assistant superintendent and steward of the city almshouse, and the keepers and assistant keepers of all cemeteries, public buildings, parks or enclosures within the city, are vested with the powers of policemen of said city, so far as the limits of their respective cemeteries, buildings, parks or enclosures are concerned. April 10, 1872.

4. If any person shall post or paste any bill or notice of any description whatever, upon any wall, building, tree-box or enclosure in the city, or paint or chalk, or in any manner deface the same, without the consent of the owner or occupier of the premises, he shall be fined not less than ten nor more than twenty dollars. June 15, 1870.

CHAPTER LVI.

CONCERNING THE SALE OF LIQUORS, AND GAMBLING.

1. If any person shall sell by retail to a person in this city, any wine, brandy, whiskey, or other ardent spirits, or a mixture thereof, to be drunk at or in the house, or other place Ordinances 1869

* Assented to by the governor of Virginia, March 26th, 1859.

Ordinances 1869 where sold, without a license to keep an ordinary, or an eating house with license to sell liquors to his guests, at the said house or place, he shall be fined not less than five nor more than twenty dollars.

2. If any licensed keeper of a house of private entertainment or public boarding house, eating house, cook shop or lager beer saloon, shall allow any gambling or play of any kind for money or other valuable thing, or shall allow any wine, ardent spirits, or a mixture thereof, to be sold upon his or her premises, he, she or they shall be fined for each offence a sum not less than ten nor more than fifty dollars: provided, that this last prohibition shall not apply to the keeper of an eating house who has a license to sell liquors to his guests, and sells it only as authorized by his license.

3. If any person not embraced in the next preceding section shall allow any spirituous or fermented liquors to be sold upon his or her premises, he or she shall be fined fifty dollars for each offence. But this section shall not apply to keepers of ordinaries, or keepers of eating houses, or merchants having a license to sell such liquors, when the same are sold only as authorized by their licenses.

CHAPTER LVII.

CONCERNING INDECENT CONDUCT, ASSAULTS, &C., IN PUBLIC PLACES.

April 28, 1873. 1. Any person who shall be guilty of lewd, indecent or disorderly conduct, or who shall exhibit any indecent representation of any subject or thing, or who shall draw an indecent picture, or write indecent language on any house, or enclosure, or post, or other conspicuous object, or who shall keep for sale any obscene picture, book or pamphlet within this city, shall be fined not less than five nor more than one hundred dollars, and of such fine one-half shall be paid to the informer.

Ordinances 1869 2. If any person shall fight or assault another in any place of public resort in the city of Richmond, or in the streets or public alleys of the city, he shall be fined not less than five nor more than one hundred dollars. Ordinances 1869

3. If any person shall appear in the streets or public alleys of the city intoxicated, or shall therein employ abusive or insulting language to another person, or use obscene language or actions, he shall be fined not less than two nor more than fifty dollars.

CHAPTER LVIII.

CONCERNING INJURIES TO THE PORT OF RICHMOND.

Deposits of Stone, &c., in Creeks or on Margin of River; Penalty.

If any person shall place or deposit, or shall attempt to place or deposit any stone, ashes, dirt, rubbish or other thing, in or near Gillie's creek or Shockoe creek, or upon the margin of the river or any island therein near the margin thereof, or between the southern limits of the city and the river, so that the same will or may be carried into the river at or below the port of Richmond, he shall be fined for each offence not less than twenty nor more than fifty dollars, one half to be paid to the informer. Ordinances 1869 Sept. 5, 1870.

CHAPTER LIX.

CONCERNING OBSTRUCTIONS AT RAILROAD STATIONS AND STEAMBOAT WHARVES, AND INTRUSION OF BOYS ON CARS.

Stations and Wharves.

1. It shall be unlawful for any agent or porter of any hotel or boarding house, for any owner, agent or driver of any Ordinances 1869

Ordinances 1869 hack or other vehicle, or for any other person, at any terminal station or wharf of any railroad or steamboat in this city, to throng or obstruct the way to any such station or wharf, or to any car or steamboat thereat, so as to hinder or prevent the free and unimpeded access to or departure from such station, wharf, car or steamboat, by passengers carried or to be carried on such car or steamboat, or of those attending or receiving them at such station or wharf.

2. It shall be unlawful for any person at any such station or wharf to make any unnecessarily loud outcry or clamor, or to solicit custom or employment in a tone louder than a conversational one, or to take hold of any passenger's person, clothing, baggage or property, unless previously requested by such passenger to do so.

3. No such porter, agent, or owner or driver of any hack or other vehicle, shall go into or upon any such car or steamboat for the purpose of soliciting custom or employment, unless previously authorized to do so by the proper person having charge of the same.

4. It shall be the duty of the chief of police to designate the limits, not less than ten feet from every such railroad station or steamboat, within which it shall not be lawful for any such hotel or other porter, or agent or owner or driver of any hack or other vehicle, to come for the purpose of soliciting custom or employment, for half an hour after the arrival of any such railroad train of cars or of any such steamboat; and every policeman on duty at such station or wharf shall be specially charged to enforce this ordinance.

5. Any person violating any of the provisions of this ordinance, and the employer of any such person so violating the same, if the keeper of a hotel or boarding house, or owner of a hack or other vehicle, shall, on conviction before the police justice, be fined for each offence not less than five nor more than ten dollars; and it shall be the duty of the chief of police, under the direction of the mayor, to have present at each of the said stations and wharves, upon the arrival of the passenger trains and steamboats stopping thereat, one or more of the city police, as may be needed for the prompt and efficient enforcement of this ordinance, and for the prevention and punishment of any violation of the same, which it shall be the duty of the police as far as practicable to prevent or report to the police justice.

Climbing of boys on cars in motion.

6. It shall be unlawful for any minor to climb or get, or attempt to climb or get upon any railroad car or machinery, while in motion, within the limits of this city; and the parent or guardian of any minor who shall be convicted of violating this section, shall be fined by the police justice not less than five nor more than twenty dollars. Feb. 14, 1870.

7. It shall be the special duty of every policeman who shall at any time be in any street where railroad cars shall be in motion, to vigilantly observe them, and to arrest any minor who may violate the preceding section of this ordinance, and promptly report such violation to the police justice, before whom the parent or guardian shall be summoned to appear, and show cause, if he or she can, why he or she should not be fined in accordance with this ordinance.

CHAPTER LX.*

CONCERNING FINES AND PENALTIES.

1. Fines and penalties for the violation of any ordinance of the city, or any order of the police justice,† given in pursuance of any ordinance, shall be recoverable by prosecution before the police justice in the police court; and when recovered shall inure to the use of the city. Sept 12. 1870.

2. Minors shall be prosecuted for breaches of ordinances in the same manner and to the same effect as adults; and if the minor be not an indentured apprentice, the fine may, in the discretion of the police justice, be imposed either on the minor or on his father or guardian; and if the offender be an indentured apprentice, upon the master or apprentice. For any violation of any ordinance by a married woman, the

* LIX in Ordinances of 1869, there being two chapters in that revisal headed as LIX.

† In the ordinance, after police justice there followed in each section the words, "or other justice," which are left out above and when used elsewhere in like connection, because by the charter, §§ 106, 107, the justices of the peace are to have no portion of the jurisdiction given the police justice as to cases arising under the charter and ordinances.

Sept. 12, 1870. prosecution shall be against her husband, and the fine imposed on him.

3. When judgment shall be rendered for any fine under an ordinance, and the same be not immediately paid, the police justice shall issue executions thereon, to be levied of the goods and chattels of the person against whom such judgment is rendered, directed to any police officer of the city, returnable within fifteen days, before the police justice. The officer who may levy such executions shall sell the property thereby taken at public auction, for cash, at one of the market houses in the city, after three days' notice of the time and place of sale, published in one of the daily papers printed in the city, to satisfy said execution, and all costs attending the levy and sale thereof.

Title 13.*

RAILROADS, AND THE JAMES RIVER IMPROVEMENT.

CHAPTER LXI.

CONCERNING THE RICHMOND, FREDERICKSBURG AND POTOMAC RAILROAD.

Whereas, the twenty-third section of the act of the general assembly of Virginia, incorporating the Richmond, Fredericksburg and Potomac railroad company, requires the president and directors thereof so to construct the said railroad across any established road or way as not to impede the passage or transportation of persons or property along the same; and whereas, various streets within the corporate limits of Richmond are thus obstructed by said railroad, and the lives of the citizens are imperilled by the passage through one of the principal thoroughfares, of the locomotives and trains of said company: Therefore, be it ordained by the council of the city of Richmond, May 13, 1872.

1. That no steam engine, tender, freight car, passenger car, or other car of any kind belonging to or used by the Richmond, Fredericksburg and Potomac railroad company shall stand, load or unload on Broad street. But any such engine, tender or car shall be carried or propelled immediately into a depot or lot adjoining said street, and there receive or discharge its load of freight or passengers, as the case may be,

*The chapters and subjects under this and the succeeding titles are not in the Ordinances of 1869.

May 13, 1872. and if the same be not done or performed on or before the first day of January, eighteen hundred and seventy-three, then and thereafter the said railroad company, for any violation of the ordinance, shall be fined not less than five nor more than twenty-five dollars for each and every offence.

2. That the Richmond, Fredericksburg and Potomac railroad company shall conform their railroad or railway track to the grade, when established and located as provided for in an ordinance passed on the thirteenth day of May, eighteen hundred and seventy-two, entitled "an ordinance to provide for the establishment of the grade of Broad street west of Ninth street,"* from Hancock street to the termination of said railroad or railway track, at the intersection of Broad and Eighth streets, and if the same be not done on or before the first day of July, eighteen hundred and seventy-three, then the said company shall be fined twenty dollars per day for every day thereafter, until said railroad or railway track shall be made to conform to the grade of said street.

Sept. 8, 1873. 3. On and after the first day of January, eighteen hundred and seventy-four, no car, engine, carriage or other vehicle of any kind, belonging to or used by the Richmond, Fredericksburg and Potomac railroad company, shall be drawn or propelled by steam upon that part of their railroad or railway track on Broad street east of Belvidere street, in said city. The penalty for failure to comply with this section shall be a fine of not less than one hundred nor more than five hundred dollars for each and every offence, to be recovered before the police justice of the city of Richmond.†

*The ordinance referred to is added as section 59 to the chapter concerning streets—the 33d chapter of this compilation.

†On the 12th of May, 1873, the preceding ordinance was suspended by the council, so far as to allow the railroad company to stop their trains on the street for the period of four days only, from the 28th day of that month, for the purpose of receiving passengers thereon and debarking them therefrom. On the 30th day of January, 1874, the third section was suspended for the period of four months from that day, to afford time to obtain a final judgment of the court of appeals as to the right of the company to use steam engines on the street; and on the 25th of May, 1874, the same section was again suspended till the 1st of August, 1874. No further suspension has been ordered by the council.

CHAPTER LXII.

CONCERNING THE CHESAPEAKE AND OHIO RAILROAD.

The council of the city of Richmond hereby offers and proposes to contract on behalf of the city, with the Chesapeake and Ohio railroad company, for the connection of the said railroad with tidewater in and near the city, according to the plan and upon the terms following, viz: Dec. 23, 1871.

1. The Chesapeake and Ohio railroad company to construct a branch of its railroad, with double track and all needful appurtenances, and to work the same with the ordinary engines and cars of the company, from its present main line in the city, as follows:

Leaving the present line near Carrington street, curving to the left or eastward, and crossing, at or near grade, Clay street west of Seventeenth street, and Seventeenth and Eighteenth streets, between Clay and Marshall streets; thence straight and by a tunnel under Nineteenth street and all intervening streets to near Twenty-ninth street, between Broad and Grace streets; thence by open cutting or embankment and on a curve to the right or southward, passing over the Richmond and York river railroad and crossing the valley of Gillie's creek, to the southern side of said valley, and thence by any practicable routes to the river front, and to the eastern limit of the city, and beyond, to the property purchased by said company of Franklin Stearns, where it will construct such wharves, warehouses, &c., as will efficiently accommodate the trade of its road and of the city in connection therewith: provided, the present depot of the company, or a depot at any point between the present depot and the James river and Twenty-sixth street, shall be the distributing and receiving depot for this city, unless the same be removed by the consent of the council.

Dec. 23, 1871. 2. To aid in the construction of this work, and to secure to the city the trade facilities to result therefrom, the city will pay to the said Chesapeake and Ohio railroad company $300,000 of six per cent. bonds of the city, having thirty-four years to run, and bearing interest, payable semi-annually from their delivery to this company, which bonds shall be delivered in monthly instalments, as the work of construction upon the tunnel progresses, and in the proportion ascertained by estimates of the engineer of said company.

3. In the construction of this branch and tunnel the said railroad company may use and occupy, permanently, any street or alley of the city on the line and within the limits indicated, or may cross any such street or alley at, under, or over its present grade, under the direction of the committee on streets, or may change such grade upon making compensation for any injury to private property caused by such change, and repairing and reinstating the public streets and crossings, and keeping the pavement in order on each side of the track for two feet. And during the construction of such branch and tunnel the said company shall be allowed, temporarily, to place needful obstructions in the streets affected by the work, and to use any such steam or other machinery as may be necessary for the efficient conduct of the work. And at the termination of the work, the company shall repair and reinstate all public alleys, streets and crossings.

4. In addition to the branch, already provided for, the said company shall have the right to construct and work under the supervision of the committee on streets generally, in like style and manner and with the like privileges, the following branches of its railroad, viz:

First. A branch from near the eastern portal of said tunnel, curving sharply to the right and passing west of the gas works to the river, with connections right and left to the tracks running along the water front of the city.

Second. A branch from near the said eastern portal, curving to the left to the line of the Richmond and York river railroad.

Third. A branch from either of the branches already named, or from the wharves and warehouses herein mentioned, by any practicable route, from the eastern limits of the city between Main street, (or a prolongation thereof, known as Rocketts and Lester streets,) and James river to

Twenty-eighth street, and thence between the northern line of Cary street and James river to near Haxall's mills, and thence between the James River and Kanawha canal and James river to the western limit of the city. Dec. 28, 1871.

The speed upon these three branches may, if it shall hereafter be found necessary, be restricted by the city council to a rate not exceeding four miles an hour.

5. The written acceptance of this offer and proposition by the Chesapeake and Ohio railroad company at any time before the first day of February, eighteen hundred and seventy-two,* shall be deemed to conclude and complete this contract.

CHAPTER LXIII.

CONCERNING THE IMPROVEMENT OF JAMES RIVER.

Sec.
1. Committee to be appointed by council and chamber of commerce.
2. Committee to elect chairman.
3. A majority of the whole a quorum.
4. Committee to have charge of property; to elect engineer and assistants, with approval of council. Funds, how kept; how paid out.
5. Meetings of committee.
6. When committee to report to council, and what.
7. If no nomination of committeemen by chamber of commerce, council to appoint without it.
8. If vacancy occur, how to be filled.

1. At the first meeting of the city council, which shall be held in the month of July of each year,† the city council shall proceed to elect five of its members, and these members of the city council, with five citizens of Richmond who are not members of the city council, who shall be certified to the president of the city council by the president and secretary of the chamber of commerce of Richmond as having been elected by that body for the purpose, shall be named and designated as the committee on the improvement of James river. August 1, 1870.

2. As soon as practicable after the formation of the committee, they shall elect a chairman from among their own number.

3. A majority of the whole number shall be a quorum for the transaction of any business relating to their duties.

---

* The foregoing offer and proposition of the city council was accepted by the Chesapeake and Ohio railroad company on the 29th day of December, 1871, as appears by the records of the city council.

† As the members of this committee are not *officers* appointed by the council, their appointment does not come under the two years' rule of chapter IV, § 2.

Nov. 21, 1870. 4. They shall have charge of all the property belonging or appertaining to the improvement of the river; they shall elect an engineer, and assistants if necessary, and employ all persons who may be necessary to the prosecution of the work; but no such appointments shall be valid unless approved by the city council. All moneys appropriated and set apart for the work, shall be under the charge and keeping of the city treasurer; and they shall be paid out on the warrants of the city auditor, which shall be issued only on the drafts of the engineer herein mentioned, attested by the auditing officer, and approved by the chairman of aforesaid committee.

August 1, 1870. 5. They shall meet once a month, and as much oftener as may be necessary.

6. The committee shall make a written report of their operations to the city council at the first regular meeting held in each month, and with this report shall submit an estimate of the amount of money which will be required for their use during the succeeding month.

7. In the event of an omission on the part of the chamber of commerce to nominate the persons mentioned in the first section of this ordinance, the city council shall elect five citizens who are not members of the city council, and they shall remain in office until the next appointment.

8. In the event of a vacancy occurring in the committee, the committee shall fill the vacancy with a member of the city council or a citizen not a member of the city council, as may be necessary to preserve the number of each stated in the first section.

Title 14.

PUBLIC PRINTING, VIRGINIA VOLUNTEERS, PUBLIC INTERESTS, RETRENCHMENT AND REFORM.

CHAPTER LXIV.

CONCERNING THE PUBLIC PRINTING, &C.

Committee on printing to contract annually; see that printing is neatly done, &c.; and examine and approve bills for printing, binding and advertising, subject to approval of council.

The committee on printing shall annually contract for all the printing, binding and advertising required to be done for the city or its officers. They shall see that all printing is neatly executed upon paper of the quality prescribed by the committee, and shall examine and approve all bills for printing, binding and advertising, subject to the approval of the city council. Sept. 19, 1870.

CHAPTER LXV.

CONCERNING THE FIRST REGIMENT OF VIRGINIA VOLUNTEERS.

1. There shall be paid annually to the first regiment of Virginia volunteers of the state militia, upon warrants drawn by its commanding officer, the sum of sixteen hundred dollars, to be used for the purpose of maintaining said regimental organization. The same shall be paid in monthly March 23, 1874.

March 23, 1874. instalments, upon the certificate of the commandant, to be filed with the auditor, that the companies composing the regiment, muster the minimum number of men required by law.

2. This ordinance shall take effect from the first day of February, eighteen hundred and seventy-four.

CHAPTER LXVI.

CONCERNING THE BOARD OF PUBLIC INTERESTS.

Oct. 22, 1874. 1. Immediately after the passage of this ordinance, and hereafter, on the first day of August, after the organization of each new council, the president of the board of aldermen shall appoint two members, and the president of the common council three members, from their respective bodies, who, together with five citizens (of whom two shall be appointed by the board of aldermen and three by the common council), and the president of the common council (who shall be chairman ex-officio), shall constitute a board, to be called the board of public interests of the city of Richmond.

2. It shall be the duty of said board to take into consideration all works of internal improvements in existence, or which may be projected from time to time; to look after the commercial, industrial and manufacturing interests of the city; to watch over and take care of its connections, means of transportation and communication with the rest of the country; and to make such reports and recommendations to the city council as will in their opinion best subserve the different interests of the city of Richmond.

3. There shall be a meeting of this board at least once a month, and as much oftener as it shall deem proper.

4. In case of any vacancy in the board from any cause, it shall be filled by the board from the class in which the vacancy occurred.

CHAPTER LXVII.

CONCERNING THE COMMITTEE ON RETRENCHMENT AND REFORM.

Appointment and duties of the committee; what reports and recommendations committee to make to city council.

There shall be selected annually, at the first meeting of the city council held in July, a committee on retrenchment and reform, consisting of five members of the city council, whose duty it shall be to inquire into any branch of the city service, the duties of officers, and all other matters connected with the same as expressed in the ordinances, and with the expenditures of the money of the city; and that they report as often as they think proper, making such recommendations in the amendments of the ordinances, or in the duties of officers and employees, as they may deem necessary to secure the faithful performance of duties required, or such changes in their requirements as may be beneficial to the city and conducive to the economical administration of the government of the city. **August 1, 1870.**

Title 15.

TEMPORARY ORDINANCES STILL IN FORCE.

CHAPTER LXVIII.

CONCERNING THE CONSTRUCTION OF A NEW RESERVOIR.

Bonds to be issued for construction of new reservoir; committee on finance to dispose of them, exclusively for this work; each bond to refer to this ordinance.

Dec. 22, 1873. For the purpose of constructing a new reservoir, there shall be issued, in the mode prescribed by the charter and the ordinances of the city, bonds of the city of Richmond to an amount not exceeding two hundred and seventy-five thousand dollars, bearing eight per cent. interest, payable semi-annually, on the first day of July and the first day of January, and redeemable in thirty-four years from the date thereof; which said bonds shall be sold by the committee on finance, at such time as they shall deem best for the interests of the city, and the proceeds thereof shall be exclusively set apart and devoted to the discharge of obligations incident to the construction of said reservoir. And every such bond shall bear upon its face a distinct reference to this ordinance, as authority for its issue.

CHAPTER LXIX.

CONCERNING THE GENERAL APPROPRIATIONS FOR 1873–4 AND 1874–5.

Sec.
1. Cancelling unexpended appropriations for 1873-4; exceptions.
2. Appropriations for 1874-5; not to be increased except by two-thirds vote; condition attached to appropriations to certain benevolent institutions; on refusal to comply, appropriation to be withdrawn.

1. All unexpended appropriations, as well as all balances in excess of appropriations, standing on the books of the auditor at the end of the past fiscal year, thirty-first January, eighteen hundred and seventy-four, except such as apply to— streets generally, two thousand six hundred and sixty-seven dollars and seventy-five cents; hands and carts, one thousand six hundred and eighteen dollars and fifty-five cents; culverts, nine thousand nine hundred and twelve dollars and seventy-three cents; St. Paul's church home, one hundred and twenty-five dollars; extension water works, eleven thousand nine hundred and twenty dollars and ten cents; compensation to judges, two hundred and forty-nine dollars and ninety cents; revision of ordinances, one thousand dollars; James river improvement, eight thousand four hundred and sixty-one dollars and eleven cents; howitzer armory, three thousand dollars; oakwood cemetery road, one hundred and ten dollars; first Virginia regiment, one thousand six hundred dollars; construction new reservoir, two hundred and seventy-five thousand dollars; and James river bridge company, two thousand dollars, shall be considered as cancelled, and the auditor is hereby empowered and directed to balance his books accordingly. March 9, 1874.

2. That there be appropriated from the funds and resources of the city, for the fiscal year ending thirty-first January, eighteen hundred and seventy-five, the following sums, and for the purposes here mentioned, and that the said sums shall not, in any case, be increased or added to, except by a vote of two-thirds of the whole council in favor of such increase or addition; said vote to be taken by ayes and noes:

Sinking fund, forty thousand dollars; discount and interest, ten thousand dollars; city hospital and board of health, nine thousand dollars; city police, eighty-four thousand dollars;

March 9, 1874. almshouse, out-door poor and fuel, forty-five thousand dollars; grounds and buildings, twenty thousand dollars; streets generally, forty thousand dollars; sewer connections—ordinance twenty-fourth June, eighteen hundred and seventy-three, two thousand five hundred dollars; hands and carts, twenty-three thousand dollars; roller and crusher, five thousand dollars; chain gang, three thousand dollars; contingent fund, thirty thousand dollars; election—May and November, five thousand dollars; courts and juries, six thousand dollars; judges of the circuit, chancery and hustings court, one thousand dollars each, three thousand dollars; oakwood cemetery, three thousand dollars; shockoe hill cemetery, one thousand five hundred dollars; friends' colored orphan asylum, one thousand dollars; female humane association, one thousand dollars; Richmond male orphan asylum, one thousand dollars; St. Joseph's orphan asylum, one thousand dollars; St. Paul's church home, five hundred dollars; St. John's burying ground, two hundred dollars; pensioners, three hundred and sixty dollars; fire department, thirty-four thousand dollars; fire alarm telegraph, two thousand five hundred dollars; stationery and printing, four thousand five hundred dollars; salary of officers, twenty-three thousand dollars; construction gas works, eighteen thousand dollars; expenses and coal for gas works, one hundred and fifty thousand dollars; construction water works, eighteen thousand dollars; expenses water works, twenty-five thousand dollars; extension water works, ; refund of taxes, one thousand four hundred dollars; school board, fifty-five thousand five hundred dollars; assessment of taxes, five thousand dollars; college dispensary, two hundred and fifty dollars; city morgue, three hundred and twenty-five dollars; James river improvement, four thousand dollars; July interest on bonded debt, one hundred and twenty-one thousand eight hundred and eighteen dollars and seventy-two cents; January interest on bonded debt, one hundred and twenty-one thousand eight hundred and eighteen dollars and seventy-three cents; July interest on two hundred and seventy-five thousand dollars reservoir bonds, eleven thousand dollars; January interest on two hundred and seventy-five thousand dollars reservoir bonds, eleven thousand dollars: provided, that the quarterly payment of the foregoing appropriations of one thousand dollars each, to the Friends' colored orphan asylum, the

Female humane association, the Richmond male orphan asylum, and the St. Joseph's orphan asylum, and of five hundred dollars to St. Paul's church home, shall authorize the council committee on the relief of the poor, to place and keep in each of the said asylums, without any additional charge to the city, a number of children not exceeding five, to be selected by said committee from such as may be from time to time admitted at the city almshouse; and in case of the refusal on the part of any of the above mentioned institutions to receive and keep any child so selected, the appropriation to such institution shall be withdrawn, and the payment thereof shall cease, upon the order of said committee on the relief of the poor, addressed in writing to the auditor of the city.

March 9, 1874.

Title 16.

RECENT ORDINANCES.*

CHAPTER LXX.

CONCERNING THE REMOVAL OF GARBAGE.

Nov. 12, 1874. 1. No person shall engage in the business of collecting and transporting garbage in this city without having obtained a permit from the board of health authorizing such person to engage in the business, in conformity with the rules and regulations of the said board. Any person violating this provision shall be liable to a fine of not less than five nor more than ten dollars for each offence.

2. Housekeepers shall deposit their garbage in water tight vessels, each having a capacity not to exceed thirty-two gallons; these shall be kept at a point on the premises most accessible to the garbage collectors. Wherever there are carriage alleys in the rear of dwellings, said vessels shall be placed in immediate proximity to the gates opening into said alleys. The definition of garbage is refuse animal and vegetable matter. No slops or dirty water, nor any other substances except garbage, shall be deposited in the garbage vessels. Any person violating this provision shall be liable to a fine of not less than two nor more than five dollars.

3. The board of health are empowered and instructed to prepare suitable rules and regulations for the garbage ser-

---

*Passed after the foregoing arrangement was completed and partly printed.

vice, and to publish the same in the Daily Dispatch, and in handbills to be distributed throughout the city. Nov. 12, 1874.

4. This chapter shall be enforced on and after the first day of December, eighteen hundred and seventy-four.

CHAPTER LXXI.

CONCERNING THE OFFSETTING OF CLAIMS DUE TO AND FROM CITY.

Auditor to deduct from bills against city amounts due by the claimants, &c.

Whenever any person to whom the city is indebted shall apply to the auditor for a warrant in his favor, and the auditor has in his possession, or has knowledge of bills against said persons for taxes, or other dues to the city, it shall be the duty of the auditor to deduct the amount due to the city from that due to the person applying, and only issue his warrant in favor of said person for the excess; and whenever it shall appear that the amount due to the city is the greater, it shall be the duty of the auditor to credit the bill of the person with the amount due to him by the city, and not to issue any warrant in his favor. Nov. 18, 1874.

Title 17.

ENACTING AND REPEALING ORDINANCE.

Approved January 15, 1875.

CHAPTER 72.

FIXING THE TIME FOR THE COMMENCEMENT OF THE FOREGOING ORDINANCES, AND REPEALING OTHERS.

Jan. 15, 1875. 1. The foregoing ordinances, as they have been hereinbefore printed and corrected, (the last in date having been approved by the mayor on the twenty-sixth day of November, eighteen hundred and seventy-four,) shall be in force on and after the first day of April, eighteen hundred and seventy-five, except such parts thereof as have been or may be repealed, superseded or substituted, either by the express words or the proper effect of ordinances approved since the said twenty-sixth day of November, eighteen hundred and seventy-four; and all ordinances and parts of ordinances, of a general nature, in force on the said twenty-sixth day of November, eighteen hundred and seventy-four, and not included in the foregoing ordinances, shall be, and are hereby ordained to be repealed on the first day of April, eighteen hundred and seventy-five, with such limitations and exceptions as are hereinafter expressed.

2. Such repeal shall not affect any act or offence committed or done, or any penalty or forfeiture incurred, or any right established, accrued or accruing, or any prosecution or proceeding pending at or on the said twenty-sixth day of November, eighteen hundred and seventy-four: except that when any penalty, forfeiture, or punishment is mitigated by provisions of the foregoing ordinances, or of ordinances amendatory thereof, passed since the twenty-sixth day of November, eighteen hundred and seventy-four, and before

the first day of April, eighteen hundred and seventy-five, such provisions may, with the consent of the party affected, be applied to any judgment to be pronounced on or after the said first day of April, eighteen hundred and seventy-five. Jan. 15, 1875.

INDEX.

FIGHTING.

FINES AND PENALTIES.

FINES AND PENALTIES—Continued.

www.ingramcontent.com/pod-product-compliance
Lightning Source LLC
LaVergne TN
LVHW010143110826
845151LV00002B/415

* 9 7 8 1 4 2 5 5 3 8 3 7 8 *